NEW YORK STATE

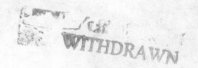

George Washington. From the bust by Houdon, 1792 in the
possession of The Hon. Hamilton Fish. Brady, Photographer, New York.

NEW YORK STATE
THE BATTLEGROUND
OF THE
REVOLUTIONARY WAR

by

HAMILTON FISH, LL. D.

Illustrated

VANTAGE PRESS
New York   Washington   Atlanta   Hollywood

Dedication

Dedicated to the early Dutch discoverers and pioneers of what is now New York State;

To those patriots who served and died in the cause of American Freedom and Independence;

To all makers of America who since the Declaration of Independence have helped to defend and build the United States into the greatest, richest, and freest nation in the world.

Published by Vantage Press, Inc.
516 West 34th St., New York, New York 10001

Manufactured in the United States of America

Standard Book Number 533-02128-6

CONTENTS

APPENDICES

Preface

The first part of this book is devoted to relating a factual history of early New York under the Dutch, English and Americans, interspersed with family reminiscences.

The motif of the book is to revise, on the basis of truth, the historical myths that have been etched for almost 200 years on the minds of the American people.

A galaxy of pre-eminent New England historians created these historical myths based on Paul Revere's Ride, the Boston Massacre, the Boston Tea Party, the Battles of Lexington and Concord, and "the shot heard around the world," that have unwittingly brainwashed the American people into believing that Massachusetts and New England not only began the war but were the main battleground and historic, revolutionary shrine of our Republic.

Every American boy or girl is familiar with Paul Revere's Ride, the Boston Tea Party, and "the shot heard around the world," and the names of James Otis, John and Samuel Adams, and John Hancock. But very few even know about New York State's participation in the war, and that it was the main battleground for seven long, harassing years, and that New York City and for thirty miles around, was under the control of British armed forces throughout the war.

Distinguished New England historians commemorated the landing of the Pilgrim fathers at Plymouth Rock on December 21, 1620. The New England Society of New York even erected in Central Park a very fine statue of a Pilgrim father, giving the date of the landing at the famous rock. There are no statues of any of the early Dutch discoverers or governors in Central Park, such as Henry Hudson, captain of a Dutch ship; Peter Minuet, who bought New York City for $24.00; or the famous and courageous last Dutch governor, Peter Stuyvesant. Why? Are New Yorkers less patriotic? No! They just did not produce such talented historians and poets as New England. Unfortunately, in 1614 the early Dutch traders to arrive at New Amsterdam (New York) found no rock upon which to establish their historic immortality.

The history of the Dutch control of New Netherlands for fifty years, 1614-1664, is even now little known by New Yorkers. Dutch New Netherlands included New York north of Albany and most of New Jersey and Connecticut. This vast territory never had more than 10,000 Dutch colonists. It is truly an epic of brave, sturdy, industrious, self-reliant, Dutch men and women, ready to take up a musket to defend their homes during Indian wars. Many of them succumbed in these wars or to brutal Indian scalping raids.

Holland had only recently won its independence and freedom from the Spanish invasion and its bloody inquisition when the Dutch settlers arrived in New Netherlands. These Dutch pioneers brought with them the stubborn courage and unconquerable qualities of their forebears. Their descendents are still among our most important families in the United States, including three presidents from New York State: Martin Van Buren, Theodore Roosevelt, and Franklin D. Roosevelt.

New York State was the main battleground of the Revolution, the center of government for the last two years, and New York City was for seven years under the yoke of the British army.

The main objective of this book, on the eve of the celebration of the 200th anniversary of the immortal Declaration of Independence, is to brush away the literary cobwebs and dust of obscurity and oblivion that covers the important part played by New York State in winning the Revolutionary War.

There is no dodging the issue. The American War for Independence was very largely a civil war. The Tories, or Loyalists, supported the king, and almost one-third of the British armed forces were composed of Loyalists. However, there was a great deal of sympathy and open support for the American cause, even in England.

Vice Admiral Keppel and General Sir Jeffrey Amherst refused to serve against the former colonists. General Harry Conway refused to "draw his sword in that cause." The Earl of Eggingham, colonel of a regiment ordered to America, turned in his commission because the duties of a soldier and a citizen "had become inconsistent." The City Corporations of both London and Dublin commended him publicly. Many of the Whig members of Parliament, such as Pitt, Burke, Fox, Barre, and Sheridan were eloquent in defense of the rights and liberties of the American colonists.

New York City, which at that time only included Manhattan Island up to the Harlem River, had a population of 22,000, including 3,500 slaves. It was almost as large as Boston, but much smaller than Philadelphia. On September 16, 1776, when the British army took over New York City, 6,000 American Patriots left as self-exiles, leaving 6,000 Loyalists and another 6,000 neutrals or fence-sitters. There were probably more than 1,000 Patriots who later escaped or were driven out of New York City as favoring the cause of freedom and independence.

This book, although based on the truths of history, is not meant to be merely another history book. It includes as a matter of public interest, family letters and reminiscences. These letters or documents are owned by the author and have been in the family for generations. This is the first time they have been published. All of them are directly connected with the early history of New York State.

In the words of Daniel Webster, "It is wise for us to recur to the history of our ancestors." He was right. We should ascertain the facts and transmit accurately the gallant deeds and glorious achievements of the Revolutionary War, to posterity.

The historical truth is that New York State was the battleground of the Revolutionary War and the symbolic center of government of the young American Republic shortly after the victory of Yorktown.

No historian will deny that Boston and New England were the hotbeds of rebellion and resistance to the king and Parliament more than a year before the signing of the Declaration of Independence. Virginia was the next among the colonies openly to defy the British governor and his Loyalist followers. It is interesting to note that both these states were considerably larger than New York in population at that time. But the Patriots in New York, despite Tory strength in the city and adjoining counties, courageously upheld the same principles that motivated New England and Virginia.

New York's revolutionary leaders, such as John Jay, Alexander Hamilton, Gouverneur Morris, Chancellor Robert Livingston, and Major General George Clinton (who served six terms as governor and two terms as vice-president), Francis Lewis, and Louis Morris (both signers of the Declaration), compare favorably with Massachusetts' famous triumvirate composed of James Otis, and Samuel and John Adams, aided and abetted by John Hancock and the brave Joseph Warren killed at Bunker Hill.

We in New York are not trying to take anything away from New England's outstanding patriotic contributions in the Revolutionary War or to minimize them in any respect. We merely want to assert and make known New York's tremendous and vital part in winning the war which has been overlooked and almost ignored.

New York State was the main battleground of the war with 92 battles, as against 19 in New England, but such was the influence of the historical legacies of the famous New England authors that the American people up to the present time have been under the impression that New England, and not New York, was the real battleground of the Revolution.

The fact is, except for the bloody defense of Bunker Hill, there was no other important battle fought in Massachusetts or even in New England, except that near Newport, Rhode Island, also a well-fought defeat.

No one seeks to deprive New England or any of the other states of their glorious part in fighting and winning the war for our independence. Pennsylvania was represented in the Congress by such outstanding delegates as Benjamin Franklin, Robert Morris, and James Wilson, and Philadelphia was the birthplace of our Declaration of Independence, the cornerstone of freedom in the United States and the Bible of freedom throughout the world. Brandywine, Germantown, and Valley Forge were all in Pennsylvania.

Virginia, the most populous state, gave that immortal galaxy of statesmen to our Republic: Washington, Jefferson, Henry, Randolph, Mason, Lee, Madison, Monroe, Marshall, and Wythe during the Revolutionary War and afterwards. The capitulation of the British army at Yorktown was in Virginia.

Maryland had its highly patriotic Governor Charles Carroll, the only Catholic at the Convention, and the distinguished delegates Samuel Chase and Caesar Rodney.

New Jersey stands high in American history with Washington's victories at Trenton, Princeton, and Monmouth, and with its astute and learned governor, William Livingston, and its delegates, Stockton and Hart, both imprisoned by the British and both died soon after being released.

Delaware, a small state, was ably represented by John Dickerson, who later became governor of Pennsylvania, and by Thomas McKean who became president of the Congress.

The North Carolina delegates were Hewes and Hooper. Its people took part in the victory at King's Mountain on its border, under Col. Sevier, who was later U.S. Senator from North Carolina and still later, first governor of Tennessee and who fought under General Green at Guilford Court House.

South Carolina had the two famous Pinckeys, the two distinguished Rutledges, and also Generals Moultrie, Marion, and Sumter, and the hard-fought battles of Charleston, Camden, and Cowpens. It stood next to New York as the battleground of the war.

Georgia was represented by Archibald Bullick, Lyman Hall, Button Gwinnett, George Walton, and by the gallant seige of Savannah.

Massachusetts has already been referred to and should be commended for a magnificent defense at Bunker Hill and for the military leadership of Gen. Henry Knox who commanded the Continental Artillery and was our first secretary of War.

Connecticut was well represented with Governor Wolcott, General Israel Putnam, Silas Deane, Roger Sherman, and its gallant record of hundreds of privateers that preyed like hawks on the British merchant ships.

New Hampshire contributed two of our best fighting generals—Sullivan and Stark. Rhode Island gave to the nation General Nathanael Greene, a former Quaker, the foremost general next to Washington, and his close associate. The battle of Newport was the second largest of the war in New England.

All of the states were bold, loyal, and active supporters of the young Republic throughout the war. But the truth after 200 years must prevail so that it will become crystal clear to all present and future generations of Americans that New York State was the main battleground of the Revolutionary War. For the last two years of the war, after the victory at Yorktown, it was also the symbol if not the actual center of the government of the young, victorious United States of America.

The battle of Bennington was actually won in New York State. One-third of all the Revolutionary War fighting occurred in New York State. New York City, including a radius of 25 miles, was continuously occupied by the British throughout the war.

Washington and his army were located within sixty miles of New York City for five years during the war. The author is only concerned with the truths of history. Massachusetts, Connecticut, Rhode Island, and New Hampshire all furnished their quota in the Continental Army and Militia that fought gallantly in New York and in other states.

Our nation was conceived and born in the war for our independence, based on the eternal truths of freedom. Two hundred years ago the main issue at the time of the Declaration of Independence was the maintenance of liberty, the equivalent of "Freedom Now." The preservation of those freedoms handed down to us by the founders of the Republic is today the most vital issue with which the American people and the free nations of the world are confronted. There is no substitute for freedom, and it is not negotiable. Freedom and independence are the rock on which the United States was founded. It is the lifeblood of the American Republic, and without it we would lose our own soul.

Patrick Henry concluded his famous speech delivered before the Virginia Convention of Delegates on March 23, 1775, in the following words: "Is life so dear or peace so sweet as to be purchased at the price of chains and slavery? Forbid it, Almighty God! I know not what course others might take, but as for me, give me liberty or give me death!"

Patrick Henry was one of the greatest American orators. In our day and generation, the same issue has been well defined by the Hon. Clare Boothe Luce: "Will mankind eventually stand in the light of freedom, or crawl in the darkness of slavery?" This makes clear the difference between Americanism and Communism, the greatest enemy of all freedom, or between democracy and a totalitarian police state.

The author does not claim to have the eloquence or rhetoric of the brilliant New England historians. But he has the clear verities of history to help revise and restore New York State as the battleground of the Revolution.

Veritas magna est et pravelebit—The truth is mighty and will prevail.

NEW YORK STATE
THE BATTLEGROUND OF THE
REVOLUTIONARY WAR

1

Early Dutch in New Netherlands 1609-1664

The Dutch claimed and partially acquired a vast territory extending from the mouth of the Delaware River, including New Jersey and most of Connecticut. This was based on the discovery of the Hudson River in 1609 by Captain Henry Hudson, an intrepid English navigator in command of the *Half Moon,* a Dutch ship. Hudson sailed all the way up to Albany on the river named after him. He was looking for the northwest passage to the Indies, but instead found the best fur-producing region south of the St. Lawrence River. It was later to become the Empire State, fabulously rich, with New York City, one of the greatest seaports in the world and a population larger than many nations.

Five years after Hudson's discovery, two enterprising Dutch sea captains, Adrian Block and Hendrick Christensen, sailed into New York harbor and up the Hudson River in order to trade with the Indians for the much sought-after furs: beaver, otter, and mink. They reached New York in 1614 and established small trading posts both at Albany and New York. This was six years before the Pilgrim fathers landed at Plymouth Rock. Block built the first small ship from the virgin forests and called it the *Restless*. It was used to survey the sound and the adjacent coasts—that is how Block Island got its name.

In 1621, the Dutch West India Company, composed of merchants in Holland and encouraged by the government, was organized to promote trade and colonization. In 1624-1625, they sent a few ships with several hundred settlers, cows, and other domestic animals under Captain Mey to New Amsterdam in the New Netherlands.

Manhattan Island, New Amsterdam (New York City), extended to the Harlem River between the Hudson and East Rivers. The following historic letter should be of interest to all who value the truths of history:

High and Mighty Lords:

Yesterday arrived here the Ship of Arms of Amsterdam, which sailed from New Netherlands out of the River Mauritius [Hudson] on September 23rd. They report that our people are in good heart and live in peace there; the women have also born some children there. They have purchased the Island Manhates from the Indians for the value of 60 guilders [$24]. It is eleven thousand Morgens in size. They had all their grain sowed by the middle of May, and reaped by the middle of August. They send thence samples of summer grain; such as wheat, rye, barley, oates, buckwheat, canary seed, beans, and flak. The cargo of the aforesaid ship is: 7,246 beaver skins, 853½ otter skins, 81 mink skins, 35 wild cat skins and a considerable amount of oak timber.

Herwith High and Mighty Lords to be commended to the mercy of the Almighty and to the States General at the Hague.

Signed your High Mightiness' obedient servant

P Schagan
Amsterdam, November 5, 1626.

Fifty-three years later, in 1679, the Labadists, a sect of German pietists, sent some of their co-religionists to seek a location in New York, fifteen years after the English took over control of New Netherlands from the Dutch. These Labadists were highly intelligent and made a comprehensive report in which they stated that "wampum, a collection of shells on a string, is more prized by the Indians than gold or silver."

The fur trade was predominant under the Dutch and for a long time afterwards under English control. Beaver skins were also a circulating medium; good merchantable beaver was worth "ten shillings per pound, black otter twenty shillings, other otter eight shillings, bear skin seven shillings, mink five shillings, grey foxes three shillings, wolf skins three shillings, raccoon one shilling and a half, deer skin half a shilling." The fur trade was the greatest exportable commodity under the Dutch, and for the first fifty years under the English control or until the influx of New Englanders to the farmlands of Westchester, Dutchess, and Long Island, mostly Presbyterians, Methodists, Baptists and Quakers. They produced vast quantities of wheat and other grains which were sent in sloops to New York, and much of it was exported.

It is interesting to note that Barbados rum sold for one shilling per gallon. It is no wonder it was the most popular drink. A hundred pounds of sugar cost 12 shillings and imported new negroes 12 pounds, and if they could speak English, 16 pounds and more in New York City. Butter was six pence per pound. The best liquors were Fayal, Pasado, and Madeira wine at two shillings a bottle. The cost of living in those days was evidently no problem.

The first director of the colony was Cornelius Jacobus Mey, the discoverer of Cape May. The second director was William Verhulst. They governed only one year each. The third director, Peter Minuit, a Walloon

3

(Protestant from the Rhineland), an able administrator, remained in office from 1626 to 1633. He established larger trading posts and settlements at both Fort Orange (Albany) and at New Amsterdam (New York).

Peter Minuit immediately—1626—entered into the greatest real estate bargain in history. He bought Manhattan Island, 20,000 acres, from the Manhattan Indians for 60 guilders, equivalent to $24, in commodities, probably blue beads, trinkets, cloth, and hatchets. The Indians thought they had made a good deal as they had plenty of land left for hunting and fishing. They did not realize how rapacious the Dutch and English would become to acquire more and more land at their expense.

He was succeeded by Director Van Twilier, an inept governor who only lasted three years. He brought with him 104 soldiers, the first military force sent to New Netherlands.

William Kief, the fifth director or governor, arrived in New Netherlands in 1638 and surrounded himself with some able counsellors, but unfortunately he hated the Indians and became involved in disastrous wars with them that resulted in the death of hundreds of Dutch farmers and almost ruined the Colony.

The Dutch Reform Church was the main religion of the early Dutch settlers and particularly of the establishment. Kief built the first substantial stone church in New Amsterdam. This however, did not prevent an acrimonious quarrel between Everardus Bogardus, an able, strong-minded Dutch dominie and Kief. Bogardus was finally sent back to Holland on the same ship with Governor Kief, who was also discredited. They both were drowned in a shipwreck on their way to Holland. Johannes Megapolensis became head of the church in 1647 and held that position for twenty years. He was one of the commissioners to negotiate the capitulation with the English in 1664. His son Samuel went to Harvard in 1657, and to the University of Utrecht, where he graduated in theology and as a doctor of medicine. On his return to New Amsterdam, he became a pastor of the church at Breuckelin and practiced medicine at the same time. Soon after the English took control of New Amsterdam he returned to Holland, but very few of the Dutch did.

The first well-known doctor in New Amsterdam was Johannes La Montagne, a learned French Huguenot who arrived in 1637. He graduated from the University of Leyden as a doctor, and married Rachel De Forrest, a member of one of the early Huguenot pioneer families. Dr. La Montagne, because of his marked ability, soon became a member of the council and assistant director at Fort Orange (Albany). His descendents, like most Huguenots, were Patriots in the Revolutionary War. Another well-known doctor or surgeon was Hans Kiersted, a German from Magdeburg, Saxony. He was a man of real ability who practiced his profession for twenty-eight years until his death in 1666. Many of his family survived and have prospered in New York and throughout the nation.

The first hospital in New Amsterdam was established in 1658 towards the end of Governor Stuyvesant's administration, through the efforts of Dr. Jacob Hendricksen Varvanger, the representative of the Dutch West India Company. This was the first hospital on Manhattan and the first in North America. The Dutch also organized the first volunteer fire department and the first public school system in America.

Breuckelin (Brooklyn)

In 1637, Joris Jansen de Rapelje, a Walloon, bought a farm on the Woal-boght, near where the Navy Yard in Brooklyn used to be. He married Cateyna Trico of Paris. She was the mother of 11 children and 149 grandchildren. After her husband's death, she was known as the "mother of Breuckelin."

It was not until 1660 that Breuckelin had a church

and a dominie of its own—the Reverend Henricus Selyns, of a distinguished Amsterdam family. The first school teacher was Carel de Beauvois in 1661, an educated French Protestant from Leyden. In 1660, Breuckelin numbered 31 families, amounting to 134 people. Most of them were farmers, growing ordinary farm products, but also they cultivated large fields of tobacco for export.

The fame of the Gowanus (Breuckelin) oysters and wild turkeys was known even in Holland. Labadist travelers who were there in 1697 said the oysters were very fine, "large and full, some of them no less than a foot long." The shells were burned for lime. The supply was abundant as great quantities were pickled and exported to Barbados, which at that time had a population of 30,000 whites and 10,000 slaves and was the largest English-speaking town in the western world.

Doctor Paulis Van Der Beeck was the first physician or surgeon in this small settlement, where he maintained a large and prosperous farm, practiced his profession, and became one of the most prominent men in the early Dutch history of Breuckelin.

Fort Orange (Albany), from its inception in 1614, became a prosperous fur-trading center. The Van Rensselaers acquired four miles on each side of the Hudson River near Albany by complying with the Dutch colonization plan of furnishing fifty colonists. Later they bought more land from the Indians and became the biggest Patroons in the Dutch colony. Together with the Schuylers, the Ten Broecks, and other large landowners, they dominated official life at Fort Orange.

Over the years, a close friendship and trading agreement was maintained with the Iroquois Indian tribes. This was mutually advantageous both for trade and for defense against incursions by the French from Canada.

There were numerous small Dutch settlements on the Jersey shore opposite New York, on Staten Island,

and larger ones on Long Island, Midwout (Flatbush), Amersfoort (Flatlands), and Waal-bogt. The other villages further out on Long Island as far as Oyster Bay were English, but under Dutch control.

All the Dutch and English villages were comparatively small and isolated communities under their own supervision, as transportation was limited to horseback, carriages, and in some places to sailboats.

A number of family names of Dutch origin have remained prominent for nearly three centuries in the affairs of Brooklyn and Long Island as well as of the state itself, such as the Wyckoffs, the Schencks, the Lotts, the Couwenhovens, Remsens, Van Sicklens, Stillwells, Stotthoffs, Van Nuyses, Ditmas, Van Pelts, Van Cleefs, Lefferts, Vanderveers, Duryeas, Cropseys, Onderdoncks, and others.

2

Peter Stuyvesant, the last Dutch governor of New Amsterdam— An Incorruptible, Irascible, Courageous, Able Administrator

Peter Stuyvesant, the son of Balthazar Stuyvesant and Margaret Hardenstein, was born in 1592 in Weststellingwerf, Holland. His grandfather, Johann Stuyvesant, lived at Dockum, one of the leading ports of North Holland. Young Peter often saw the Dutch fleet sail in and out of that harbor. The Dutch had recently freed themselves after many years of domination by the cruel and bloody tyranny of Spain and its Inquisition. It had since become one of the foremost maritime powers. Its ships, smaller, but faster, were more than a match for the huge Spanish galleons, many of which, loaded with the spoils of Mexico and Peru, were captured and ended up in Dutch ports.

The adventuresome Dutch sailors were the heroes of those days. Peter Stuyvesant was early embued with the same spirit of adventure. He probably, like his father, had a college education. At 21, he entered the service of the Dutch West India Company, recently formed, and was sent to Brazil, then under the control

Governor Peter Stuyvesant, after the portrait by Van Dyke

of the Dutch. He remained there until appointed governor of the Dutch island of Curacao in 1633. While governor of Curacao, he lost a leg in battle while aiding the Dutch colonists on the island of San Martin against the Portuguese.

He had to return to Holland to have a wooden leg fitted. On his arrival there, he stayed at the home of his brother-in-law, Samuel Bayard, the husband of his sister Anne. Here he met, courted, and wed Judith Bayard, his sister-in-law, on August 15, 1645, in the French Church at Breda.

The author is a direct descendant of Judith Bayard and Peter Stuyvesant. It is very likely that she was a collateral descendent of the famous French Chevalier Bayard, *sans peur et sans raproche,* as he had three brothers and lived in a section of France where there were many Calvinists a generation later. Her father was a Huguenot and a Protestant minister whose family had lived at Breda, Holland, for a long time. Whether this can be completely substantiated is immaterial, as the descendents of the young Bayards who came over in the same ship with Peter Stuyvesant when they grew up, held important positions under both the Dutch and the English.

Soon after Stuyvesant's marriage, he was appointed governor-general of New Netherlands, with his headquarters at New Amsterdam.

Stuyvesant left Texell on December 24, 1646, accompanied by his wife, his widowed sister, Mrs. Samuel Bayard, and her three sons. He stopped at Curacao, as it was part of his domain, and arrived in New Amsterdam on May 27, 1647. There he replaced Governor Kief whose administration had all but ruined the Dutch colony by causing disastrous Indian wars.

Most people forget that little Holland was the greatest maritime nation in the world when the Dutch established a trading post in New Amsterdam. In the

17th century, Holland had 15,000 vessels, and over 100,000 sailors that carried the commerce of most of Europe. The Dutch possessions in the East Indies, Java and Sumatra, were highly profitable. New Amsterdam, on the other hand, was far from being a financial asset for the Dutch West India Company or the States General of Holland. That is why the Dutch government exchanged the New Netherlands colony 58 years later for Surinam (Dutch Guinea) on the northeast coast of South America, in the worst business deal in all history.

Peter Stuyvesant, the one-legged, incorruptible, tempestuous governor of New Netherlands, who was criticized in his time, actually was by far its greatest administrator. He was its last governor and a firm upholder of the Dutch Reform religion and the Dutch West India Company. He treated the Quakers harshly and quarreled with the Lutherans, Mennonites, and Jews, but yielded and complied with the instructions from Holland for complete religious toleration.

When Stuyvesant arrived at New Amsterdam, the population was 600. The houses were of wood and poorly built, numbering 150. The streets were unpaved and filthy, and cattle and pigs wandered wherever they wanted. Seventeen years later, under his governorship there were 300 houses and a population of 1,400. Most of the streets were paved, and many houses were of brick and wood. Cattle, pigs, and garbage were no longer to be seen on the streets. Colonel Richard Nicolls, who captured New Amsterdam in 1664, called it the fairest of His Majesty's possessions on the Continent. It had become, as a result of Stuyvesant's administration, a thriving, clean, Dutch settlement with a church, a school, a hospital, a government office, a fort, and docks.

A few slaves from the West Indies were brought to New Amsterdam by the West India Company and served there as laborers for the company. It was not until 1654 that a cargo of slaves from Africa arrived at

New Amsterdam. At the end of Stuyvesant's administration, slaves were generally used as domestic servants and treated well by the Dutch citizens.

The Van Cortland's had fourteen slaves; the Bayard's, nine; the Loockerman's, eight; the Kipp's, eight; the DePeyster's, five; the Stuyvesant's, five; the Van Dam's, five; the Van Horn's, four; the Provoost's, three; the Beekman's, three; and the Van Schaick's, three.

Stuyvesant, soon after he was settled in New Amsterdam, evidently liked the prospects so much that he started buying land several miles beyond the city limits. *The History of New Amsterdam* by Professor A. Davis, published in 1854, states that "Governor Stuyvesant bought his farm of 1,000 acres extending from the Bowerie to the East River for $2,500. It had on it, a fine house, a barn, two horses, six cows and two negroes." The actual date of purchase is not given in any book, but it must have been around 1652. He was probably tired of being cooped up in his house in New Amsterdam and bought this large farm as a summer residence where he could get away from the perpetual controversies. His Bowerie home, made of stone and wood, of three stories with projecting rafters, was located 150 feet east of Third Avenue and 40 feet north of 12th Street. It had a carefully laid-out Dutch garden. Stuyvesant planted orchards of apples, pears, and peaches. The famous old pear tree on the corner of 13th Street must have stood northwest of his home. It gave fruit for 200 years, protected in its old age by an iron railing. About 1840, the author's grandfather, Hamilton Fish, while walking with his uncle, Peter Gerard Stuyvesant, asked him where the governor's house had stood. Mr. Stuyvesant was surprised that he did not know, as he had been born and brought up within a half mile of it. Consequently his uncle showed him the site where in his childhood he had seen the remains of the governor's house and then showed him a pile of stone where the old well had been.

Stuyvesant's grandson built another, more sumptuous house on 11th Street not far from where St. Mark's Church stands today. This was known as Petersfield, and his son, Petrus Stuyvesant, built an even larger and finer house just east of 2nd Avenue and 9th Street where British high officials and officers were entertained during the war, while the city was under the control of the British army for seven years. All three of these houses have disappeared without a trace, and some historians have confused the two later houses with the Bowerie Farm of Governor Peter Stuyvesant.

Not even a windmill left
Nor a garden plot they knew
And but a paling marks the spot
Where erst the pear-tree grew

—Edmund Clarence Stedman

The Dutch Colony prospered under Governor Stuyvesant's strong but sometimes arbitrary government. He made peace with the Indians. He defeated the Swedes on the Delaware. He protected the Dutch settlers at Esopus (Kingston) from Indian raids, and kept on friendly terms with the English settlements in Connecticut and on Long Island. He turned New Amsterdam in seventeen years from a cow pasture into a clean, well-organized, prosperous, peaceful, lovely little town. This was not done by wishful thinking. Stuyvesant was a vigorous and able administrator, loyal to the Dutch West India Company and to Holland. He was by far the best of the Dutch governors of New Netherlands. He stood fearlessly for law and order in his day, and some present-day mayors might well profit by his example.

He took over the dying, bankrupt Dutch colony, and through courageous, constructive leadership, breathed new life into it, and restored it into a happy, orderly community. That is the test of real leadership. Let the record speak for itself.

13

When the British fleet, under Colonel Nicolls, appeared before New York in 1664, Stuyvesant indignantly declined to surrender despite the fact that he had neither the soldiers nor the powder to withstand such a superior English force, aided and abetted by English settlers in Connecticut and Long Island. His council, the merchants, and the women combined and insisted on entering into peace negotiations. His historic statement, "I would rather be carried out dead than surrender," was overcome by the entreaties of most of his council and most of the people.

Stuyvesant's insistence on defending New Amsterdam by a show of force enabled him to obtain very fair terms for his Dutch compatriots, who were permitted to maintain their property and language, and were given equal rights and protection under the law. After a few years' visit in Holland and in England, where he arranged for the merchants of New York to secure free trade with Holland, he returned to his Bowerie Farm. He lived there in peace, tranquility, and honor until his death on January 29, 1672, at eighty years of age. He was buried in a tomb at St. Mark's Church at 10th Street and 2nd Avenue in New York, which was on his property, not far from his Bowerie Farm.

His critics depicted Stuyvesant as a harsh, arbitrary, autocratic ruler. This was far from the truth. It was only the image of his puny, jealous enemies who for selfish reasons opposed his constructive reforms. He was intolerant towards those he believed to be opposed to the existing government and to the Dutch Reform Church. But in the latter part of his administration, he was respected and admired by the people for his courage, his integrity, and his sound, dedicated leadership.

On the eastern wall, under the second window from the porch of St. Mark's Church, there is a marble tablet which reads as follows:

In this wall lies buried
  Petrus Stuyvesant
Late Captain-General and Governor-
in Chief of Amsterdam
In New Netherlands—now called New York,
And the Dutch West India Islands,
  died in A.D. 1670½

The date of Governor Stuyvesant's death given on his tombstone as 1670½ is on account of the old and new style. In England, until 1753, the legal year began on March 25th, so that all dates between January 1st and March 25th fell in different years, according to the style employed. Governor Stuyvesant died in February, 1671, according to the old style, 1672 according to the new.

Stuyvesant left a wife, two sons, and the largest estate in New York City, that was, to a considerable extent, preserved in the family for 250 years. Stuyvesant's widow, Judith Bayard, lived at the Bowerie Farm until her death in 1687, fifteen years later. By her will, she founded St. Mark's Church. She had two Stuyvesant sons: Balthazar, born in 1647; and Nicholas William, born in 1648. Balthazar went to the West Indies where he died, leaving a daughter. Nicholas William first married Mira Beekman and secondly Elizabeth Schlectenhorst. He lived his entire life in New York City. When he died, he left two sons and one daughter and the property was divided among them.

Although the British took over the government of the new province of New York in 1664, the Dutch remained predominant in numbers and language for several generations. A number of the old Dutch merchant and political families, and some Huguenots, intermarried with them and held offices under the British: Bogarduses, Brevorts, Brinkerhoffs, Cuylers, DeWitts, Dows, DuBoises, Kipes, Melyns, Remsens, Roosevelts, Rutgers, Schuylers, Strykers, Stuyvesants, Suydans,

Swartwouts, Ten Broecks, Van Burens, Van Cortlands, Van Dams, Van Gilders, Van Pelts, Van Rensselaers, Van Schaicks, Van Zandts, Ver Planks; and five Huguenot families: the Bayards, Cortelyous, DePeysters, Provosts, and Rapeljes, the Philipes (Bohemians), the Crugers (Danish), and the Beekmans, Kiersteds, and the Leislers (Germans). The Costers, VandenHeuvels, Gebhards, and Graveses—all Dutch—arrived at New York soon after the end of the Revolutionary War.

The following constitute one hundred, in addition to the above, of the active and prominent Dutch families of New Netherlands: the Abeels, Anthonys, Banckers, Bergens, Blauvelts, Bleekers, Bogarts, Brashers, Broncks, Byvancks, Clasons, Couwenhovens, Creigers, Croliuses, Curtiniuses, Cuylers, Deckers, Degroats, De-Vries, DeWints, Duychincks, Dyckmans, Eckers, Elmen-dorfts, Eltings, Everts, Gansevoorts, Hagermans, Hams, Hamtramcks, Hardenburghs, Hendricksons, Houghtal-ings, Jans, Jensens, Ketelases, Klocks, Knickerbockers, Kupters, Lefferts, Lockermans, Losings, Mynderses, Neviuses, Opdycks, Outwaters, Phoenixs, Polhemuses, Quackenbosses, Roosas, Schemerhorns, Schoonmakers, Silyns, Slechtenhorsts, Storms, Steenwycks, Stouten-brughs, Ten Broecks, Ten Eycks, Tienhovens, Van Alans, Van Alstynes, Van Anthwerps, Van Clefs, Van Corlers, Vanderbergs, Vanderbilts, Vanderlips, Vander-pools, Van der Veers, Vanderventers, Van Dorns, Van Dusers, Van Dykes, Van Ettens, Van Hatens, Van Hornes, Van Inwegens, Van Kleecks, Van Keurens, Van Nesses, Van Norstrands, Van Ransts, Van Ruyvens, Van Schaicks, Van Schoonhovens, Van Scoyks, Van Vechtens, Van Vliets, Van Vorsts, Van Wagenens, Van Wycks, Voorhees, Vredenberghs, Vrooms, Waldrons, Wendells, Wyckoffs, and the Wyncoops.

These Dutch families intermarried with the Huguenots, Germans, English, and Scottish, and are scattered throughout the United States in every walk of life.

16

The most remarkable feature of the fifty years of Dutch government in New Netherlands is that so few, less than 10,000, Dutch settlers controlled such a vast territory. This extended from the Delaware River up to the Hudson to Albany and a part of Connecticut and Long Island.

In addition, under the Dutch rule there were probably 2,000 English in Long Island and parts of Westchester and Dutchess Counties, and several hundred Huguenots, Germans, and 100 Jews and fewer Catholics.

It seems almost impossible, looking back, how so few accomplished so much and at the end of fifty years had established law and order over such a large region with very little help from either the Dutch West India Company or the States General in Holland.

The reason is that the New Netherlands was not a financial asset. If it had been, the Dutch government would have sent thousands of new settlers and provided the colony with both ships and armaments to protect themselves against encroachments by the New Englanders and attacks by the English fleet. Those few early Dutch settlers who created the history of New Netherlands prospered both under the English and American governments in New York State and served as mayors and aldermen, and in Congress and the legislature.

In 1787, a few years after the end of the Revolutionary War, there were six aldermen of Dutch origin out of fourteen, showing the continued prominence of the Dutch in the early part of the history of New York under the Americans. This is a list of Patroon Stephen Van Rensselaer's funeral 19th of October, 1769, at Albany, seven years before the Declaration of Independence. In those days friends expected a formal invitation to the funeral of any important person and to be asked to the funeral of a patroon was in the nature of a royal command—even British ships dipped their colors when they passed Renssalearwick on the Hudson River. The

17

list of 280 names begins with Margaret Ten Broeck and Margaret Livingston; then came Van Schaick, Lansingh, Wendell, Delancy, Bogaert, Ganesvort, Kip, Pruin, Yates, Staats, Edgar and many others. It ends "all the Tenants of the Whole Manor, Robert Livingston and family and Judge Livingston. Relations at Claverack. Minister and particular friends at Schinectady, Sir William Johnson and family, Bearers of the Pall—Lucas Van Veghten, Philip Van Veghten, John Van Schaick and spouse, Abraham C. Cuyler and spouse, Abraham Schuyler and spouse, Rutger Bleecker and spouse, Henry Jacobse Ten Eyck and spouse, Henry Glen and spouse."

The Dutch custom of asking women to be pall-bearers probably did not last very long after this, for it was commented on as an odd feature of a funeral twelve years later.

The funeral of the old Dutch Patroon Van Rensselear one hundred years after the English had captured New Amsterdam, shows that the influence of the Dutch was still strong in Albany and throughout New York State.

3

The Early Jews under the Dutch in New Amsterdam and in New York prior to and during the Revolution

Some Jews actually arrived in New Amsterdam from Holland before 1650. The famous historical French ship from Brazil reached New Amsterdam in 1654. The first congregation was founded the next year called Sharith Israel ("Remnant of Israel"), a good name for the beginning but not for New York City today with 2½ million, and with nearly six million Jews in the United States. The first rabbi, Paul Pardo, presumably from Portugal or Spain, actually came from Newport, Rhode Island.

The Dutch had heroically fought for their freedom and independence for thirty years against Spain, the blood-thirsty Duke of Alva and the cruel inquisition. The people of North Holland had suffered the horrors of brutal religious persecution for many years and as a result, developed a tolerance for others being persecuted for their religious beliefs. The persecuted Jews from Spain and Portugal were allowed to settle in Holland, build their synagogues, and engage in trade. The few Jews who had migrated from Holland to New Amsterdam had encountered no racial or religious difficulties. The situation changed when the Dutch West India Company began to lose the control in Brazil to the Portuguese. Some Jewish exiles from Portugal, fearing further persecution, arranged to leave Brazil for New Amsterdam.

In 1654, a French ship brought 27 Jewish refugees to New Amsterdam. The captain of the ship claimed he had not been paid for their fare. Consequently he began a lawsuit and won. The Jewish refugees appealed for help from their co-religionists in New Amsterdam, who being Dutch or German, were not interested.

The Dutch dominie complained to the authorities in Holland, asking them not to permit any more Jews to come to the New Netherlands as there was plenty of trouble already with the Quakers, Mennonites, and Catholics. Governor Stuyvesant was told by the Dutch West India Company to leave religious issues alone and to permit the Jewish emigrants to trade in furs in any part of his province, provided they looked after their own people. The arbitrary old Dutch governor changed his tune and posted on the cabin doors of the emigrant ship the following notice: "No man shall raise or bring forward any question or argument on the subject of religion on pain of being placed on water and bread for three days in the ship's galley and if any difficulty shall arise out of such disputes, the authors shall be arbitrarily punished." This could not have happened without Stuyvesant's tacit approval.

The Jews, comparatively few in number, assembled for a number of years in homes or designated places for religious worship, since their arrival in 1654 at New Amsterdam.

The first Jewish synagogue was erected about 1700 on the north side of Mill Street (South William). It was replaced in 1730 by a new stone building 35 feet wide and 58 feet long on the same site, and it remained there for 100 years. It was here that the famous Gershon

20

Seixas of Portuguese descent, born in New York in 1745, was the rabbi of the congregation. He succeeded Rabbi Pinto in 1766 and held office for fifty years. He preached the first sermon in English in the Jewish synagogue.

When the British army under General Howe was about to capture New York, Rabbi Seixas closed his synagogue, took the scrolls of the law and the tablets, and, followed by most of his congregation, left New York as war refugees for seven agonizing years.

Soon after the American army under George Washington marched into New York on November 25, 1783, King's College was renamed Columbia University. Rabbi Seixas was named as one of the trustees as he was very highly regarded by everyone.

Mario Gomez was a much-respected real estate man and money lender. The *Daily Gazette* contained his obituary as follows: "He was religious, hospitable, humane and generous and a staunch friend of freedom as was evidenced by his relinquishing a very considerable property and residing among the friends of the Revolution during the late war."

Another member of the congregation was Hyman Levy, probably a descendent of Asher Levy, the pioneer emigrant known as "the battling butcher of New Amsterdam." Hyman Levy was an honest and successful merchant. He was one of the great fur dealers of the time. It was in his store that John Jacob Astor learned the fur business. During the Revolution, he retired to Philadelphia. He was a true Patriot and a friend of the United States. Rabbi Seixas, Gomez, and Levy were buried in the Jewish burying ground bounded by Oliver, Madison, and James Streets, within the new Bowery. New York graveyards or cities of the dead have not been untouchable or sacred from the hands of time or the foot of progress. About 1830, congregation Shearth Israel moved to Crosby Street near Spring Street, and thirty years later it again moved to a synagogue near the northwest corner of 19th Street and Fifth Avenue.

When the English took over from the Dutch in 1664, the Jews were tolerated in the quiet profession of their religion and business. Such was not the case with Catholics, who were regarded with suspicion in New York with its 99 percent Protestant population. Strange as it may seem, the Catholics were not permitted, under British rule, to have their own church—such was the religious prejudice in those days.

On the other hand, in New York, generations of native American Jews became wealthy long before the Declaration of Independence, and owned large estates. They were active in shipping, commerce, and in the fur trade. They were among the foremost realtors and merchants, and enjoyed the rights and liberties of other British subjects.

As we approach the 200th anniversary of the Declaration of Independence, the nation owes a debt of gratitude to a young Jewish emigrant from Poland, Haymen Solomon of New York. Imprisoned by the British in New York, he secured his release by translating German documents, but later was again arrested for spying and fortunately succeeded in escaping to Philadelphia. There, with the help of friends, he became active in a security house and made a considerable fortune. He was highly patriotic and helped Robert Morris, who was in charge of the government's financing, to raise money to conduct the war. He loaned much money of his own and, probably due to his imprisonment and active participation in the war, he died at an early age, before the government had made restitution on his loans. He was a martyr to the cause of liberty and American independence. Most of the New York Jews were Patriots during the Revolutionary War. The few Loyalists were the Nathans, Hendrickses, and a part of the Gomez family. Col. Isaac Franks and Maj. David Franks served in the Continental Army with honor and distinction from New York.

Among other Jewish officers of distinction in the Revolutionary War were Major Benjamin Nones, Capt. Jacob de la Motta, and Capt. Jacob de Leon, who were attached to Baron de Kalb's staff at the battle of Camden, South Carolina.

When the huge and brave general of German origin was wounded mortally from a half a dozen wounds and deserted by most of his troops, it was these three Jewish officers who, at the risk of their own lives, carried him off the battlefield.

Among Jews who distinguished themselves in the Revolutionary War were: Lt. Col. Solomon Bush, who was cited for valor after having been severely wounded, and a member of his family, Capt. Lewis Bush, was killed in the battle of Brandywine. The three Pinto brothers of New Haven left Connecticut to fight for American independence.

The earliest known New York Jews were of Portuguese origin from Brazil: the Ascostes, the Benjamins, the Cardozas, the Cordobas, the Gomezes, the Hendrickses, the Levys, the Mendozas, the Nathans, the Pintos, and Rabbi Sexias.

New Amsterdam in 1654 was the first port of entry for the Portuguese Jewish refugees from Brazil, but three years later a score of Jewish families arrived in Newport, Rhode Island. This was a colony under British rule, far more tolerant than any of the others. The Jewish emigrants there built their own synagogue and established one of the most ancient of all Jewish settlements in the United States.

The following is part of a letter from George Washington to the Hebrew congregation at Newport, Rhode Island:

Gentlemen:

While I received, with much satisfaction your address, replete with expressions of affection and esteem, I rejoice in the opportunity of assuring you, that I shall always retain a grateful rememberance of the cordial welcome I experienced in my visit to Newport from all classes of Citizens.

The Citizens of the United States of America have a right to applaud themselves for having given to mankind examples of an enlarged and liberal policy, a policy worthy of imitation. All possess alike liberty of conscience, and immunities of citizenship.

May the children of the stock of Abraham who dwell in this land continue to merit and enjoy the good will of the other inhabitants, while everyone shall sit in safety under his own vine and fig tree and there shall be none to make him afraid. May the father of all mercies scatter light and not darkness in our paths and make us all in our own several vocations useful there, and in his own due time and way, everlastingly happy.

G. Washington

It is interesting to note that there was more tolerance for Jewish emigrants under the Dutch in New Amsterdam than in New England, except Rhode Island. Holland was a sanctuary for religious and civil rights even in the 17th Century. Later New York City, under the British and American governments, provided the Jewish inhabitants with equal rights and security. This was long before the French Constituent Assembly in 1791 made Jews citizens without restrictions. This act broke the century-old chains of discrimination and persecution not only in France but throughout Western Europe. (See Appendix D on Jewish Builders of America.)

4

New York under the British 1664-1783—
English, Scots, Huguenots, and Germans

After the capture of New Amsterdam by Col. Richard
Nicolls, there was very little immediate change there except for the name of New York and an English government. Nicolls remained as governor for two years. He
treated the Dutch fairly and permitted them to retain
their property and their language, and to have equal
rights under the law. He was recalled, having made an
honest and honorable record as governor, to fight England's perpetual battles in that era and was killed in the
service of his country within a short time.

The English colonists from Connecticut quickly
spread into Long Island, Westchester, and New York City.
After the British took over the government of the
new province of New York, the Dutch still remained
predominant in numbers and language. However, the
Dutch and Huguenots soon married into English and
Scottish families. Thus New York became gradually a
predominantly English Colony.

The English governors were usually selected from
among the king's favorites and only a few could be clas-
sified as good. Most were poorly qualified and quite a
few were corrupt, inebriates, and tyrannical. The Colony

of New York continued to grow as Scots, both Irish and Highlanders, and Germans seeking freedom in the New World came to New York in increasing numbers.

The origin of the cosmopolitan population of New York City just before the American Revolution was 45 percent British and Welch, 10 percent Scottish, 14 percent Dutch, 9 percent German, 3½ percent Huguenot, 1½ percent Jews, 1 percent Irish Catholics, ½ percent Spanish, Cubans, Mexicans, and other Latin Americans, ½ percent Swedes, Danes, Norwegians, and other nationalities, and 15 percent slaves.

In the province of New York just prior to the Revolution, the population was 180,000 including 22,000 Negro slaves, or approximately one-eighth. In New York City, Manhattan up to the Bronx, the population was approximately 22,000, of which 3,500 were slaves.

Among the one hundred prominent Revolutionary War New York families of English and Welch origin were the Allens, Alsops, Asks, Atkinsons, Baches, Baldwins, Bards, Bartles, Bedlows, Belknaps, Bensons, Blackwells, Bradhursts, Browns, Budds, Bruens, Bulls, Burells, Burrs, Churchs, Clintons, Codwises, Coles, Coopers, Cornells, Cuttings, Dales, Delafields, Dennings, Deuers, Dodges, Duanes, Dunscombes, Elliotts, Fishes, Flloyds, Frenches, Ganos, Gardiners, Gelstons, Gilberts, Haights, Halseys, Hammonds, Hathorns, Herrings, Hicks, Hitchocks, Hopes, Howards, Kisams, Kents, Kingslands, Knapps, Lambs, Lansings, Lashers, Lawrences, Ledyards, Leonards, Lewises, Lotses, Lushes, McVickars, Merrills, Minturns, Morrises, Newbolds, Ogdens, Osgoods, Pells, Pitchers, Piersons, Platts, Posts, Primes, Purdys, Randalls, Reeces, Reeds, Renwicks, Sackets, Sandes, Sheffields, Slidells, Smiths, Steels, Stevenses, Stillwells, Stoddards, Stouts, Stringhams, Strongs, Scudders, Thomases, Throups, Varicks, Waddingtongs, Walkers, Whites, Willets, Woodhulls, Woodwards, Wrights, Yateses, and Youngs.

The Scotch-Irish and the Highland Scots in New York

The Scotch-Irish living in North Ireland (Ulster) were staunch Presbyterians. They were discriminated against by the dominant English Anglicans. Serious crop failures added to their troubles. One hundred thousand fled from Ulster to America during the first half of the 18th century with hatred of England in their hearts. An inscription in the Shenandoah Valley, Virginia, tells the story: "Here lies the remains of John Lewis who slew the English Lord, settled Augusta County, located the Town of Staunton and furnished five sons to fight the battles of the American Revolution."

The Irish Scots in New York were firm Patriots. They migrated in large numbers to New York and many settled in Ulster and Orange Counties, N.Y., along the Hudson River. The largest number migrated to western Pennsylvania where their sons joined the American army fighting both the British and the Indians during the Revolution.

An estimated 25,000 Scots from their own Highlands migrated during a score of years before the war. The Highland Scots were scattered all over the colonies from Boston to Savannah. A number settled along the Mohawk Valley, N.Y., as tenants of Sir William Johnson, the superintendent of the Iroquois Indians. Others settled on farms in nearby Delaware and Schoharie Counties. These Highlanders were largely on the side of the Loyalists. They joined the British Rangers under Col. John Butler and his son Walter Butler. They volunteered to serve with the Royal Green Regiment under Sir John Johnson.

The greater part of the Scotch Highlanders remained loyal to King George, probably because many of them were recent emigrants and were friendly to the Johnsons. However, the most important Scotish family in New York State, the Livingstons, who owned vast tracts of land in Columbia, Dutchess, and Ulster Counties, were very largely with the Patriots. Philip Livingston signed the Declaration of Independence. Robert R. Livingston was a member of the committee that drew up the Declaration, and William Livingston, of New York, became governor of New Jersey and was a militant Patriot. There were three Livingston colonels in the Patriot Army from New York. However, Philip John Livingston, the sheriff of Dutchess County, and his entire family fled to the Loyalist sanctuary in New York City, where his sons became officers in the British army and he became the British superintendent and manager of confiscated rebel (American) estates within the British lines. Gilbert Livingston was a captain in Arnold's American Legion, and John W. Livingston was a captain in Fanning's Loyalists.

During the Revolutionary War, many churches were destroyed and desecrated. The Old South Church in Boston was used as a riding school by the British Cavalry and so was one of the Dutch Reformed churches in New York City, while another was used as a hospital. The Presbyterian churches suffered the most as the Presbyterians were almost all Whigs or Patriots. The Presbyterian Church at Newtown, Long Island, had its steeple sawed off and was used as a prison and guardhouse until it was torn down and its boards used for soldiers' huts. This was the Fish family church for eighty years. The property upon which the church was built was given in 1700 by the author's ancestors who were devoted Presbyterians until the end of the Revolutionary War.

The Presbyterian Church at Crumpond and Mount Holly were burned. The Presbyterian Church at Princeton was stripped of its pews and gallery for fuel by the Hessians. The church at Babylon, Long Island, was torn down by the British, and that in Elizabeth, New Jersey, was burned. Of the two Presbyterian churches in New York City, one was made into a prison and the other was used by the British officers for stabling their horses. More than fifty churches of various denominations throughout the country were entirely destroyed by the British during the course of the war.

At a meeting of the General Assembly at the end of the war, a sermon was preached by President Stiles in which he predicted that the United States would be dominated by three denominations: Congregationalists, Presbyterians, and Episcopalians. Two generations later, the Catholics were number one, Methodists seconds, and Baptists third.

The Presbyterian clergy in New York and their congregations were ardent Patriots. Gen. John Morin Scott was the fearless, outspoken leader of the Sons of Liberty, along with Isaac Sears and General McDougal. The three Patriot Presbyterian clergymen, Rodgers, Mason, and McKnight, were constant as the North Star in their denunciations of British usurpations by Parliament and the autocratic King George III. They joined the band of American refugees from British military bondage for seven long years.

There was a Scottish farmer living in a western township of Ulster County, N.Y., who was a staunch Presbyterian and believed in the doctrine of predestination. During the Revolutionary War, he carried his musket while tending his farm. One of his friends said to him, "Why do you, believing in predestination, bother taking your musket?" He replied, "Friend, I don't want to disappoint the Lord when I shoot a predestined Indian."

Among the American patriots of Scottish origin in New York State besides the Livingston family were Alexander Hamilton; General Richard Montgomery of Rhinebeck, killed in the attack on Quebec; General Alexander (Lord Sterling); General Alexander McDougal; General John Morin Scott; the Hon. John Sloss Hobart; the Hon. Samuel Mitchell; the Rev. Dr. Johnson Mason;

the Rev. John McKnight; the Rev. Dr. John Rodgers; and the Rev. Tillery.

The following is a list of sixty mostly American Patriots of Scottish origin: the Armstrongs, Bairds, Bethunes, Bradfords, Broomes, Bruces, Buchanans, Burnses, Campbells, Chrysties, Clarksons, Cochrans, Douglases, Erskines, Fentons, Finchs, Fosters, Fultons, Furgusons, Giles, Grahams, Haddens, Haldanes, Halletts, Hammersleys, Harpers, Harrisons, Hazards, Humes, Irvings, Jaukes, Johnsons, Jonses, Kings, Kirks, Malcolms, Maxwells, Mckessons, Mckinstrys, Millers, Montroses, Mortons, Neilsons, Nicholls, Palmers, Patersons, Phoenixes, Pophams, Robinsons, Rutherfords, Sears, Shippens, Spratts, Stebins, Stewarts, Talbots, Thompsons, Williamses, and Wilsons.

Soon after the end of the Revolutionary War, the Gracie, Lenox, Sloan, and Watson families settled in New York, and later on the Carnegies, Armors, and Mellons in other parts of the nation.

Captain John Waddell, was one of the first members of the Masonic Society of the City of New York. He was one of the original twenty-three whose certificates of membership are all dated the same day, viz.: January 8, 1770. That list deserves to be preserved. No. 1 was Captain Leonard Lispenard; No. 2 was John Leake; No. 3, Linus King; 4, Robert Benson.

Thomas Randell was No. 5; Thomas Witter, 6; Daniel Stiles, 7; David Dickson, 8; William Mercier, 9; Henry Law, 10; William Masterson, 11; Anthony Rutgers, 12; Peter Berton, 13; John Finglass, 14; Isaac Sheldon, 15; James Wright, 16; Robert Dale, 17; Israel Munds, 18; James Nicholson, 19; William Thompson, 20; Thomas Doran, 21; Joseph Rose, 22; John Waddell, 23; Patrick Dennis, 24; Henry Benson, 25; Thomas Farmer, 26; Daniel Tingley, 27; Thomas Randall, Jr., 28; Roger Richards, 29; James Prince, 30; Alexander Kidd, 31; John Stevenson, 32; Geo. Fowler, 33. All of them were famous sea captains in their day, and most of Scottish origin.

The French Huguenots in New York

The Huguenots, persecuted in France because of their Protestant convictions, were compelled to flee from their native land to save their lives. They sought safety in Holland, England, and other nations after the revocation of the Edict of Nantes. But like most refugees they were without funds or influence and a number became a burden to Holland and England. Consequently, they were encouraged to seek a new homeland in America.

The Huguenots were generally well educated, of strong character, industrious, and helped by integrity and ability in business, political, and governmental life of both New Amsterdam and later New York under the British rule.

The Bayards, Delanceys, DePeysters, Cortelyous, Jays, DuBoises, DeForrests, Delaplanes, LaMontagnes, Prases, and the Raplejes played a prominent part under both the Dutch in New Amsterdam and the English in New York.

The Huguenots under the British settled in New York City, Long Island, New Rochelle, and in New Paltz, Ulster County, N.Y. There were among them able men with great gifts of leadership such as John Jay who became chief justice of the U.S. and governor of New York, and was one of the leaders of American Patriots from the very beginning of the American Revolution. Most of the Huguenots were staunch Patriots: Berriens, Boudinots, Careaus, Dekays, Goelets, Izards, Ezra l'Hommedieu, LaMontagnes, Leroys, Peirets, Pintards, Sicards and Tiebouts.

Among the Loyalists were the Desbrosses, Gerards, Lispenards, DeForests, Gautiers, and the Duryees. Some of the most important Huguenot families, the Delanceys, the Bayards, and the dePeysters, held office under the British military government during the Revolutionary War.

The Huguenots flourished under the Dutch rule and continued to be prominent and successful under the English in New York.

In 1680, a small group of Huguenots settled near Charleston, South Carolina, for the purpose of cultivating silkworms and vineyards. These Huguenot families prospered: they owned rice plantations and many of them became leaders in South Carolina society. Such families as the Laurens, Marions, Pingrees, Petigrus, Hugers, Ravenels, deSaussures, Legares, Simons, Manigaults, and Pochers were mostly on the side of the Patriots during the war.

The Huguenots succeeded in establishing a unique and historic small settlement at New Paltz about 1677, thirteen years after Peter Stuyvesant was forced to surrender New Amsterdam to the British. There were twelve patentees, most of whom built solid, comfortable, greystone houses which are still well preserved. Two of the patentee families, the DuBoises and Crispells, came to New Amsterdam in 1660, then governed by Peter Stuyvesant. The other patentees arrived in New York fifteen years later under British rule. The families of these patentees have played important roles for generations in county and state affairs: DuBois, Hasbrouck, Lefevre, Deyo, Bevier, Crispell, and Frere. Other Huguenot families who lived in New Paltz were the Cantines, Rutans, Cottons, and Leroys, and many, like the Roosas, Eltings, and Schoonmakers of Ulster County, are intermarried with the original New Paltz families.

In the early days of the Republic, the Congress elected a president or presiding officer who was actually the head of the government and was virtually the president of the United States with strictly limited powers. Among the first half-dozen presidents of Congress were three French Huguenots: Henry Laurens of South Carolina (Huguenot); John Jay of N.Y., who was afterwards chief justice of the U.S. and also minister to both Spain and Britain (Huguenot); and Elias Boudinot (Huguenot) of N.J. and N.Y., who was the U.S. commissioner in charge of the exchange of prisoners, and a friend of Washington's. Lawrence Washington, George Washington's grandfather, married a French Huguenot.

Although the Huguenots were few in numbers compared to other immigrants, they held very important positions in our government. Four descendents of the Bayard family, one of the oldest Huguenot families, became U.S. senators, which is still a record. The Gerards were one of the Huguenot families under the Dutch rule in N.Y. However, like the Bayards, they were Loyalists during the Revolutionary War. The Hon. James W. Gerard was our ambassador to Germany at the time of World War I, and Col. James W. Gerard, his nephew, was President-General of the Order of Lafayette, and past-president of the Sons of the American Revolution of New York State.

Paul Revere and Fanueil of Boston were both Huguenots and active Patriots at the start of the war.

Huguenots prospered in all walks of life and, although comparatively small in numbers, have helped to build the United States. The following is a list of 47 Huguenot families, mostly Patriots, omitting those already mentioned: Alliers, Beviers, Bontecous, Briells, Bouchards, Boutilliers, Canons, Daubennys, DeGrushes, Delanoes, Demarests, Denyses, Depeaus, Deyos, Desiles, DuBoises, Dumonts, DePuis, Franchots, Garniers, Gouveneurs, Guinos, Hasbroucks, Kortrights, Legrands, Lamoureauxs, Lefevres, LeQuiers, Lamberts, Mesiers, Michels, Neufvilles, Noels, Perrins, Parmentiers, Pelletreaus, Raynals, Richards, Rolands, Romanies, Roberts, Rombauts, Roosins, Sanfords, Tiebouts, Vignauds, and the Vincents.

The Early Germans in New York

There is some question whether Peter Minuit, the Dutch director of the New Netherlands Colony in 1626, was German-born in the Rhineland, or a French Huguenot. If he was a German, he was the first one of distinction in New Amsterdam (New York). It was Minuit who purchased the entire island of Manhattan from the Indians, for 60 guilders ($24 in gold), the greatest real estate deal in history. He built a stone fort at the tip of Manhattan, now called the Battery. He, however, became involved with the large feudal landowners and after seven years was recalled by the Dutch West India Company. He subsequently persuaded the Swedish government to establish a colony of Swedes on the Delaware River near the present city of Wilmington.

Minuit was appointed the governor and built Fort Christiana, where he died and was buried in 1641. The Germans claim him as one of their own and so do the Huguenots. The reader can take his choice.

Later on, Peter Stuyvesant, the governor of the New Netherlands, with his Dutch troops had no trouble in capturing Fort Christiana and taking possession of the territory occupied by the Swedes.

The first really great undisputed German who had a distinguished career under both the Dutch and English was Jacob Leisler, who was born in Frankfort and joined the Dutch West India Company as a soldier. He became a highly successful trader and shipowner, and married into one of the more important families in New York. He eventually became lt.-governor during the transition period in England from James II to William and Mary in 1688. Leisler antagonized the rich landowners by his advocacy of the political rights of the middle-class Dutch and English against the prevailing autocracy and plutocracy of the influential proprietors. They brought charges of treason against him with Governor Sloughter, who condemned Leisler and his son-in-law Milborne to death in what is now considered a disgraceful miscarriage of justice. History indicates that Leisler's enemies persuaded Governor Sloughter when he was drunk, to sign his death warrant. A few years later the English Parliament, realizing the great injustice done, restored all property and civil rights to his family. Leisler was the first champion of freedom, democracy, and civil rights in New York State. He was the first American martyr in support of those freedoms later inscribed in our Declaration of Independence.

Twenty thousand persecuted Palatine Germans whose lands had been devastated by war fled in 1708 to England and to Holland where relief was provided. But they, like other refugees, were shipped to the unpopulated lands in America. Most of them went to Philadelphia, but some reached New York in 1709 and were provided with homesites near Newburgh and on the west side of the Hudson. They stayed there for a number of years clearing land and planting corn. They fished and hunted deer, turkeys, and other game for food. There was an abundance of wild strawberries, raspberries, grapes, and nuts. These German refugees received very little help from the New York officials who finally told them that they had no legal right to some of the land which they had improved. Embittered by this mistreatment, they decided to move to the more hospitable province of Pennsylvania. Some trekked over the hills to William Penn's province, and others went north to Schoharie and to the Mohawk River where a number settled. Their descendents joined the Patriotic Militia under General Herkimer in fighting against the English and Mohawk Indians. Many of the Palatine Germans moved down the Susquehanna into the promised and friendly land of Governor Penn. Thirty-five thousand German exiles settled in Pennsylvania. By the time of the American Revolution, the number had doubled.

These Germans largely entered America by way of Philadelphia. Thousands of Germans went to Virginia and the Carolinas and into the interior, mixing with the pioneer Scots and English.

During the Revolution, many of the Germans, particularly in Pennsylvania, remained neutral, whereas in New York State most of them entered the militia and served on the side of the Patriots against the Indians.

George III, king of England, was of German origin and due to the large number of Hessian soldiers in New York City German was recognized as a second language there as well as in Philadelphia. Just before the Revolution, the Germans comprised ten percent of the population of New York State. Among their leaders who sided with the Americans after the Declaration of Independence were General von Steuben, the great drillmaster; General DeKalb, killed in the Battle of Camden; General Muhlenburg, of Pennsylvania; and General Nicholas Herkimer, killed in the battle of Oriskany.

Among the early Germans in New York and New Jersey at the time of the Revolution were the Arculariuses, Col. Sebastian Bauman, Beekmans, Bashes, Brans, Fischers, Flaglers, Frosts, Grims, the Rev. Daniel Gross, Hoffmans, Kierstedes, the Rev. Dr. Kunze, Laights, Leislers, Lorrilards, Luckers, Ludwigs, Malecks, Markses, Merkels, Meirs, Oertleys, Rockefellers, Schultzs, Shemeds, Snyders, Spies, Stamlers, Tillmans, Travers, General von Steuben, Waddels, Webbers, Weises, Wiegands, Wilmerdings, Col. Weisenfels, Wills, Wisners, and Zengers. The Astors, Schieffelings, and Doctor Anthon arrived in New York just after the end of the war.

At the time of the Revolutionary War, there was a large German farm population along the Mohawk River in Tyron County. They suffered terribly from the cruel raids of Butler's brutal Rangers and Joseph Brandt's Indians. General Nicholas Herkimer led a militia force of 800, mostly Germans, to the relief of Fort Stanwix. Both

36

sides suffered heavy losses. General Herkimer had his horse shot and he was seriously wounded. He was propped up on his saddle on the ground facing the enemy, which he insisted on, and continued to encourage his German riflemen. Although surrounded and outnumbered, they stood their ground until the Indians retired from the battle due to heavy losses. General Herkimer, the valiant old soldier, was taken to his nearby home on the Mohawk, and died there a few days later of his wounds.

When the American colonies revolted in 1776, it is estimated that there were about 18,000 Germans in New York State out of a population of 180,000. Most of them were farmers on both sides of the Hudson River all the way to Albany, and also along the Mohawk and Unadilla, and throughout Tyron County. They were not anti-British, but were generally opposed to kings and royalty which inclined them to support the American cause. (See chapter on German builders of America in appendix.) There are more Germans now in America, except British, than any other ethnic group.

5

The early Irish, Polish, Italian and Scandinavians in America

The Irish were divided between the Protestant Irish and the Catholic. But there were not more than 100 Irish Catholic families in New York City before the Revolution. On July 4, 1776, the birthday of our nation, there was not a single Catholic church in New York City. The city was 96 percent Protestant, 1 percent Irish Catholic, 1 percent Latin American Catholic, 1 percent Jews, and 1 percent other nationalities. Today, 199 years later, Protestants compose only 20 percent of the population, compared to 45 percent Roman Catholics, 30 percent Jews, 3 percent Greek Orthodox, 1 percent other sects, and 10 percent no religious affiliations.

The first Roman Catholic congregation in New York was formed in 1783 when the British abandoned New York to Washington's army. In 1785, the cornerstone of the first Catholic church was laid at the southeast corner of Barclay and Church Streets. The building was completed in November, 1786, and was known as St. Peter's Church and stood there until the present church was erected in 1888.

Until the building of St. Patrick's Cathedral, it was the only Catholic church in the city. In the early days, it received most of its financial support from the Spaniards, Cubans, and South Americans. In 1789, there were 22 churches representing various denominations: Episcopalians, Dutch Reform, Presbyterian, Lutheran, Huguenots, Baptists, Methodists, German Reform, Quakers, Moravians, Jewish, and Catholic.

Anti-Catholicism was prevalent in all the states except Maryland, Pennsylvania, Delaware, and Virginia for many years after the Revolution. Nine of the thirteen states had a clause in their Constitution that no one but a Protestant could hold public office. Strangely enough, New York, Connecticut, and Massachusetts did not revise these restrictions for a generation or more, New York in 1806, Connecticut in 1818, and Massachusetts in 1833, which now has the highest percentage of Catholics in the U.S.—over fifty percent.

Much earlier, General Washington had outlawed the "ridiculous and childish custom of burning the effigy of the Pope during the celebration of Guy Fawkes Day," but anti-Catholicism was too deeply rooted to be banished by such gestures. It endured for many decades. It had numerous bitter enemies among the Huguenot exiles from France such as John Jay, governor of N.Y. and chief justice of the United States, who opposed concessions.

Redpath's *History of the United States* states that in 1784 there were 30,000 Catholics in America out of a population of over three million. There were 16,000 Catholics in Maryland, 600 in New England, and 1,700 in New York State. Charles Carroll of Maryland, a Catholic, signed the Declaration of Independence and was the leading citizen of that state for many years.

The Roman communion in 1785 counted only 24 priests and 30,000 souls, mostly in Maryland and Philadelphia. The first mass to be celebrated openly in Boston was in November, 1788, by a former chaplain of the French navy. The small number of Roman Catholics in the colonies were under the jurisdiction of a bishop in London. At the end of the Revolution, Pope Pius VI in 1784 appointed the Rev. John Carroll of Baltimore to represent him. He was consecrated six years later as a bishop and his see covered the whole United States.

In 1683, Col. Thomas Dongan, the first Catholic governor of New York, which was then 98 percent Protestant, was looked upon with considerable suspicion due to religious grounds. However, his administration was one of the best in the long line of British governors. He was responsible for having had enacted a Charter of Liberties and Privileges, creating an assembly that had supreme legislative authority, and provided that there should be no taxation without its consent. It was the beginning of home rule in New York City, and of civil liberty. Unfortunately, Governor Dongan was recalled because his royal master, James II, did not approve of popular government or of being deprived of the power to tax.

There were numerous sailing ships between New York and Irish ports just before the Revolutionary War. They regularly traded with Cork, Dublin, Londonderry, and Belfast, and brought back Irish wool, linen, beef, butter, livestock, salmon, whiskey, and emigrants.

The Irish for centuries have been real fighters and seldom dodge a good fight. Although few in numbers, except in Maryland, they were mostly on the side of the Patriots and served courageously throughout the war. General Sullivan of New Hampshire, who led our armed forces in the invasion of the Iroquois Indian-territory in New York, and Commodore Barry were outstanding officers.

The following is a list of forty Irish Catholics living in New York at the time of the Revolutionary War or who, as Patriot exiles, returned when the British evacuated the city: Shiel Allay, George Barnwell, Thomas Bebe, Thomas S. Brady, James Brown, Gibbon

Burke, John Chambers, William Constable, William Edgar, John Flack, Sampson Fleming, Hugh Gaines, John Haggerty, Jacob Hankey, Jacob Harvey, Cornelius Heeny, William Hill, Felix Ingolesby, Joseph Kernochan, Henry Laberty, Dominick Lynch, Alexander Macomb, General Maunsel, James McBride, Daniel McCormick, Dr. McNever, William Mooney, Andrew Morris, William Niblo, the Rev. Nugent, Thomas Prendergast, the Rev. William O'Brien, Carlisle Pollock, Thomas Roach, John Shaw, James Steward, Thomas Suffern, Charles Taylor, Oliver Templeton, Robert Waddell, and Robert White.

They were so few that they were not an important factor. The reason why there were so few Irish Catholics in New York under the British rule was simply because Catholics were very generally persona non grata at that time. The advent of Irish Catholics to New York began soon after the evacuation of the city by the British army in 1783. It was not until the potato famine in 1845 that the influx of Catholic Irish began on a big scale and continued steadily for the next fifty years, until today there are as many Irish Catholics in New York City as in Dublin.

Generals Kosciuszko and Pulaski: Two Brave Polish Volunteers Who Fought for American Freedom and Independence

There were very few people of Polish origin in New York City before the Revolutionary War. That war, based on freedom and independence, appealed to two great freedom-loving Poles who came over to join Washington's army as volunteers.

Thaddeus Kosciuszko, a young Polish engineer officer who was already known as a fighter for freedom in Poland, added to his fame during our War for Independence. Washington was very much impressed with him and made him a brigadier general of engineers. He designed the fortifications of the American army at Saratoga and thereby helped beat back Burgoyne's army when they made their final attack. Later on, he had charge of the fortifications at West Point. His plans made it into the most powerful fortress in our country. He became a friend of Washington and was highly respected by all the American officers. Later on, he was to become the commander-in-chief of the Polish army and, with limited numbers and armaments, he sought to maintain the independence of Poland against the might and numbers of the Imperial Russian Army. But before he was finally defeated and captured, he became enshrined in the hearts of the Polish people as one of their greatest heroes.

When Empress Catherine died, he was released from prison, along with his friend Count Julian Ursyn Niemcewicz, provided that they would go to France or America. He and Neimcewicz came to the United States about 1800. Kosciuszko received a hero's welcome throughout the nation as one of the greatest living freedom-fighters. After a short time, he returned to Europe and later to Poland to continue the struggle for freedom. Niemcewicz stayed in America and became tutor to Peter Kean, the son of the author's great-great-grandmother, Mrs. Susan Livingston Kean whose husband, John Kean, a former member of Congress, had died a few years before. The old story was repeated, but whether Niemcewicz fell in love with her first or she did with him is unknown. But at any rate, they got married and lived at the famous Liberty Hall, her uncle's mansion while he was governor of New Jersey, during the Revolutionary War.

After five years of married life at Elizabethtown, now Elizabeth, New Jersey, he informed his wife that he had to go to Poland to recover his family estates, as Napoleon had freed Poland. Niemcewicz, who was one of the foremost writers, poets, and statesmen of Poland, was welcomed back by the government and his property was restored. But when Napoleon was driven out of Poland by the Russians, Niemcewicz retired to Paris, the mecca of exiled Poles, where he spent the next thirty years of his life. His devoted wife back in Elizabeth sent him $100 a month, which was equivalent to $1,000 today. He lived comfortably on this remittance the rest of his life, urging the restoration of the freedom and independence of Poland. He ranks with the top Poles of history. The author has inherited most of his letters written to his wife and members of his family which are now considered historic. Niemcewicz claimed he adopted his stepson, and that his descendents would also be Polish citizens.

There was another very gallant Pole who volunteered his services in the American cause of freedom—Casimir Pulaski. He was commissioned as a young general of cavalry under General Lincoln in the southern campaign. His command was known as Pulaski's Legion. He was a brave and able officer who was tragically killed leading his soldiers in the seige of Savannah.

The names of these two valiant Polish officers—Kosciuszko and Pulaski—are part and parcel of American history. The seven million Poles who live in the United States today have every reason to be proud of these two great, heroic freedom-fighters. Strange as it may be, there was another Polish officer, Count Grabowski, who served as a major in the British armed forces and was killed leading his grenadiers in the capture of Fort Montgomery, New York. No matter whether he was on the wrong side, he was certainly a courageous officer who was wounded three times in the attack and died shortly afterwards.

Since the American Revolution, millions of Poles, persecuted by the harsh military government of Imperial Russia and more recently by the brutal Communist dictatorship at Moscow, have sought freedom in the United

States. Here they have helped to build America and to live in peace and freedom. They are among our most loyal citizens.

Famous Italian Navigators Discovered America and New York

There were few Italians in the United States until after the Civil War, but no one played a more important part in the discovery of America and of New York harbor than native Italian navigators in command of ships under foreign flags. First there was Christopher Columbus, born in Genoa, who ranks as one of the greatest discoverers in history. He commanded a small fleet of three ships in 1492 flying the flag of Spain under Ferdinand and Isabella. Next came Amerigo Vespuci, born in Florence who, in command of a Portuguese ship, discovered a large part of the South American continent in 1498. One of the most important map-makers at that time, gave his first name to the American continent.

Another Italian, Giovanni Verranzano, discovered New York harbor while captain of the French ship *Dolphin* in 1524, eighty-five years before Henry Hudson, an English navigator in a Dutch ship, sailed up the Hudson River as far as Albany. John Cabot, also of Italian origin, from Venice, was captain of an English ship that surveyed New York and the adjacent coast in the year 1498. Verrazano actually entered New York harbor and anchored there. He left a description of the harbor and of the Indians who flocked to see his ship. These Italian navigators were the advance guard of millions of Italians who followed their footsteps 100 years ago, and today, both in New York State and other parts of the nation, represent the third largest group of Europeans in the United States. The first being British, then Germans, and next Italians, followed closely by the Irish.

Americans of Italian origin have had a tendency to

congregate in the larger cities. There are over one million in New York City, and almost as many in Philadelphia and Chicago, and large numbers in Los Angeles and San Francisco. Utica, New York, is predominantly an Italian city. Fiorello LaGuardia and Vincent Impelliterri were former mayors of New York. The present mayor of Philadelphia is Frank L. Rizzo, and that of San Francisco, Joseph Aliota.

Fordham University in the Bronx, which was for many years a citadel of Irish dominence, has changed recently and Americans of Italian origin now outnumber all other students. In Brooklyn, the largest borough of New York City, the son of an Italian barber now presides over the large Catholic community. The most outstanding American of Italian origin, Mr. A. P. Giannini, was born in San Jose, California in 1870. He founded the Bank of America, which is today the largest bank in the United States and probably in the world. Mr. Giannini succeeded from a small beginning because he always had faith in the destiny of America.

Americans of Italian origin over the years have contributed by their industry in helping to build the United States into the greatest, strongest, and freest nation in the world. Their sons served in the American armed forces in World Wars I and II in greater proportions than any other ethnic group. They brought to the United States the knowledge and love of music and cultural arts, and have held high positions in all aspects of American life.

Scandinavians in America

It is historically true that about the year A.D. 1000, blond-bearded Norsemen, in their Viking ships from Iceland, discovered the northeastern part of America. They called it Vineland, because it abounded with wild grapes. Their settlements, however, were bleak, cold, and unprofitable. They were of short duration and were soon forgotten except in Scandinavian saga and song.

Eric the Red of Iceland was the heroic discoverer. If these Vikings had landed in New York, it might have been a different story. This was 500 years before Christopher Columbus discovered America and established a settlement in Hispaniola which was enduring.

The first Swedish settlers arrived in America in 1638 and founded a small colony on the Delaware River near Wilmington, called New Sweden.

Peter Minuit, the former governor of New Netherlands, was their director. He built Fort Christiana, and in 1641 this adventurous leader died and was buried there. The settlement was small and unsupported from Sweden. The one-legged Dutch governor, Peter Stuyvesant, had no trouble in capturing Fort Christiana and shipping its military defenders back to Sweden. Some of the Swedish colonists remained, as did some of the old Swedish names of places and families. Some of these early Delaware Swedes were prominent in the Revolutionary War: John Hansen was president of the Congress in 1781, and John Morton was a signer of the Declaration of Independence. His vote made the necessary majority in the Pennsylvania delegation for the Declaration of Independence. Captain Jacob Loper was prominent under the Dutch.

Although there were few Americans of Swedish origin who fought in our Revolutionary armed forces, there were many who served as volunteers in the French army under Rochambeau. One of these was Count von Fersen, who distinguished himself as an aide to Rochambeau in the seige of Yorktown. He and another Swedish officer, Colonel Curt von Stedingk, were elected to the Order of the Cincinnati, composed of officers who served under Washington in our armed forces. There were also others who served in that war with honor: Baron von Fock, who distinguished himself at

Yorktown; Baron Nordenskjold, who was active in the seige at Savannah and later became vice-admiral in the Swedish navy; and Carl Raab, who was killed in the battle of Savannah.

In the last 100 years, millions of Scandinavians from Sweden, Norway, Denmark, and Iceland have migrated to the United States. Most of them moved out to the northwestern states, particularly Minnesota and Wisconsin where they are predominant. The author served in Congress for 25 years and knew the Americans of Swedish, Norwegian, and Danish origin who were members of Congress, and admired them. They were able, industrious, and highly patriotic, whether Democrats or Republicans, both in the House of Representatives and the Senate of the United States.

6

The Capture of Quebec by the British in 1759 ended French control of Canada

There were four Anglo-French intercolonial wars prior to the Declaration of Independence, actually involving the American colonies and Canada. The first three of these wars originated in Europe and extended to North America as incidents of European conflicts. They unleashed, in New York and other colonies, a bloody "open season" between Frenchmen and Englishmen and their respective Indian allies. The fourth war, known as the French and Indian War, started in 1754 as a preliminary of the Seven Years' War, 1756-1763, the most titanic conflict the world had seen up to that time. It was fought not only in America, but in Europe, the West Indies, Africa, on the high seas, and as far east as the Philippines. The principal adversaries in Europe were England and Prussia on one side, arrayed against France, Spain, and Austria. The bloodiest fighting was in Germany, where Frederick the Great won his title by defeating the French, Austrian, and Russian armies. The British played a comparatively small part, but provided Frederick liberally with gold and needed supplies. Fortunately for the British, the French were so involved in this protracted European war that they were unable to send adequate forces to protect and defend Canada and their colonial empire in the West Indies. "America was conquered in Germany" was a shrewd observation by Britain's William Pitt.

In 1754, the British held an Intercolonial Congress at Albany, New York, near the Iroquois territory. The Indian chiefs were loaded with presents and urged to keep their scalping knives sharp and be ready to participate in the oncoming war with the French Algonquin Indians. The real purpose of the Albany congress was to unite the colonials in a common defense against the French and their Indian allies along their northern and western boundaries.

The beginning of the Seven Years' War was disastrous for the English colonials. General Braddock, an experienced British officer in European warfare, with a strong detachment of British regulars and colonials amounting to 2,000 soldiers, including George Washington, started out from Virginia to capture Fort Duquesne (Pittsburgh) on the fork of the Ohio. Braddock's army was ambushed by a small French and Indian command. The Indians fighting from behind trees poured a murderous fire into the ranks of the Redcoats. George Washington, the fearless aide of General Braddock, had two of his horses shot and General Braddock was mortally wounded. His defeat had tragic results for the American colonists as it inspired the Indians and their French allies to take the offensive all the way from North Carolina to New York. To offset Braddock's defeat, the British war ministry in London ordered a full-scale invasion of Canada in 1756 as the war in America merged into a world conflict.

Fortunately for the British, they had a powerful, dynamic leader, William Pitt, known as the "Great Commoner," who believed in upholding the interests of his country. Pitt was the active organizer of British victory in Canada. He ordered an expedition against

Lewisburg, the foremost fortress of the French in Canada. Its capture was the first significant British victory since the defeat of the British army at Ticonderoga in New York. It was soon followed by the intrepid 32-year-old General James Wolfe, who out-maneuvered and defeated the French army at Quebec under the equally gallant commander, General Montcalm. Both Wolfe and Montcalm were killed in the fighting.

The battle and capture of Quebec ranks as one of the most important victories in British and American history. It swept France out of America, and made the British the sole dominant power in North America and the strongest naval and colonial power in the world.

7

New York City just prior to the Revolutionary War was a small attractive replica of London, its 18th-century life and customs

Nature gave New York City one of the finest harbors in the world. With that inheritance, it was inevitable that New York would become a thriving and important market for the goods, not only from Europe and the West Indies, but from all parts of the world. Shipping was and still is one of the major factors in the growth and prosperity of New York. For the first 200 years, sailing ships of all types and sizes carried commerce to and from the Port of New York.

The early Dutch realized the need of small trading vessels to conduct commerce with the West Indies and New England. Ship-building was begun by the Dutch, and developed and enlarged later by the British. The surrender of New Amsterdam in 1664 by its courageous, irrascible, peg-legged governor, Peter Stuyvesant, to the British under Colonel Nicolls, was an unexpected boon to New York. It enhanced its overseas trade and that with New England and the West Indies. Britannia then ruled the waves, and its merchant ships, protected by the British navy, dominated the sea lanes. New York soon became the most active and largest port in America, and has maintained that supremacy until the present day.

New York, at the beginning of the Revolutionary War in 1775-1776, was a small, compact town of 22,000, built largely on the East River opposite Brooklyn, because of better harbor facilities there that afforded protection for the numerous sailing ships. It was essentially a seaport town within the finest harbor on the eastern coast.

The buildings extended from the Battery opposite Governor's Island to the Commons, the present City Hall Park, a distance of about one mile. In breadth, it was a little more than half a mile from the banks of the Hudson to the East River.

The houses were mostly built of brick and two stories high. Many had balconies on the roof where the occupants could enjoy the views of the opposite shores and the cooling breezes in the summer. Most of the streets had rows of trees on each side to provide shade from the summer heat. In the summer, there were numerous birds chirping in the foliage and quantities of singing tree-toads or frogs that made an incessant racket, much to the annoyance of the homeowners. The streets were paved but, except for Broadway and one or two others, they were generally narrow.

The city was clean and neat because most homeowners took pride in their gardens. The Dutch inhabitants retained the formal Dutch gardens, but the wealthy English merchants perferred the English style of landscape gardening. There were also French and Italian gardens, and in some cases the famous grottos of English estates were emulated.

New York society, despite many prominent Dutch and Huguenot families, was fundamentally based on English customs and habits. New York was actually a small replica of London. It was a prosperous and attractive small town. Both Boston and Philadelphia were larger and continued to be until 1800. English ships brought English goods of all kinds, including the latest London fashions, to New York.

The most important and fashionable residential streets were lower Broadway, Wall Street, Crown Street (Liberty), Maiden Lane, Little Queens (Cedar), King Street (Pine), and William and Nassau Streets. The chief business centers were Queens Street (Pearl), Water, Little Dock Street, and Hanover Square.

The center of social and cultural life was at Fort George at the Battery (Bowling Green), where the governor's mansion was located. Prior to the fighting at Lexington, Concord, and Bunker Hill, all social and army life revolved around the colonial governor, representing the king. The court was composed of his counsellors, judges, army officers, Anglican ministers, the president and staff at Kings College, and prominent Tory families: the DeLanceys, DePeysters, Stuyvesants, Bayards, Coldens, Crugers, Waltons, Watts, Ludlows, Philipses, Beverly Robinson, Roger Morris, and Captain Kennedy, who had a very large house at One Broadway. It was at the governor's mansion that dinners, dances, and other festivities were regularly held on the king's or other royal birthdays, and receptions for the important visitors to New York.

Political tensions had become so acute just prior to the Revolution that the great Whig families—the Livingstons, Gouveneur and Lewis Morris, Jays, Van Cortlands, Beekmans, Clintons, Duanes, Lewises, Scotts, McDougals, and the Alexanders—were no longer invited to the governor's receptions or to Loyalist festivities.

Fifteen percent of the population of New York were slaves and served as domestic servants or in the shops.

The period from the advent of George I in 1714 to the Revolutionary War is known as the "Golden Age" of New York. Among the most prominent members of the mercantile and social life of that period were the Stuyvesants, Waltons, Verplanks, Beekmans, DePeysters,

Alexanders, Philipses, Van Cortlands, Duanes, Livingstons, Jays, Morrises, Bayards, Lispenards, Rutgers, Delanceys, and Roosevelts. There are today in New York many descendents of these old merchant families. Half of them, when the Declaration of Independence was signed, joined the American or Patriot side, and the rest remained either neutralists or pro-British.

This chapter depicts largely the life of the more affluent merchants and officials, but the wage-earners also lived well in smaller but comfortable houses, less ostentacious, but well provided for in the necessities of life. The only means of getting around in New York was by walking, by carriage or horseback. The distances at that time were short, so people were naturally accustomed to walk to business and to the markets. The more prosperous had stables on their property. Almost everyone who could afford it had a horse, as riding was not only a pastime, but a necessity.

It is all very well to speak of New York as being in its "Golden Age" during the 18th century. It was truly a small, clean city of trees, flowers, and gardens, with an abundance of fresh air. Surrounded by rivers on two sides and on the south, it touched the bay, and on the north it extended for fourteen miles of meadows, lakes, woods, and farms to the Harlem River. However, New York City today, despite its maddening crowds and polluted air, enjoys many conveniences unknown in the 18th century. There were no gas or steam heat for heating or cooking, no electricity for lighting; candles and lamps were the only means of lighting. There were no telephones, no automobiles, no trains, no airplanes, no steamships and, more important than all, no running water, which made bathing and toilet facilities primitive.

On the other hand, the social life in New York City 200 years ago was very pleasant, and much more restful and peaceful. The manners, culture, and the dress of women and costumes of men, furniture, china and silverware were very fine and compared with the best in London.

The New York 18th-century lady, like her present-day descendent, spent a great deal of time at her dressing table, covered with numerous bottles of perfume, jars of facial cream, rouge, powder, and skin unguents. The use of cosmetics was indulged in so extensively that a number of the reigning beauties became victims of it in London.

Horace Walpole, after taking his beautiful niece and her friend to dinner said, "They had just refreshed their last layers of red, and looked as handsome as crimson could make them."

The 18th-century beauties and matrons of New York followed very closely the customs, modes, and fashions of London. The arrangement of their hair for many year prior to the Revolution was most elaborate. In the reign of George III, until 1780, it became ever increasingly higher and more eccentric. For many years before the Revolution, there were forty wigmakers and hairdressers registered in New York. In view of the complicated, fashionable hair towers in vogue, it was impossible for the New York ladies to dress their own hair. It was an absurd fashion, but prevailed both in New York and London, despite contemporary ridicule, until the end of the Revolutionary War.

The most distinguishing part of women's dress was the hoop. This was a great bell-shaped petticoat lined with whalebone and made of rich and flowered brocade. Jonathan Swift, the famous English satirist wrote in 1730:

> Five hours (and who can do it less in?)
> By haughty Celia spent in dressing.
> The goddess from her chamber issues,
> Arrayed in lace, brocade and tissues.

The young ladies of the 18th century were schooled

in sewing and embroidering, and had that advantage over the present-day fair sex. However, they had several things in common—they loved to shop and dress well, and practiced economy at home by sewing and repairing their own clothes, perhaps by necessity as it may have been difficult to secure that type of help then, as it is in our generation.

The luxury, extravagance, and frivolities of the wealthy gave offense to some of the old-fashioned and more sedate people. One writer, in 1739 apparently believed that New York "was going to the dogs." The return to a much simpler and less extravagant way of life took place immediately on the reoccupation of New York in 1783, and lasted until Washington was inaugurated there six years later.

Women who live in New York today, representing all elements, spend a great deal of time and money on hairdo's. But 200 years or more ago in New York, hairdressers and peroq makers did a very extensive business.

There were some differences from today's social activities. The young ladies of those days were carefully instructed in manners, etiquette, and courtseying. They spent considerable time in paying social courtesy calls and, of course, attending social and family tea parties. They carried fans, wore gloves, and used lace handkerchiefs. Some even indulged in gold snuff boxes, just as cigarettes today are smoked by both sexes. Religion and church attendance was part and parcel of the family life. No festivities or sports were permitted on the Sabbeth.

In the fashionable society of New York prior to the Revolution, the wife or mother of the children took a great deal of interest in their education. Boys of fourteen were well versed in Latin, Greek, and French, and generally entered college at fifteen. She managed the home, servants, and slaves fairly and intelligently, entertained generously, drove in handsome carriages, and enjoyed the prevailing gaieties and balls.

Newspapers, in announcing weddings, usually had something complimentary to say about the bride, as in the quoted statement of 1759: "Saturday night Mr. John Lawrence of this City merchant, was married to Miss Catherine Livingston, daughter of the Hon. Phillip Livingston, Esq., late of this City, deceased, a very agreeable young lady with a handsome fortune"; "Wednesday night last, Mr. Thomas Marston, son of Mr. Nathaniel Marston, merchant of this City, was married to Miss Kitty Lispenard, daughter of Leonard Lispenard, Esq., of this place, merchant; a most agreeable young lady, possessed of all those good accomplishments that render the married state completely happy."

The New Yorkers of that time apparently were very fond of pets, and particularly of dogs of various breeds. In 1769, Lord Rosehill lost his small "black and white dog of King Charles breed," for which he offered 20 shillings; and in 1773 another dog-lover lost his silver and white pointer that "answers to the name of Ponto." Birds were also popular as pets. Parrots were favorites, and there was a constant importation of parrot cages, as announced in the advertisements of those days.

In 1759, there was a statement in the current newspaper that an innkeeper of Kingsbridge wanted to "dispose of a large collection of canary birds in full plumage and song," and another advertisement was "to buy some Virginia nightingales."

The course of human nature in hundreds of years, and maybe thousands, has not changed very much, as in 1735, a distressed lady in New York, who signed herself as "Mrs. Nameless," wrote to the editor asking advice since she was head over heels in love: "But custom and modesty of my own sex forbids me to reveal it to the dear man I adore." Affairs of the heart and the business of getting a husband formed quite an important part in fashionable New York before the Revolution. In a town where every energy was devoted to money-making, a portionless girl had a small chance of making a desirable match. Many of the young English officers and sons of merchants were fortune-hunters, and the native New Yorker was accustomed to go where money was.

Old New York, for many years before the Revolution, was a gay, pleasure-loving town. It was then, as it is today, filled with gaieties, amusements, and entertainments as well as sports and various pastimes. However, the main similarity is that the same race for wealth that blankets New York today was very much alive there 200 years ago.

A contemporary visitor of New York in 1748 said: "I found it extremely pleasant to walk in the town for it seemed like a garden. The trees are chiefly of two kinds; the water beech is the most numerous and gives an agreeable shade in the summer, by its large and numerous leaves. The locust tree is likewise frequent with its odoriferous scent and there are lime trees and elms."

Georgian New York, before the Declaration of Independence, was a charming, uncrowded city. Most of the houses had their own gardens. The houses were often located in meadows or on the waterfront, unsurpassed in beauty anywhere. These homes were filled with every convenience and stocked with wine cellars containing large assortments of wines from France, Spain, Portugal, and Madeira. The latter was the most popular drink and took the place of modern-day cocktails. Luxuries were brought from the ends of the earth to satisfy the tastes of the well-to-do New Yorkers, and many of them were highly prosperous.

The three largest and finest houses of New York were the Walton, the dePeyster and Alexander homes. They were surrounded by gardens, stables, outhouses, and were larger, and three stories in height. The earliest of these houses belonged to the well-known dePeyster family, built in 1695 on Queen, near Pearl Street, and remained until 1859. It was luxuriously furnished, and later on became the historic residence of Governor Clinton and the headquarters for George Washington.

The Walton house, built in 1744 was the home of Henry Walton, the richest and most successful merchant in New York. My ancestor, Lewis Morris, married his daughter there in 1749. A magnificent entertainment on a great scale was held at the Walton house in 1759 in honor of the victorious British officers who had returned from the battleflields in Canada. The Waltons were Loyalists and remained in New York throughout the war, and so did the dePeysters and the Stuyvesants.

The James Alexander house was the center of social activity prior to the war. He was one of the city's foremost lawyers, and was the father of Lord Sterling who became a general in the Continental Army. It was probably the most luxurious house in New York, filled with all the newest furniture, china, and paintings that London could produce.

How did these rich merchants make their money? In counting houses, in all kinds of commerce, shipping, trade in furs, investments in real estate, farming, or in any trade for profit. Some of them also were engaged in privateering, including the famous Livingston family. The lawyers also, even in those days, made ample fortunes and lived well. The royal governor lived in the greatest luxury and style at Fort George, and his home was the center of all social activity. Governor Burnett had nine Negro slaves, sixteen horses, a chaise, a coach a barge, a four-oared boat, and numerous staff and assistants.

The most fashionable and popular amusement in New York City prior to the Revolution, continued by the British during the war, was dancing. The dances were dignified and rather elaborate. The requirements were to dance well, dress well, look well, and entertain well. In many respects, old New Yorkers lived in a simpler and more courteous way. The hurry and fever of our modern life was unknown. The dances were introduced from England, and were stately but of a lively character, with swift movements of the feet. The round dance was unknown. The country dance (contra) was the favorite. The young ladies generally had dance cards. The present-day jazz music and the twist were non-existent. Snuff-taking seems to have been prevalent and deprevalent among ladies, and formed a favorite subject for the lampooners in New York. "This silly trick of taking snuff is attended with such a coquette air in some young women as to be disagreeable and offensive."

It is only fair and proper, having described the female dress of those days, to mention briefly the costumes of the men. Most of them wore wigs. The usual apparel was black satin breeches with silk stockings and gayly decorated shoes. The waistcoats or vests were generally long and often of white silk embroidered in colors. The coat was always well trimmed and of various colors, open at the front, and the hat a cocked beaver. Men were usually very fastidious about their clothes, and often carried either a sword or a tasseled cane. The only part of their apparel that might have a popular appeal today would be the vests, which were far gayer and more attractive than the somber and colorless vests worn by men of this generation.

The New Yorkers, from 1730 up to the Revolution, lived well and ate well. The Dutch and English brought various native seeds for planting in the new world. The New York gardens were well supplied with beans, corn, peas, turnips, cabbages, parsnips, carrots, potatoes, beets, endives, spinach, radishes, onions, artichokes, asparagus, and a variety of fruits. The pumpkin, thought little of in England, was held in high esteem in New York for use in making pies. They also made a beverage from it. Gardening in old New York was almost a universal pastime.

Fruit trees were cultivated with equal assiduity. The best of English and Dutch stocks were imported and often grafted on the native trees, which produced new and hearty varieties. The consequence was that, in many cases, New York City orchards lost nothing by comparison with the best in Europe. An advertisement in 1769 stated that William Prince of Flushing had the following varieties of fruit trees for sale: English cherries, nectarines, plums, apricots, peaches, pears, apples, and numerous varieties of all of them. Rich New York also imported fruit from the West Indies; oranges and pineapples were regularly on the market. Watermelons were cultivated near the city and grew very large, and it was claimed that they were better than in any other part of North America, though planted in open fields and not in hot beds. Watermelons weighed up to fifty pounds. In August, 1774, an item read, "A watermelon last night was cut at a gentleman's table in New York City [Manhattan up to the Harlem River] that grew in his own garden on this island, that weighed no less than 50 pounds."

There is no question but that the early New Yorkers ate well, drank well, and lived well.

Comparisons are often odious but sometimes interesting and beneficial. The men of the Revolutionary War period in New York drank as much as those of today. They had more time to drink as there were not as many social activities such as present-day theaters, operas, radio, television, and movies. The main difference was there were no cocktail parties. They did not drink as much hard liquor, but consumed quantities of Madeira, port, sherry, and wines, and suffered from gout and rheumatism. The popular drink among the wage-earners was rum, which was imported from the West Indies on a large scale. Whiskey, brandy, gin, and beer were all available in the taverns.

The women of the 18th century in New York drank wines, port, sherry, and Madeira, and there were no alcoholics among them.

In our modern age, the continuous rounds of

61

cocktail parties among the well-to-do have resulted in far too much drinking among American men and women. Cocktail parties have replaced the old tea parties with a vengeance, and with dire results.

Both men and women drink fairly consistently in this club-and-cocktail age. Unfortunately, however, some of both sexes become heavy, consistent drinkers and addicts to alcohol. They are not exactly ornaments at home for peace and harmony of the family and as examples for the children. The ever-increasing divorce rate bears testimony to this. There were virtually no divorces in New York in the 18th century.

Reference has been made to the terrible yellow fever epidemics in New York during the latter part of the 18th century that caused a large number of deaths among the rich and poor alike. In spite of the great progress in medical science, cigarette smoking on a vast scale by men and women is causing numerous deaths by cancer annually. A quarter of a million Americans die every year from cancer from pollution of the air, of the water, and of the food. The cancer death toll each year is fifty times larger than the casualties in the Vietnam War, or almost as much as the entire population of New York State during the Revolutionary War.

There had been very little change in eating or drinking over the 200 years since the Declaration of Independence. The food and drinks are very much the same except for the advent of cocktails, vodka, canned food, ice cream, and hot dogs.

No comparison in women's dress is possible as their styles change frequently.

All that remains of the clean, attractive, little old New York with its trees, flowers, and gardens has gone forever. Only the memories remain, but the same indominable spirit that existed then still remains, and makes New York the greatest financial market and money-making city in the world. The problems are different—

overcrowding, crime in the streets, high cost of living, pollution, and taxation. But there are advantages—easier traveling, electricity, gas for heating, and a steady supply of running water and modern toilets.

It would be puzzling and difficult to express a preference between New York 200 years ago and the great metropolis today. New York before the Revolution was a clean, attractive little city with numerous trees, flowers, and gardens. It was in the midst of its golden age of leisure, tranquility, security, prosperity, and peace. Old New York had an abundance of fresh vegetables, dairy products, and cattle from nearby farms in Queens, Westchester, and northern New Jersey. It also had a great abundance of fresh fish from the Hudson River, nearby streams filled with trout, and from the ocean. It was a fishing and hunting paradise. In addition, the finest commodities from most of the ports of the known world filled New York shops.

The country estates and taverns were only a few miles drive from the present City Hall. It all made for a very alluring, appealing, and liveable city. If you had a wishing stone, which would it be? The small, lovely city, or the great big, modern city of New York with all its conveniences, despite its being overcrowded and saturated with a polluted atmosphere and surrounded by drug addicts, male and female of all ages, in and out of schools and colleges. Would all the modern conveniences outweigh the prevailing corruption, black mail, racial tensions, and threats of violence and bloodshed? The modern conveniences might indicate a favorable balance unless the menace of the world Communist conspiracy with its nuclear weapons, like a devastating red cloud hanging over the Free World, would cause an agonizing reappraisal.

8

New York 1725-1783

The Zenger Trial, Weekly Newspapers

In November, 1734, John Peter Zenger, of German origin, was arrested and imprisoned by order of the Council for printing seditious libels against Governor Cosby, and was brought to trial eight months later. His own lawyers had been disqualified on technicalities, so Andrew Hamilton, a famous lawyer from Philadelphia, was secretly engaged and appeared unexpectedly to represent the prisoner. He was an eloquent, fearless, and able advocate, and managed the case before the unfriendly court with such skill that the jury was out only ten minutes before returning with a verdict of not guilty.

Andrew Hamilton was hailed as a champion of liberty, and was presented by the New York Corporation with the freedom of the city for "his learned and generous defense of the rights of mankind and the liberty of the press."

Zenger was released from his long confinement in prison. Many years later, Gouverneur Morris stated that it was his conviction "that the trial of Zenger in 1735 was the germ of American freedom—the morning star of that liberty which subsequently revolutionized America."

Lewis Morris, who had previously been chief justice,

had been removed by Governor Cosby before the Zenger trial. He went to London to protest his removal and was upheld, but instead of being restored to office of chief justice, he was appointed governor of New Jersey, where he had large land interests.

James DeLancey had been made chief justice in his place, and the second judge was Frederick Philipse, both openly against Zenger. Lewis Morris, after his removal as chief justice, became a candidate for Representative from Westchester County and was violently opposed by the DeLanceys, Philipses, and all their Tory retainers, but was elected. From that time on, he became, along with Rip Van Dam, who had been acting-governor, the head of the Whig Party in New York City, with the Livingstons, and James Alexander and William Smith, two of the ablest lawyers in New York.

William Bradford, a Quaker from Philadelphia, introduced the art of printing in New York and in 1725 published the *New York Gazette,* a weekly, and the only newspaper in New York. Bradford was not only the first publisher and editor in New York, but a man of the highest character, industry, and probity.

The second newspaper in New York was the *Weekly Journal,* published in 1733 by John Peter Zenger who had been apprenticed for a number of years to Bradford. This was the same Zenger who wrote caustic lampoons against Governor Cosby and helped to win a great victory for the freedom of the press. After he was freed from prison, he became a popular hero and publisher.

On February 26, 1750, another New York weekly, the *Post-Boy,* announced a performance by a Philadelphia company of Shakespeare's *King Richard III.* This is believed to be the first notice of play acting in New York. The advertisement ran as follows:

By His Excellency's permission, at the theatre on Nassau Street, on Monday the Fifth of March next, will be presented the historical tragedy of Richard III. This play re-

65

lates the death of King Henry VI; the artful acquisition of the Crown by King Richard; the murder of the two Princes in the tower; and the landing of the Earl of Richmond and the Battle of Bosworth Field.

Tickets, five shillings; gallery, three shillings. To begin precisely at half an hour after six o'clock and no person shall be admitted behind the scenes.

Dinner in those days was around five o'clock and even earlier, probably because it was then the custom to go to bed at nine and get up by six—daylight.

Just prior to the Revolution, there were four articulate and able editors in New York: John Holt, a Virginian with a vigorous personality and a dedicated Patriot, published the *New York Journal*. It was the spokesman for the Patriot cause. However, because of his openly expressed principles he was compelled to join the other exiles from New York. After the war, he returned to New York where he died the next year, a great loss to the American cause.

Hugh Gaine, an Irishman, was entirely a different type. He tried to play with both the Whigs and the Tories. He did his best to remain neutral and, as a result, ended by belonging to both sides. His paper, the *New York Mercury*, during the war, was an outright British propaganda sheet. After the war he was permitted to remain in the printing business. His newspaper failed, but he continued as a printer of almanacs and books for many years.

The third publisher was James Loudon, also an Irishman, who was an outspoken supporter in his *New York Packet and Advertiser* of the American Patriots. He was forced to flee from New York, and continued to print his paper at Fishkill throughout the war. On his return to New York, he changed his paper into a daily. He also published *Loudon's Magazine,* the first of its kind in New York City.

The fourth and best-known publisher was James Rivington, who in 1773 brought out the *New York Gazette*. This was the mouthpiece of the Tories and Loyalists. It was violently pro-British before and during the war. It was more loyal than either the governor or the king, and filled with libels and falsehoods against all patriotic Americans.

In 1775, a group of angry Patriots from Connecticut wrecked Rivington's shop twice, destroying his presses and melting the type into bullets. After the war, Rivington published an abject apology. It did not avail him anything. His truthful *Gazette*, replacing his lying *Gazette*, lasted only one month after the return of Washington's army into New York.

The *New York Evening Post*, thirty years before the Revolutionary War, was edited by Henry DeForest, the first printer known to have been born in New York. It was a weekly, like all New York newspapers until the end of the Revolutionary War. Advertisements were, at that time, few and quite odd. The following is one of them: "To be sold, a Negro wench, that can do all manner of housework, fit for town or country. She has had the smallpox."

Taverns

The Province Arms, the most famous of all New York taverns, was housed in the former spacious mansion owned by Lt. Governor James DeLancey and built by his father in 1700. It was acquired in 1754 by Edward Willet and opened as a tavern. In this tavern, numerous brilliant public and social dinners were held. The most historic was the patriotic signature by 200 New York merchants of the famous non-importation agreement in 1765 against the Stamp Act. It was at the Province Arms that a celebrated duel was fought between Captain Tollemache of His Majesty's Ship *Zebra* and Captain Pennington of the Coldstream Guards. Captain Pennington had written a sonnet which Captain Tollemache thought reflected on the wit of his lady; swords were the weapons, and a few days later Captain Tollemache was buried in the Trinity Churchyard.

It is impossible in a limited space, to give a history of the numerous taverns, inns, and coffee houses in New York during the 18th century. They flourished like Green Bay trees: the Blue Boar, St. George the Dragon, the Three Pigeons, the Fighting Cocks, the Merchant's Coffee House, Jamaica Arms, and Griffin Tavern (privateering), Cart and Horse, Bull's Head Tavern (for horse racing), and the Black Horse Inn for social life, balls, concerts, dinners and it was there that the Masonic Order held its meeting. It was at one of these taverns that the large celebration was held in May, 1766, when the repeal of the Stamp Act was known in New York. At this large celebration dinner, 28 toasts were drunk; one of them to William Pitt and another to "perpetual union between Great Britain and her Colonies." This was ten years before the Declaration of Independence.

Fraunces' Tavern

In 1765, Sam Francis bought the old DeLancey house, which was then being used as a storehouse, and established a tavern there. He was an ardent Patriot and joined Washington's army after the Declaration of Independence. When the war was over, he returned and, for some unknown reason, assumed the name of Fraunces, and the tavern has since been known as Fraunces' Tavern, located at the corner of Broad and Pearl Streets and still in existence. It was at the long room in Fraunces' Tavern that Washington bade farewell to his officers. This event gave great renown to the tavern which has never been forgotten. The long room was 38 feet long and 19 feet wide, its length extending along Broad Street as it does today.

On the morning of December 3, 1783, Washington and his officers met at Fraunces' Tavern for the last time as soldiers of the Revolutionary Army. No complete record exists as to who was present on this memorable occasion, but it is understood that there were forty-four. Only eighteen of them are known by name. Among these were: Generals Green, Knox, Wayne, Steuben, Carroll, Lincoln, Kosciuszko, Moultrie, Gates, Lee, Putnam, Stark, Hamilton; Governor Clinton; and Colonels Talmadge, Humphreys, and Fish (as published in *Old Taverns of New York* by Balis). Col. Nicholas Fish served throughout the war and was the youngest there—aged twenty-five.

The American army officers had been assembled for a short time when General Washington entered the room. His emotions were too strong to be concealed and were evidently reciprocated by all present. After partaking of a slight refreshment, followed by a few moments of silence, the general filled his glass with wine and turned to his officers and said: "With a heart full of love and gratitude, I now take leave of you. I most devotedly wish that your latter days may be as prosperous and happy as your former ones have been glorious and honorable."

After the officers had responded in a glass of wine, he requested that each one of them should come and take him by the hand. General Knox, who was nearest him, turned and grasped his hand and they embraced each other in silence. In the same affectionate manner, every officer parted from the commander-in-chief, who then left the room without a word. From there he went to Annapolis to surrender his commission to the Continental Congress.

9

Horse racing and fox hunting under British rule in New York.
Sports, Amusements, Hunting and Fishing

From the very beginning of the English rule in New York, horse racing and fox hunting became popular and fashionable sports, particularly among the people of means. In those days there were plenty of horses, foxes, and imported fox hounds.

Governor Nicolls, the first British governor, established a race course on Hempstead Plains which soon became the most important around New York and well known through all the colonies, as well as in England. There was another race course on Long Island, at Beaver Pond near Jamaica. There were two race courses in New York City: one on the west side on the estate of Sir Peter Warren where Greenwich Village is today; and the other on the east side, only a short distance north of City Hall.

There were also a number of race tracks in New Jersey: at Paulis Hook, Perth Amboy, Elizabethtown, and Morristown, which were well attended by sportsmen from New York City. Most of the races were limited to American-bred horses.

A New York newspaper published that "on June 1,

1750 there was a great race on Hempstead Plains for a considerable wager that attracted many people; and that the horses on the Plains of the race far exceeded a thousand." This presumably refers to those who attended on horseback. It is only natural that horse racing should be very popular in those days, as almost everyone who could afford it owned a horse. No Englishman could be long in New York without importing his own race horse and hunters.

Individual races and trials of speed were often arranged on a basis of personal wagers. Thus we read on the day of April 29, 1759, that "Oliver DeLancey's horse ran from one of our Palisade Gates, Wall Street and Broadway, to Kingsbridge and back again being upwards of 30 miles in a hour and 47½ minutes." A few years later there was "a race on the New York course for 20 pound value by any horse, mare or gelding carrying ten stone (saddle and bridle included). The best of three heats, two miles in each heat."

One advertisement stated that in January, 1774, a race would be run on the first day of March "between a mare called Ragged Kate, belonging to Mr. Peter DeLancey and a horse called Monk, belonging to Hon. William Montague for 200 pounds."

Horse racing continued as a popular sport throughout the war. The *Royal Gazette* of November 4, 1780, announced three days' sport at Ascot Heath, formerly Flatlands Plains. On the second day, the first event was the ladies' subscription purse of fifty pounds; the second race by women, quarter-mile heats; the first to get a Holland smock and chintz gown, full trimmed of four guineas value, the second, a guinea, and the third, a half-guinea. This only goes to show that women participated in the horse racing of those days. This was natural, as women owned their own horses.

The *Royal Gazette* of August 8, 1781, contained the following advertisement:

Gentlemen that are fond of fox hunting are requested to meet at Loosley Tavern on Ascot Heath on Friday morning next between the hours of five and six as a pack of hounds will be there purposely for a trial of their ability. Breakfasting and relishes until the races commence. At 11 o'clock will be run for an elegant saddle etc., value at least 20 pounds for which upwards of 12 gentlemen will ride their own horses. At 12 a match will be rode by two gentlemen. Horse for horse. At 1 a match for 30 guineas by two gentlemen who will ride their own horses. Dinner will be ready at two o'clock after which racing and other diversions will conclude the day with pleasure and harmony.

In November, 1781, there was another advertisement: "Brooklyn Hunt—the hounds will shove off at Denyse Ferry at 9 Thursday morning, a guinea or more will be given for a good strong bag fox, by Charles Loosley."

In April, 1782, a sweepstakes of thirty guineas was won by Jacob Jackson's mare Slow and Easy over Mercury and Goldfinder on Ascot Heath.

English officers were brave and good fighters, but nevertheless they insisted on their horse racing and fox hunting throughout the war.

In early New York, horseback riding through the numerous lanes that by-passed the main highways on Manhattan Island was the favorite pastime. "The lady and her escort often shared the same stead, the fair rider being mounted on a pillion behind, and maintaining her position by passing her arm along her companion's waist."

On the corner of 50th Street and Second Avenue, there was a quaint stone bridge, famed as a kissing bridge, spanning a little clearwater brook, that went babbling down to the East River. On crossing this bridge in a chaise or pillion, the young gentleman was privileged to claim a kiss from his companion.

The Reverend Mr. Burnaby, who visited the city about 1748, says:

> The amusements are balls and sleighing expeditions in winter and in the summer going in parties upon the water and fishing or making excursions into the country. There are several houses, pleasantly situated up the East River near New York where it is common to have turtle feasts (terrapin). These happen once or twice a week. Thirty or forty gentlemen and ladies meet and dine together, drink tea in the afternoon, fish and amuse themselves until evening and then return home in Italian chaises (the fashionable carriage in this and most parts of America) a gentleman and a lady in each chaise.

There is no mention in the press of the British soldiers in New York playing football, soccer, or rugby. Football in England is of ancient vintage. Richard Mulcaster, first headmaster of Merchant Taylor's School in 1582, said: "Football strengthens and brawneth the whole body. It helpeth weak hames by much moving and simple shankes by thickening of the flesh, no less than riding doth." But for some strange reason it did not reach the United States until the 1870s. There was no golf or tennis in early New York either. There were a number of competitive sports: cricket, boxing, foot racing, jumping, and, of course, horse racing and fox hunting. Shooting matches seem to have been a favorite with the people. They lasted for several days and for big prizes such as real estate. Each shot cost a shilling or more, and at the end of the match the champion won the big prize and also the acclaim of the people.

The Commons where City Hall is today was used for outdoor games. On Monday, April 28, 1751, a great match of cricket was played there for a considerable wager by eleven Londoners against eleven New Yorkers. The newspaper account states that "the game was played according to the London method—The New Yorkers went in first and got 81; then the Londoners went in and got 43; then the New York went in again and got 86; then the Londoners finished the game with getting only 37 more."

The game of bowls was very popular in New York in the 18th century. At the further end of the smooth ground, a white ball was placed called the jack and the bowlers endeavored to roll the balls as near as possible to the jack. Bowling Green in lower New York got its name from this game.

Cock-fighting was also a popular sport. At the Fighting Cocks Tavern, the best birds could be bought and steel and silver spurs purchased. Cock-fighting in the North has almost disappeared and so has the cruel sport known in those days as bear-baiting and bull-baiting. Bear-baiting became rare as those animals became scarce in the vicinity of New York, but bull-baiting continued right up to the Revolutionary War. It evidently had to do with attacks by dogs upon the bull.

Backgammon, which is still played throughout the United States, apparently was in vogue in New York during the 18th century at the taverns and coffeehouses. It also had its critics, for in a letter dated June 13, 1768, the writer says: "They have a vile practice here, which is peculiar to the City; I mean that of playing at backgammon which is going forward at the public coffeehouses from morning til night—frequently a dozen tables at a time."

Prior to the Revolutionary War, hunting and fishing were by far the greatest pastimes and sports for almost the entire population of New York City and vicinity. The ponds, lakes, and streams teemed with trout and freshwater fish. The woods and forests, which then covered a large part of the land within twenty miles of New York, were filled with deer, turkey, and all types of wild fowl. Everyone in New York who could afford it had a horse and a gun and, within an hour's ride, there was abundant hunting of every description. In the nearby hills there were bears, wolves, and wildcats. The fishing on the Hudson River, then unpolluted, was enough to make any fisherman's mouth water. In those days there was salmon, sturgeon, shad, an abundance of bass, and every kind of saltwater fish available in the nearby ocean. Strange as it may seem, there were numerous whales off Long Island. Most of the whaling ports were at New Bedford, Salem, and Nantucket, but there were whaling stations far up the river at Hudson and at Sag Harbor. The Legislature granted a man with a French name the sole right for a number of years to fish for dolphins. It would be interesting to know whether people appreciated eating fried dolphins.

Reference has already been made to the fact that the coves of Manhattan, then known as New York City, were filled with the finest oysters in the world, and so were the opposite shores in Brooklyn. Lobsters were very plentiful and of enormous size: from one foot to three feet. Another delicacy that was then very common were terrapins, now almost extinct. The New York Market gives the best picture of New York as a game center. Its market listed bear, deer, raccoon, rabbits, hare, dead or alive; turtles: green turtles, snapper, and terrapin; shell fish: oysters, lobsters, clams, crabs, shrimps, prawns, scallops, and mussels. The largest list is under the heading of birds and enough to make a hunter delirious: wild turkeys, heath hens, partridges, quail, woodcocks, and wild pigeons which were in great abundance and very large; wild fowl: wild goose, brant, black duck, grey duck, canvas back, wood duck, wigeon, cormorant, snipe, and plover; fish: salmon, sturgeon, shad trout, pickerel, pike, bass, sole, codfish, mackerel, herring, smelt, haddock, and eel.

The fishing was excellent all the way up the Hudson River. Great quantities of bass were caught a few miles south of West Point and brought in fresh to New York.

It is hard for crowded New Yorkers today to realize that the immediate vicinity of old New York at the time of the Revolution was a paradise for hunting and fishing. The following is taken from an advertisement published in 1772:

Little Bern Island at public auction belonging to the estate of Mr. St. George Talbot, deceased, situated opposite New Harlem Church, in the out-ward of this City, containing upwards of one hundred acres of land and meadows. It abounds with wild fowl, as ducks, geese, pigeons, quails, etc., and has the advantage of a fine seine fishery, and blackfish, oysters, lobsters, etc. Being in the vicinity of New York, the produce may be brought to the Fly Market with the tide of ebb and the winds will waft the craft home.

This is enough to make any modern spotsmen's mouth water with envy. Little Bern Island was located near the Harlem River. Sportsmen today would go many hundreds of miles for any such opportunity to hunt and fish, but unfortunately there are few left anywhere in the United States.

Only the small sturgeons from the Hudson River were eaten. The roe was highly prized as caviar by the English. Sturgeon and lobsters were pickled for the market. In 1765, John Alexander's company advertised New York pickled sturgeon and vaunted its superiority both as to the quality of the fish and the richness of the pickle. Some lobsters were of enormous size. New York oysters were exceptionally fine. They were eaten raw and cooked in as many ways as they are today. Every tavern had pickled oysters on its bill of fare and they were exported in large quantities. Fresh oysters at low cost were available to all elements of the population and, like lobsters, were of large size. Caviar and terrapin were plentiful and popular in early New York.

10

Causes of the War

The history of the Revolutionary War from the Stamp Act of 1765 to the evacuation of New York City by the British on November 25, 1783, would be incomplete without a sketch of the activities of the Tories and Whigs there.

From the beginning of the British Colonial history in 1664 until 100 years later, there were two colonial parties in New York: the party of conservatives (Tory), supported by the wealthy landlords, the Anglican Church, the military establishments and the officials of the government and Crown; and the other, a progressive party (Whigs), composed of some of the big landowners such as the Morris, Livingston, Van Renssalaer Beekman, and Schuyler families, but mostly by lawyers, the Presbyterian and non-conformist clergy, the small shopkeepers, mechanics, and laborers. These political divisions continued until the end of the War for Independence with different names, such as Loyalists and Patriots.

The partisans on both sides were English, Holland-Dutch, Scottish, French Huguenots, and Germans. The Dutch, Huguenots, and upstate Germans were predominantly Whigs, and later Patriots.

The Irish Catholics numbered only 1500 in the entire state and probably around 400 in the city. They were, during the war, divided in their allegiance, but predominantly on the side of the Patriots.

The Jewish population in New York City and vicinity was also approximately 400, but under the leadership of Rabbi Seixas, were very largely Whigs and Patriots.

The ten-year period before the Declaration of Independence was truly a time that tried men's souls. The year 1765 has been appropriately called a critical or red-letter year in American history. The passage of the Stamp Act early in that year was not an oppressive measure, but, because of the principle involved, created a spirit of liberty and almost of rebellion among many citizens in New York. It increased the bitterness and enmity between the Tories and the Whigs, causing tumults and riots.

The Stamp Act merely provided that all deeds, receipts, and legal papers, including marriage licenses, had to be printed on stamped paper sold by the Customs Collectors, as part of the revenue to be collected from the colony. The American colonists regarded this tax as a violation of the English Constitution. There was a fundamental principle involved. They claimed that the tax was illegal, unconstitutional, equivalent to a forced loan, and levied without their consent. The colonists realized that if the Ministry had the power to lay this type of tax, they could make additional ones whenever they wanted. There was no possible compromise except by the integration of the American colonies into the British Empire with representation in Parliament. King George III and his Tory ministers were too obstinate, arrogant, and narrow-minded to make the only concession that could have saved the British Empire from dismemberment.

Public resentment flared up in all the American colonies, and particularly in New York, against the Stamp Act. Rebellion was in the air and stalked the streets. The

22,000 inhabitants of New York City were divided into Loyalists or Tories, in support of the British government and King George III, with almost blind devotion, and the Whigs or Rebels, who openly resisted in every way the opppressive encroachments in what they called the "tyranny of the King and Parliament." Resistance and scurrilous verses were spewed forth by annoymous writers on both sides. There were three newspapers in New York: Holt's *Journal,* supporting the Whigs; Gaine's *Mercury,* trying to be neutral; and Rivington's *Gazette,* for the Tories. All of them were rabble rousers, fanning the flames of dissension and hatred.

There were, however, a substantial group of moderates in the Tory party who insisted on the American interpretation of the British Constitution of no taxation without representation. In the British Parliament itself, such Whig leaders as Pitt, Burke, Fox, and others, upheld the views of the American colonists. Partisanship was increasing rapidly in New York and it was obvious that it would not be extinguished without peaceful conciliation of fair representation in Parliament. The ultraconservative wing of the Tory Party was led by that staunch old Tory and irreconcilable autocrat, Lt. Governor Cadwallader Colden, the astute Dr. Myles Cooper, president of King's College, and Judge Thomas Jones who, with the royal officials and a coterie of Tory friends, believed that Parliament and the king could do no wrong and that their edicts must be enforced.

By the time of the Tea Tax in 1770, every important political controversy became a party issue between the Tories and the Whigs. They in turn were gradually giving way, prior to the outbreak of the Revolution, to Loyalists and Patriots. These became the standard names by 1774. The Loyalist leaders were, in addition to Governor Colden, most of the big landowners and merchants, such as the DeLanceys, Bayards, DePeysters, Waltons, Philipses, Watts, Ludlows, Crugers, Roger

Morris, the Anglican church, the army, and a substantial number of merchants, storekeepers, and farmers in Long Island, Staten Island, and Westchester.

The Patriots were led by the Livingston and Morris families, John Jay, James Duane, George Clinton, Philip Schuyler, the Van Renssalaers, John Morin Scott, and later by the youthful Alexander Hamilton. The radical Liberty Boys were led by Marinus Willett, Captain Isaac Sears, Alexander McDougall, and John Lamb.

The pre-Revolutionary period was the time of pamphlets, poems, diatribes, sermons, letters in the newspapers, and speeches by both sides to arouse public opinion. They were the only means of communication in those days, before the telephone, telegraph, radio, and television.

New England historians have made much of the so-called massacre on the Boston Common in March, 1770, in which British soldiers shot and killed members of the Boston mob which had been trying to disarm them. They actually built this bloody riot up into being the first battle or cornerstone of the Revolutionary War. Two months before this so-called Boston Massacre, the Sons of Liberty in New York City called a protest meeting of citizens, on January 19, 1770, in defense of their rights against the lawlessness and brutal conduct of the British soldiers garrisoned in New York. The next day, eighty of them, belonging to the 16th Infantry, faced an equally numerous group of Liberty Boys on Golden Hill near what are now John, William, and Fulton Streets.

Here a battle took place with several thousand citizens as onlookers. Blood ran freely on both sides. The British discharged their muskets and then, using their bayonets, fled to their barracks, followed by a barrage of stones and all available missiles. One citizen, a Quaker, was shot through the head, and three were wounded by bayonets. They were the first victims of British armed might, and the first to shed their blood for the cause of liberty in America. Five soldiers were disabled and carried to their quarters. In reality, the Battle of Golden Hill was the spot where the first blood of the Revolution was shed, and not in the so-called Boston Massacre. The truth is that the Boston fight between a mob and a party of soldiers should never have been characterized as a massacre. It involved no contest for principles as did the conflict with the Sons of Liberty. The firing on the mob in Boston was justified by verdict of a jury of citizens of Boston, and the British captain who gave the order to fire was defended by such patriots as Josiah Quincy and John Adams and was exonerated. Lastly, the Boston encounter did not occur until two months after the Battle of Golden Hill. But such is the power of propaganda and of historians' pens that every American schoolboy has heard of the Boston Massacre and few, if any, have heard of the Battle of Golden Hill.

As the crisis increased, efforts were made to keep it cool and under control, as evidenced by the following committee of prominent citizens almost equally divided between Whigs and Tories, or Patriots and Loyalists. However, within the next year, the news of the battle of Lexington added immediate fuel to the flames of dissension and all efforts at compromise came to an end by the issuance of the Declaration of Independence, July 4, 1776.

At a Meeting at the Exchange, 16th May, 1774, ISAAC LOW, chosen CHAIRMAN.

1st Question put, Whether it is necessary for the present, to appoint a Committee to correspond with the neighbouring Colonies, on the present important Crisis? Carried in the Affirmative by a great Majority.

2d. Whether a Committee be nominated this Evening for the Approbation of the Public?—Carried in the Affirmative by a great Majority.

3rd. Whether the Committee of 50 be appointed, or 25?—Carried for 50, by a great Majority.

The following Persons were nominated:

John Alsop,
William Bayard,
Theophylact Bache,
Peter V. B. Livingston,
Philip Livingston,
Isaac Sears,
David Johnston,
Charles McEvers,
Charles Nicholl,
Alexander McDougall,
Capt. Thomas Randall,
John Moore,
Isaac Low,
Leonard Lispenard,
Jacobus Van Zandt,
James Duane,
Edward Laight,
Thomas Pearfall,
Elias Desbrosses,
William Walton,
Richard Yates,
John De Lancey,
Miles Sherbrook,
John Thurman,
John Jay,
John Broome,

Benjamin Booth,
Joseph Hallett,
Charles Shaw,
Alexander Wallace,
James Jauncey,
Gabriel H. Ludlow,
Nicholas Hoffman,
Abraham Walton,
Gerardus Duyckinck,
Peter Van Schauck,
Henry Remsen,
Hamilton Young,
George Bowne,
Peter T. Curtenius,
Peter Goelet,
Abraham Brasher,
Abraham P. Lott,
David Van Horne,
Gerardus W. Beekman,
Abraham Duryee,
Joseph Bull,
William McAdam,
Richard Sharpe,
Thomas Marston,
Francis Lewis, added *nem. con.* May 19th.

Election of Committee of 50(51)

The Whigs called the Tories "Ministerial Hirelings," and aristocrats, and the Tories retaliated by calling the Whigs "fomentors of sedition," mobility, and, of course, rebels and traitors. The Sons of Liberty were denounced as being composed of drunks, bandits, and Puritan ministers "who belched from the pulpit Liberty and Independence." The Whig writers were just as bitter and sarcastic. They defined a Tory as "a man whose head is in England, whose body is in America and whose neck ought to be stretched."

All the colonies joined in organized resistance to the

82

Stamp Act. The stamp tax collectors were so intimidated that they were compelled to resign, including James McEvers, a merchant from Hanover Square, appointed from New York.

The growing spirit of liberty was jet propelled by the rebellion against the Stamp Act. The principle of no taxation without representation became enshrined in the hearts of the American people. Every attempt by the Parliament and King George to suppress American rights and liberties engendered more bitter opposition and more open attacks on the Crown. The Stamp Act and the tax on tea were the firebrands that caused the conflagration to spread throughout all the colonies, and to drive deeper the wedge between the Tories and the Whigs. Ultra-Patriots such as the Liberty Boys resisted the Stamp Act with such violence that they temporarily alienated the middle-of-the-roaders among the bigger merchants, professional men, and some large landowners who opposed the Stamp Act and other unwise oppressive measures. The principles of the two parties, Tories and Whigs, were well developed a decade before the Revolution; only their names were changed, to Loyalists and Patriots.

Such was the bitter feeling aroused by the Stamp Act that it caused a political and social upheaval in New York which, by the time of the tax on tea five years later (1770), resulted in open dissension between the rich and social Whig and Tory families and a spirit of resistance among the more radical Sons of Liberty.

Pitt, speaking in favor of the repeal of the Stamp Act, said: "I rejoice that America has resisted," pointing out that successful tyranny in the colonies might lead to tyranny at home. There was a temporary breathing spell when, as a result of pressure throughout the colonies and by the Whig leaders in Parliament, headed by William Pitt, the odious Stamp Act was repealed a year afterwards.

The people in New York and in all the colonies

83

were jubilant and grateful to both Pitt and King George. An equestrian statue of King George III was erected in Bowling Green and also a statue of Pitt.

Ten years later, the same people celebrated the Declaration of Independence by dragging down the statue of King George from its pedestal and sending it to Litchfield, the residence of Governor Oliver Wolcott of Connecticut. From this statue of the British king, Governor Wolcott's wife and daughter manufactured 42,000 bullets "to assimilate with the brains of the adversaries."

The statue of William Pitt remained untouched until the occupation of New York by the British under General Howe. The bitterness against the memory of Pitt because of his friendship for the American colonists was so great among the British armed forces that his statue was decapitated.

Present-day Americans do not realize that the war against the American colonies was so unpopular in England that it was difficult to enlist British troops to fight against the Americans. Pitt withdrew his oldest son from the army to prevent his serving against the colonists. To a very great extent, it was the king's war and not the people's. The Tory Ministry took orders from George III, who at that period was a forceful, domineering sovereign. Unable to raise sufficient troops in England, the Ministry tried to hire soldiers from Russia. Failing there, it succeeded with some of the petty German princes who sold their subjects like beef for slaughter to pay their debts.

The eloquence of Pitt, Burke, Fox, and Barre was powerless in preventing the hiring of German serfs to fight freedom-loving Americans, the sons of Englishmen.

Chatham (Pitt) in the House of Lords did not mince words over the hiring of German mercenaries: "You may traffic and barter with every little German Prince that sells his subjects to the shambles of a foreign power;

your efforts are forever and forever in vain and impotent—If I were an American as I am an Englishman, while foreign troops were landed in my country, I never would lay down my arms, never, never, never."

The landgrave of Hess-Castell furnished 12,000 Hessians out of a total of 20,000 German soldiers that were sold to the British by a half a dozen German principalities; a third of these mercenaries either died, were killed in battle, or remained in America where they helped to build the nation they were hired to destroy.

W. E. H. Lecky, the great historian, wrote: "The conduct of England is hiring German mercenaries to subdue the extensively English population beyond the Atlantic made reconciliation hopeless, and the Declaration of Independence inevitable."

Charles James Fox, with all the charm and force of his oratory, declared in the British Parliament: "I have always said that the war is unjust, and the object of it unobtainable—In order to induce the Americans to submit you pass laws against them, tyrannical and cruel in the extreme. When they complain of one law, your answer is, to pass another far more vigorous than the former."

The Tories, now known as Loyalists, were greatly disappointed in the first Continental Congress which they had hoped would be conciliatory and restore peaceful relations with England.

The First Congress held in 1774-1775 did submit a list of grievances to the king which were ignored. However, it did recommend a stronger union among the colonies and encouraged resistance to the usurpation by the Crown. After the news of Lexington, it appointed George Washington to command the Continental Army. He succeeded in driving the British army out of Boston. For the next eight years, Washington was the inspirational American commander-in-chief. During the same period of time, George III was the real prime minister of Britain. Washington was the providential leader of the United States whereas King George III, who caused the war by his autocratic policies, was a catastrophe for his own country and a blessing and a cause of glory for our Republic.

11

New York State—The Battleground of the Revolutionary War, 1776-1783

New York State was the greatest battleground of the Revolutionary War beginning with the battle of Long Island, August 27, 1776 (an American defeat at Brooklyn) until the evacuation of New York by the British on November 25, 1783.

Five times as many battles, skirmishes, and raids were fought in New York State than in all of New England. Eight thousand British and Hessian soldiers were captured in New York State during the war. Less than half that number of Americans were captured there by the British. These figures include what is now Vermont, which was then a part of New York State. Very few British soldiers were captured in Massachusetts and all of New England. Yet the American people have been brainwashed into believing that Massachusetts, which started the war, also won it because of the overemphasis placed by its able historians on Paul Revere's Ride, the Boston Tea Party, Lexington, Concord, and the "shot heard around the world." No one denies that Bunker Hill, although a defeat, was a Pyrrhic victory.

The author, too, was one of the brainwashed who believed in New England's Revolutionary War propaganda as he spent his early years in St. Mark's School and Harvard College in Massachusetts where he graduated with honors in history. The blame rests more on the dearth of well-informed New York historians than on the slanted writings by a galaxy of New England authors. Once the pattern had been established, lesser historians followed in the footsteps of Bancroft, Fiske, Channing, Hart, Windsor, and Frothingham.

It is never too late to present the truth of history to the American people. The fact is that New York State did participate in the war and suffered far greater losses than any other state. New Yorkers of this generation and in the future, as well as all Americans, have a right to know the truth about the very great part played by New York State and its people in winning our War of Independence.

It is the purpose of the author to try, on the basis of truth, as we approach the 200th anniversary of the Declaration of Independence, to dispell the historical myth etched on the minds of the American people by New England historians.

There were one-third as many military encounters in New York State as there were in all the rest of the states combined. This is evidenced by the fact that General Washington had his headquarters at Newburgh, and a few miles away at New Windsor and elsewhere in New York for a period of three years in order to prevent the British from carrying out their plans to control the Hudson River and divide the New England States from the middle and southern states.

For another two years of the war, Washington had his headquarters in New Jersey within a radius of sixty miles from New York City. No other city in the revolting colonies suffered so disastrously, because it endured a British military occupation for seven harassing, war years. Besides it was, and still is, the only outlet to the sea for most of New York State.

88

In addition to the original 6,000 Patriot self-exiles, when the British seized New York there were thousands of other Patriots sympathetic to the American cause whose properties were later confiscated and who were driven out of New York City into Westchester and New Jersey as poor and destitute refugees. They only survived through the help of Patriot farmers and a pittance of state aid. Even if New York State had not been the battleground, the tragic extermination of American prisoners in the British prison hulks and jails in New York City, the harsh and brutal treatment of Americans who were in the least bit sympathetic to freedom and the cause of the Patriots, and the sad plight of the 6,000 refugees, should place New York State automatically in the forefront of those states which made the greatest sacrifice in sweat, blood, and tears in behalf of American independence.

The British strategic plan made New York State the battleground throughout the war. When the British army was forced to leave Boston, it went to Halifax, where it received large reinforcements, armaments, and supplies. They then proceeded in a vast armada to Staten Island at the entrance of the Port of New York to await additional forces composed of Hessian mercenaries, sold by the avaricious petty rulers of German states for money, as sheep to the slaughterhouses.

This army under General Howe was composed of 22,000 British and 12,000 Hessians at the beginning of the war. It constituted the largest British expeditionary force in history up to World War I. Later during the war, it was increased by 10,000 British and 10,000 more Germans, and 15,000 Loyalists.

General Howe, with his large, well-equipped and well-trained army, had no difficulty at the outset in carrying out the British strategic plan of defeating Washington's army, occupying New York City, and making it the British stronghold in America, and the base for its operations. The British objective was to control the Hudson River and divide the middle and southern colonies or states from New England.

This plan was drastically upset by the defeat and capitulation of General Burgoyne and his entire army of 6,000 at Saratoga in New York State on October 17, 1777, in the most decisive battle of the war. Burgoyne led his army down from Canada expecting to join up with the British army from New York at Albany. Shortly before the surrender of General Burgoyne, American troops under General Stark had defeated and captured 900 Hessians near Bennington, but actually across the border in New York State.

About the same time, General Nicholas Herkimer, of German origin, in command of American militia, mostly Germans from the Mohawk Valley, fought a bloody battle at Oriskany, New York, trying to relieve Fort Stanwix. It was being besieged by General St. Leger, with British troops and his Indian and Loyalist allies. The brave old Herkimer was badly wounded during the battle, but insisted on being placed facing the enemy to encourage his troops to withstand the British and Indian ambush. This he did until the Indians withdrew after losing ninety warriors and some chiefs. General Herkimer was taken to his home nearby and died a week later of his wounds.

What Herkimer failed to do, Col. Benedict Arnold, with American Continental troops, succeeded in accomplishing by putting to flight St. Leger's Army which had been designed to join up with Burgoyne at Albany.

The gallant General Herkimer who died from wounds received at the battle of Oriskany was not the first New York general to die in defense of his country. General Jesse Woodhull of Long Island and president of the N.Y. Provincial Assembly was killed, after he was forced to surrender, in a most brutal manner. He was hit with a saber on his head and a bayonnet run through his arm, and died of his wounds. He was a great loss to the American cause. General Richard Montgomery of Rhinebeck was killed leading the assault on Quebec on January 31, 1775, six months before the Declaration of Independence. He was the first American general killed.

These three brave, combat generals from New York were killed during the early part of the war. No other state had three of its fighting generals killed during the entire war.

It would take too long to describe all the battles, raids, and skirmishes in New York State. The following list is enough to prove without fear of contradiction that New York State was the main battleground of the Revolutionary War. Ninety-two battles were fought in New York State including Ticonderoga, Crown Point, Brooklyn, Harlem, White Plains, Fort Washington, Oriskany, Fort Stanwix, Freeman's Farm, Bemis Heights, Saratoga, Bennington, Stony Point, Sullivan's campaign against the Iroquois Indians, Forts Clinton and Montgomery and the naval battle on Lake Champlain. It also included numerous raids by Indians and armed Tories, along the Mohawk.

Even before the Declaration of Independence, there had been active fighting in northern New York. Colonel Ethan Allen and Colonel Benedict Arnold captured Fort Ticonderoga and sent the captured guns and ammunition to Washington's army at Boston. Colonel Seth Warner took Crown Point. General Richard Montgomery commanded 1,200 troops from New York and Connecticut that invaded Canada and captured Montreal. On December 31, 1775, General Montgomery was defeated and killed trying to take Quebec by assault. A fateful shot because, if Quebec had fallen, Canada might have become part of the United States.

The American troops withdrew to Montreal, and, when they did not receive the expected reinforcements, were forced to abandon Canada. On the retreat, there

Richard Montgomery, after the painting by C. W. Peale

were numerous minor encounters, including a naval battle on Lake Champlain, fought against a well-equipped invading British fleet. The American flotilla was built and manned by Col. Benedict Arnold. These make-shift American ships fought bravely in the first naval battle with the British in the war. They were out-gunned and out-numbered, and were forced to beach their ships. This naval action delayed Sir Guy Carlton's plans to capture Fort Ticonderoga which, in the meanwhile, had become so strengthened that he did not have a sufficient force to capture it.

The next year the Americans were gradually driven southward by Gen. Burgoyne's army as he marched toward Albany before his final defeat at Saratoga, the decisive battle of the war.

The Mohawk Valley in New York State was subjected to violent Indian raids and massacres by the combined Tories under Colonels Johnson and Butler, and Indians under Brandt.

The British had a few minor successes in the captures of Forts Montgomery and Clinton, fifty miles up the Hudson River, over our militia troops. They were overwhelmed by a surprise attack by superior British forces. They fought well and many of them escaped during the night, including Gen. George Clinton and his brother Gen. James Clinton, to fight again.

These forts were soon abandoned by the British. However, in retaliation, General Washington ordered Gen. Anthony Wayne to storm Stony Point, which was sixteen miles south on the west side of the Hudson River, and heavily fortified and garrisoned. Wayne's surprise attack was successful and resulted in the capture of 500 British troops, including two sons of Beverly Robinson, the colonel of the American Loyalist Regiment in New York who had six sons in the British army as commissioned officers. Gen. Lewis Morris, the author's direct ancestor and a signer of the Declaration of

93

Independence, was reputed to have had six sons in the American army.

These were some of the battles that were fought in New York State. There were also scores of skirmishes and raids that were conducted in lower Westchester, Long Island, Staten Island, and in and around the western frontier, and the northern sections of New York State near the Canadian border.

There were many more Patriot American soldiers killed in these numerous skirmishes and raids than there were in all of New England. Besides, more than 1,000 farmers, settlers and other civilians—men, women and children—were killed in Indian raids, adding to the wartime casualty list in New York State.

12

British Loyalists versus American Patriots in New York 1775-1783

Just prior to the war, the Provincial Congress of New York in 1775 established local committees to organize resistance. The main function was to divide the sheep from the goats, or, the Patriots from the Loyalists. All citizens were forced to sign as Patriots or be publicly held up to scorn as enemies of the country.

It took drastic steps to suppress the Loyalists in New York City and throughout the state, and many were arrested. The treatment of these Loyalists was generally firm but not harsh. Some of them were dismissed on parole, some were put on bond, and others were exiled or imprisoned. There were, however, a few instances of Loyalists who became victims of excessive patriotic fervor. They were ridden on rails, tarred and feathered, their livestock and their printing presses destroyed, but they were not seriously injured. The bitterness between the Loyalists and Patriots was unrelenting in New York during the war and for years afterwards.

The Declaration of Independence was proclaimed by the Second Congress on July 4, 1776. It was dreaded more than death itself by the Tories as it gave a finality to the position of all Loyalists. They were now forced to take definite sides. They openly avowed their allegiance to England and fought independence with pen and sword. They denounced separation from Britain as the height of folly, a wicked and evil act, and suicide for Americans. They claimed to believe that British armed might was unconquerable and that independence was impossible to attain. There was no middle ground and no compromise. Every American had to be loyal to his country or a British subject; a traitor to his country or vice versa.

The die had been cast and there was no turning back. The Patriots representing American liberties despised the Loyalists who were obliged to support the stupid follies and blunders of the British government. With the Loyalists, the supreme issue was the unity of the British Empire.

The surprising fact is that large numbers of Americans remained loyal to the Crown, despite the autocratic actions of Parliament and the king.

On December 23, 1776, Major Nicholas Fish, then only nineteen years of age, was assigned to take charge of a sloop under a flag of truce, at Verplank's Point, just south of Peekskill on the Hudson River, for the purpose of escorting certain prominent Loyalists back to their families in New York. This was done on the order of the N.Y. Provincial Congress. Among the Loyalists were: Mrs. Inglis, wife of the Rev. Dr. Inglis; Mrs. Livingston, wife of Philip John Livingston, former sheriff of Dutchess County and then British superintendent and manager of rebel estates; Mrs. Moore; the two Misses Lakes; Mrs. Bruce, by birth Judith Bayard; and eighteen or twenty children of the above, together with Mr. Alexander Wallace and Mr. Miles Sherbrook. They were all important New York Loyalists.

When the sloop reached New York, it anchored near the British warship *Asia*. Major Fish went on board to report, but in the meanwhile a violent storm arose and the sloop on which he had conveyed the Loyalists, was blown from its anchorage down the harbor. Fish was obliged to stay overnight on the *Asia*. During the delay, his father and sister came on board and told him that his mother was dying and wanted to see him. He asked permission to visit her and offered to go blindfolded, but his request was denied unless he would resign his Continental commission and accept a similar commission in the British army. Despite the urging of his father and sister, he refused to submit to this blackmail and later was publicly commended by General Washington for his loyalty and patriotism.

Governor Tryon, the British governor, remarked that he knew him and said, "He was a bonnie lad and kind hearted and would rather see his mither than run the risk o'being hanged." His mother died shortly afterwards. He delivered the Loyalist prisoners and brought the sloop back safely. A mission well done by a young American officer at the outset of the war.

British Loyalists

New York City, under British army rule for seven long years, was the center of British Loyalists in America. They flocked to New York City from all over New York State, New England, New Jersey, and even from Philadelphia, after the British had abandoned that city. Southern Westchester, Queens, and Richmond were overwhelmingly Loyalist. The population of New York City, despite the loss of thousands of Patriot exiles, increased to 30,000.

Life under General Howe and Sir Henry Clinton was even more socially glamorous, despite the two terrible and disastrous fires. All kinds of entertainments were the vogue for the officers: dinners, dances, masquerades, and theatricals. English sports were popular: horse racing, cricket, fox hunting, and shooting small game in the nearby woods, but not for the refugee Loyalists who swarmed into New York City.

Once the British armed forces had taken possession of New York, Long Island, southern Westchester, and nearby parts of New Jersey, the Loyalists volunteered by thousands in both the militia and in the regular British army to fight for the king and unity with Britain. The occupation of New York City by the British army was welcomed with joy by all the Loyalists, as their only hope lay in the success and victory of the king's army.

Young Loyalists from upstate, Long Island, Connecticut, and New Jersey reached New York by devious ways to join the Redcoats in the battle against independence. Sixty thousand people living in southern New York, one-third of the population of the entire state, were under British rule. Although New York City remained throughout the war under martial law, the civil courts were reopened and the property of the Patriots or rebels was confiscated.

Within one year, four regiments of Loyalists were organized. There were other Loyalist corps on the Canadian border with Burgoyne's army and in the attacks made by Sir John Johnson, John and Walter Butler, and Brandt, at Oriskanny, Cherry Valley, Wyoming, Minisink, Schoharie, and the entire Mohawk Valley.

The enlistment of Loyalists was never-ending throughout the war. The record discloses that approximately 15,000 Loyalists served with the British Regulars and 8,500 with the militia. One-third of the British army in New York were Loyalists. The remaining two-thirds were made up of British and Hessians. Most of the spies were Loyalists.

King's County contributed 300 pounds for Colonel Fanning's royal battalion, and New York gave 2,000 pounds in two weeks for Loyalist regiments. The Loyalist women of New York City raised funds for an armed privateer called *Fair America*. The Loyalist farmers of Queens County and lower Westchester provided a steady supply of farm products, vegetables, poultry, and beef for the British troops.

Long lists of Loyalists were sent to the king, who promised them land grants and the property seized from the revolutionists for help in crushing the insurrection. It is comparatively easy even today to obtain lists of all the Loyalists in New York City during the Revolutionary War. On the other hand, it is extremely difficult to secure even a limited list of Patriots who left New York City and remained in exile while the British occupied it. The author has spent considerable time in research trying to compile a list of Patriots, but it is far from complete. There is, unfortunately, no available list of the New York Patriots who sacrificed their fortunes, homes, property, and often their lives in defense of their country. There were no greater patriots in the history of the United States.

Soon after the arrival of General Howe in New York, he inaugurated a policy of enlisting Loyalists into the British army or mustering them into active militia companies. Loyalists were offered numerous inducements to enlist, which were unnecessary owing to the destitute situation of most of those who had sought the protection of the British armed forces in New York. Commissions in the regular army at the same pay as the British officers and soldiers were granted. Staten Island, a hot bed of Loyalists, raised a provincial corps and troop of cavalry. Two thousand Loyalists from Long Island joined the British army under Howe, and 1,500 more signed up with the Loyalist militia. Westchester supplied that ardent Loyalist James Delancey with a troop of light horses and, in 1778, he invaded Suffolk County, New York, with 1,000 Loyalist troops. Oliver Delancey was commissioned a brigadier general in charge of 1,500 Loyalist troops. The loyal American regiment was raised in New York in March, 1777, by Col.

Beverly Robinson, a Loyalist and wealthy Dutchess County landowner. Many of the recruits were his own tenants, people from Dutchess and Westchester Counties. The volunteers of Ireland, or the second American regiment, created in March, 1778, was composed of Irish-born Americans and was commanded by Lord Rowdan.

There were not many people of Irish origin in New York at that time, and they were divided in their allegiance. It was estimated that there were fewer than 1,500 in New York State, less than one percent of the population. Irish emigration began a few years before the Revolutionary War, but increased steadily afterwards.

The Loyalists who sought refuge in New York City had to sacrifice their homes and property and endure privations and dangers in reaching the British lines. Once there, they found that New York City was no paradise. It was overcrowded and was not the sanctuary they had expected. Most of them had to live in huts or tents. They had difficulty in securing accommodations and, worse still, employment. Many Loyalist refugees were without any resources of any kind and had to be provided with both food and board by the British authorities. Contributions were raised from the residents of the city for the relief of the new arrivals. Fifteen thousand Loyalists enlisted in the British army and 8,000 in the militia in Kings, Queens, Richmond, and Westchester Counties, where they took over the farms of the Patriot refugees. Service in the British army solved their living conditions during the war, but forced them to join the army of exiles and depart from New York when the British left on or before the evacuation day, November 25, 1783.

The returning American refugees to New York denounced service in the British army as synonymous with treason. The Loyalists had no choice except to escape, bag and baggage, before the embittered and victorious Patriots gained control of the city. Over 30,000 refugees went to Canada and Nova Scotia, and 10,000 to England and the West Indies, where they continued to endure the same hardships as refugees everywhere.

During the war, the New York Legislature, on October 22, 1779, passed a law which attainted 59 notorious Loyalists and confiscated their properties. Commissioners of the Forfeiture were appointed and authorized to sell forfeited lands at public sale. New York State realized three million six hundred thousand dollars by sale of the confiscated property. Here are the names of the first Loyalists attainted:

John Murray; Earl of Dunmore, formerly governor of the Colony of New York; William Tryon, Esq., later governor of the said Colony; John Watts, Oliver Delancey, Hugh Wallace, Henry White, John Harris Cruger, William Axtell, and Robert Morris, Esq., late members of the Council of said colony; George Duncan Ludlow and Thomas Jones, late justices of the Supreme Court of said colony; John Tabor Kempe, late attorney general of said colony; William Bayard, Robert Bayard, and James Delancey, now or late of the city of New York, Esquires; David Matthews, later mayor of the said city; James Jauncey, George Folliot, Thomas White, William McAdams, Isaac Low, Miles Sherbrook, Alexander Wallace, and John Wetherhead, now or late of the said city, merchants; Charles Inglis, of the said city, clerk, and Margaret, his wife; Sir John Johnson, late of the county of Tryon, knight and baronet; Guy Johnson, Daniel Claus, and John Butler, now or late of the said County, Esquires, and John Joost Herkimer, now or late of the said county, yeoman; Frederick Philipse and James Delancey now or late of said county, gentlemen; David Colden, Daniel Kissam the Elder, and Gabriel Ludlow, now or late of Queen's County, Esquires; Philip Skeene, now or late of the County of Charlotte, Esq.; Benjamin Seaman and Christopher Billop, now or late of the County of

101

Richmond, Esquires; Beverly Robinson, Beverly Robinson the younger, and Malcolm Morrison now or late of the County of Dutchess, Esquires; John Kane, now or late of said county, gentleman; Abraham C. Cuyler, late of the County of Albany, Esquire; Robert Leake, Edward Jessup, and Ebenezer Jessup, now or late of the said county, gentlemen, and Peter DuBois and Thomas H. Barclay, now or late of the County of Ulster, Esquires; Susannah Robinson, wife of the said Beverly Robinson, and Mary Morris, wife of the said Roger Morris; John Rapalje, of Kings County, Esquire; George Muirson, Richard Floyd, and Parker Wickham, of Suffolk County, Esquires; Henry Lloyd, the elder, later of the State of Massachusetts Bay, a merchant; and Sir Henry Clinton Knight.

Later on, a large number of other active Loyalists, particularly those who left New York either with the British army, or prior to its departure, November 25, 1783, had their properties confiscated. It is estimated by most writers on the Loyalists in New York, or America, such as Flick, Ryerson, Sabine, and Thomas Jones, who was a notorious Loyalist, that the number of Loyalist exiles was approximately 40,000 from New York, which included those from New Jersey, Connecticut, and some from Pennsylvania, and 35,000 from all the other states. This is about 2½ percent of the population, which is not very much considering that at least one-third of the people were opposed to the separation from England until the Declaration of Independence was signed, and many took no sides.

The lot of refugees, however, is generally difficult and unfortunate and such was the case of those who were exiled to Canada and Nova Scotia. The English government spent 15 million dollars in compensating these exiles for their losses. Some of the wealthier ones fared very well—those who had influence and could afford adequate presentation of their claims—but many got very little. Three-quarters went to Canada and Nova Scotia from New York, and others to England, Scotland, Bermuda, Nassau, Jamaica, and Barbados. Many refugees left Boston in the early part of the war, and many migrated from New England to Canada during the war. The refugees from Virginia, the Carolinas, and Georgia either went back to England, to Florida, or to the West Indies, and those from Maryland, Delaware, and Pennsylvania went mostly to Canada or England.

A few years after the war, a number of refugees, particularly those who had left behind families and property and who had intermarried with prominent patriot families, managed to return to New York, such as the Barclays, Bayards, Crugers, Coldens, Cuylers, dePeysters, Gerards, Kissams, Lloyds, Lows, Ludlows, Philipses, Pells, Beverly Robinson, Schieffelines, Wattses, Whites, Wichams, and the family of Thomas Jones.

After the war in 1784, the law disfranchised all voters guilty of bearing arms against the patriotic cause. Most of the Loyalists in the British army went into exile, but the militia remained. This act affected two-thirds of the voters in New York, Richmond, and Kings County, only one-fifth of those in Suffolk County, and three-fourths of those in Queens County and in the Borough of Westchester. Queens County was the greatest stronghold of Loyalists. Every town, with the exception of Newton (Elmhurst), was overwhelmingly on the side of the king. This was true because a great many American Patriots fled across the sound to Westchester or to Connecticut when Lord Howe's army landed on Long Island and took over control of New York, Queens, and Kings Counties.

13

The Declaration of Independence—
The charter and bible of freedom
throughout the world

The early pioneers in New England, New York, and the other colonies, lived in the heroic age of America. At the risk of their lives, they traversed the seas in small sailing ships and landed in the wilderness of a yet unknown country. They cut down the forests for homes and farms. They hunted for food. They planted the rocky soil. They built their own houses. They made their own clothes. They brought up large families. They were self-sufficient and self-supporting. In addition, they were deeply religious and, at times, intolerant. They were also trained, armed, and ready to lay down the plow to take up the musket to repel the Indians.

They were, in truth, the heroic founders of America who laid out enduring foundations based on hard labor, courage, determination, and devotion to the preservation of freedom and civil liberty.

We present-day Americans, with every convenience at our disposal, owe a debt of gratitude to our sturdy pioneer ancestors for preparing the way for us, based on freedom and civil liberty. They are the unsung heroes of our Republic. Their sons and grandsons, 75 percent of

John Hancock

British origin, took up their muskets in the cause of liberty and independence against the arbitrary and tyrannical acts of a British king, George III. They resented being ruled from London, 3,000 miles away, by the king and Parliament where they had no representation. Their grievances took months by sailing ships, the only communication. They were bitterly opposed to direct taxation by the Parliament and, as a result, the slogan "taxation without representation" became the political doctrine of the Whigs in America and also of the prominent Whigs in Parliament, including Pitt, Burke, Fox, Sheridan, and Barre. King George III, who dominated Parliament, largely by bribery, refused even to consider the American grievances and the request for representation.

Two years before the Declaration of Independence was written, the American Whigs changed their name to Patriots and the Tories to that of Loyalists. The colonies, including New York, were generally divided into three equal parts: Patriots, Loyalists, and neutralists. At the time of the skirmish of Lexington, April 19, 1775, when British Regulars shot down some brave Patriot militiamen, it ignited a spark of rebellion to the king and his armed forces that spread into a flame of resistance throughout the colonies. Emerson, in his famous poem, immortalized Concord as the place where the shot was fired that was heard around the world. But even after Lexington, Concord, and the bloody Battle of Bunker Hill, the majority of people, although against taxation without representation and the British armed forces, were not in favor of severing relations with Britain or for independence.

The first official appeal for independence did not come from New England or from New York, but from Virginia, the largest in population of the colonies. Then from Pennsylvania, the second largest colony, came an unofficial revolutionary appeal entitled "Common Sense" by Thomas Paine, in favor of immediate independence.

Who was Thomas Paine? He was an exile and an obscure Englishman who arrived at Philadelphia two years before the Declaration of Independence. But on January 10, 1776, he wrote and issued a political pamphlet, clear and concise with bold and outspoken arguments for liberty and immediate independence. It attacked the British tyranny of the king and the House of Lords. It was a tremendously powerful propaganda appeal for independence and was read immediately by 120,000 Americans. No printed pamphlet ever had such an instant effect on the history of our country and perhaps of the world. The number of outspoken supporters for independence doubled in a short time. Washington publicly approved of the sound doctrine and unanswerable reasoning of the pamphlet. Edmund Randolph, the first attorney general of the United States, claimed that "the Declaration of Independence was due, next to George III, to Thomas Paine."

Before the demand ceased, half a million of Paine's pamphlets had been read by the American people. The equivalent circulation would be forty million on the basis of our present population. According to the contemporary newspapers, "Common Sense" turned thousands in New York to independence who could not endure the idea before. It is difficult to name any human composition which had such an electric and inspiring effect and "so instant, so extended and so lasting."

In "Common Sense," the American colonists saw and realized the light of liberty and independence. It was truly the greatest propaganda contribution and asset for the cause of independence and the consummation of the Declaration of Independence.

On June 7, 1776, Richard Henry Lee, a delegate from Virginia, moved that "these united colonies are, and of a right ought to be, free and independent states." Lee's resolution was referred to a committee composed of Thomas Jefferson of Virginia, Benjamin Franklin of

Pennsylvania, John Adams of Massachusetts, Chancellor
Robert Livingston of New York, and John Sherman of
Connecticut. This was a committee of outstanding ability, elected by the convention. Jefferson, then 33 years of
age, received the highest vote and acted as chairman. He
possessed both political experience and talent for prolific
and creative writing. Franklin, the oldest and perhaps
the best known for his abilities as a writer, a statesmen
and scientist, still ranks as one of our greatest Americans. John Adams, later to become president, was then a
leader in the cause of freedom and independence.
Robert Livingston, the highly talented chancellor of New
York, was one of the ablest lawyers among the American
Patriots. He was a collateral ancestor of the author. His
direct descendents claim he said that he had written a
considerable part of the Declaration. John Sherman was
a Connecticut Patriot who had held various high offices
with distinction and ability.

It would be historically wrong not to give each
member of the committee credit for helping to formulate the views and sentiments of the Declaration. However, Thomas Jefferson deserves the greatest praise and
commendation for his magnificent and untiring part not
only in formulating the views, but for his great and clear
facility in phrasing the remarkable document that sowed
the seeds of freedom throughout the world. Even the
eminent Massachusetts historians were unable to claim
parentage for our final separation from Britain.

The highest honors belong historically to the mastermind and political genius of the Declaration, Thomas
Jefferson. He was the chief draftsman of it, and realized
that however long the list of grievances against King
George III and the British Parliament might be, something more constructive had to be announced to the
world than merely a rebellion. Jefferson and his col-
leagues had the sound and wise judgement to see that a
new theory of government should be explained, particu-

Thomas Jefferson, painting by Rembrandt Peale

larly a political philosophy which provided the people the right to establish their own government and to control it. That is what made it the cornerstone of our Republic and the symbol of liberty everywhere.

"These were the times that tried men's souls." It took strong moral courage to write, sign, and publicly issue the Declaration of Independence. In 1776, all kings claimed to rule by Divine Right and there was no right of rebellion.

The signers were well aware that placing their signature on that famous Declaration might well mean the loss of their property, imprisonment, and the gallows. The threat and power of the royal judges, and military and other agents of King George III was very real. It was that master statesman, philosopher, and scientist, Benjamin Franklin, who, just before signing the Declaration, reminded his fellow delegates of their mutual peril by stating: "Gentlemen, we must hang together or surely we shall all hang separately."

The records confirm that the agents of King George III were prompt in their retaliation and punishment. New Jersey signer, John Hart, was hunted by the British for months, but he refused to leave his native state to be near his ailing wife. He was captured and imprisoned, and died shortly thereafter. Richard Stockton, another New Jersey signer, was arrested shortly after signing. Francis Lewis, a New York signer, had his home burned by the British. His wife, imprisoned for many months, was released on the intercession of Washington, but died a week after release from her imprisonment. The homes of fourteen signers of the Declaration were destroyed and their personal property confiscated. The fate of other signers was grim throughout the war. The closing lines of the Declaration are perhaps the most significant in American history. Certainly they are a source of real inspiration to all freedom-loving Americans:

Benjamin Franklin

We, Therefore, the Representatives of the United States of America, in General Congress assembled solemnly publish and declare that these United Colonies, are, and of right ought to be, Free and Independent States. . . . And for the support of this declaration, with a firm reliance on the protection of Divine Providence, we mutually pledge to each other our lives, our fortunes, and our sacred Honor.

The 56 signers of the Declaration took an awful risk of being hanged as traitors to the king and Parliament in case the armed might of Britain won the war. With the greatest navy in the world and an army composed of well-trained and battle-experienced regulars, supported by the Loyalists who constituted one-third of the population, victory was uncertain and dim for the American Patriots.

There is still an unanswered question whether Henry Wisner, a New York delegate, voted for the Declaration. It is possible he voted on the roll call but was not counted because the colonies were supposed to vote as a unit. Several weeks later, four of the New York delegates signed: Francis Lewis, Philip Livingston, William Floyd, and Lewis Morris.

John Alsop, also a New York delegate to the Second Continental Congress, resigned his seat on July 16, 1776, rather than sign the Declaration.

The Declaration proclaimed that all men are created equal and endowed with certain unalienable rights such as life, liberty and the pursuit of happiness, which it is the purpose of all government to secure; and that "whenever any form of government becomes destructive of these ends, it is the right of the people to alter or abolish it."

In a general order of July 9, 1776, General Washington communicated the Declaration to his army in New York. The order read:

The General hopes that this important event will serve as an incentive to every officer and soldier to act with fidelity and courage as knowing that now the peace and safety of his country depend under God solely on the success of our arms; and that he is in the service of a state possessed of sufficient power to reward his merit and advance him to the highest honors in a free country.

At the time of the Revolution, the word "liberty" was used as synonomous with "freedom" today. Patrick Henry closed his historic oration in the Virginia Assembly with the words: "Give me liberty or give me death." It is just as true as it was 199 years ago, and probably more so. Today in the U.S., subversives, cowards, and faint-hearts would sacrifice their freedoms on the altar of slavery and tyranny. The slogan "Better Red Than Dead" would have been angrily denounced by our founding fathers: Washington, Jefferson, Adams, Franklin, Hamilton, Lee, and all the others.

We are rapidly approaching the 200th anniversary of the Declaration of Independence, the greatest event in the history of the United States and one of the most important in the world. It not only set forth the reasons for our separation from Britain, but proclaimed to the world a new doctrine of freedom. It was, and has become, by time and tradition, our birthright and Bible of freedom. It was dedicated to the fundamental truths, concepts, and ideals of freedom.

The 200th anniversary of the Declaration on July 4, 1976, will be and should be the greatest and most important celebration in the history of the U.S. That immortal document proclaimed to the world a revolutionary form of government by the consent of the governed. It denounced British tyranny in the strongest terms. It affirmed, pioneered, and breathed a living flame of freedom, not only for Americans but for all people everywhere for ages to come. It is the cor-

113

nerstone of the foundation of freedom everywhere. It is still the hope and aspiration of the struggling masses of mankind, and particularly those behind the Iron Curtain in Communist-dominated nations. It is the Bible of freedom and has had more influence in all free nations than any other political document.

What do we mean by freedom? Free speech, a free press, freedom of religion, free and untrammeled elections, self-determination of nations, freedom to travel, freedom of assembly and protest, freedom from fear of concentration and slave labor camps and from despotic tyrannical totalitarian governments and police states. Freedom is the password and symbol of every loyal American and of all the free nations.

The preservation of freedom which was vital to our ancestors is even more important in our day and generation. The world Communist conspiracy and totalitarian forces seek to undermine and destroy our free institutions and free enterprise, and those of all free nations. The preservation of those freedoms is the paramount and single greatest issue in the world. It transcends all partisanship. It amounts to the survival of our country, of free Americans, and civilization based on our heritage of freedom. There is no substitute for freedom, and it is not negotiable.

President Richard M. Nixon added his outspoken endorsement of the preservation of freedom in a television address of November 3, 1969: "The defense of freedom is everybody's business. . . . The wheel of destiny has turned so that any hope the world has for the survival of peace and freedom . . . will be determined by whether the American people have the moral stamina and the courage to meet the challenge of free world leadership."

The Hon. Clare Boothe Luce made the issue crystal clear when she said, "Will mankind eventually stand in the light of freedom or crawl in the darkness of slavery?"

We Americans living under a government based on those freedoms provided by the sacrifices of the signers of the Declaration of Independence, guaranteed by the armed forces under Washington and later by the Constitution of the United States, the greatest charter of human liberty ever devised by the mind of man, do not propose to surrender one iota of our liberties and freedoms for any form of Nazism, Fascism, Communism, or any foreign totalitarian government.

The immortal Declaration which proclaimed our independence to the world was nothing but a scrap of paper until a government was established, through the leadership, courage, determination, and faith of George Washington and the Revolutionary Army. This was the beginning of our representative form of government based on freedom and democracy. Thirteen years later, when our present form of constitutional government was adopted, it became in time the oldest single continuous form of government in the world. It was founded on the fundamental principles of freedom, based on the rights of man, and approved and first inaugurated by the American people.

After the Constitution and Bill of Rights were adopted, freedom became synonomous with Americanism. It is today the guiding star of all oppressed and enslaved people living in Communist-dominated and totalitarian nations.

At the time of the Declaration of Independence and the adoption of the Constitution, there were very few nations in the world with a democratic form of government. The British government at the time of the Revolutionary War had a more representative form of government, including an elected Parliament, than almost any other nation, despite the fact that King George III was an out-and-out autocrat who believed in the Divine Right of kings. If it had not been for the sheer stubbornness and despotic leadership of King George III, there might not have been an American Revolution, or a Declaration of Independence.

Our wage-earners are the best paid, the best fed, the best clothed, best housed, and the most contented and freest in the world. If there is any country worth living in, defending, fighting or even dying for, it is the United States of America, the birthplace and homeland of freedom.

In celebrating the anniversary of the Declaration of Independence, the American people should reaffirm their faith in the U.S. as the fortress of freedom and hold high the torch of freedom so that its flames may be seen throughout the world.

The author hopes to be alive to witness the 200th anniversary celebration of our great and free nation, and to see the slanted Revolutionary War history revised in order to place New York State, on the basis of truth, as the battleground of the Revolutionary War.

14

The unsuccessful battle to defend New York City

When the British army under General Howe evacuated Boston, General Washington wisely and correctly anticipated that New York would be the next British target, in order to control the Hudson River and divide the American Colonies. From April, 1776, until the British army won the battle of Long Island on August 29th of that year, and forced the American troops back across the river into New York, that city had been turned into a beehive of fortress workers. The defenses were extensive, but not formidable.

Nicholas Fish, a militia major not yet 18 (an ancestor of the author), described the situation in a letter dated April 6, 1776, to his young friend, Captain Richard Varick, later to become mayor of New York and after whom Varick Street was named. He gives an interesting and vivid account of the military activities of the American army in New York.

Picture to yourself the once flourishing city, evacuated of its members (especially the Fair). Business of every kind stagnated; all its streets that lead from the north and east River blockaded and nothing but military operations are current employment. [He speaks] of being busy on fatigue duty, building a redoubt around the hospital.

This did not agree well with the tender hands and delicate texture of many, but it was executed with amazing ability and neatness. Another fort superior in strength was built at Bayard's Mount and rechristened Mount Montgomery as a monument to the great hero. The Battery was strengthened and forts were built on Long Island. We worked every day in the week including Sundays. All days are alike. Generals Putnam, Sullivan, Heath, Thompson and Lord Sterling are in town and Washington is hourly expected. There are about 14,000 troops and fresh arrivals from Cambridge daily. On Sunday before, an English landing party in search of water for the fleet in the narrows was driven off with the loss of about 24 men killed, wounded and captured.

The author has the original letter, which is much longer. They were prolific letter writers in those days.

Manhattan, which was then known as New York City, took in only Manhattan Island from Bowling Green to the Harlem River, as the Bronx at that time was a part of Westchester County.

The near disastrous defeat of the Revolutionary Army in the battle of Brooklyn, August 27-29, 1776, the rout at Kip's Bay, September 15, 1776, and the subsequent victory of Harlem Heights are all a part of what might be termed the unsuccessful battles to defend and maintain New York. This all occurred at the beginning of the Revolutionary War—within three months after the signing of the Declaration of Independence.

The British army, under Sir William Howe, landed on Staten Island in July of 1776 and remained there awaiting reinforcements, both British and Hessian. By the end of August, it was the largest expeditionary force Great Britain had ever assembled and approximated 32,000 well-trained, professional soldiers, supported by a fleet of thirty warships and 140 transports. It was reported that "there were so many masts in the lower harbor that the bay looked to one observer like a forest of pine trees."

Admiral Esek Hopkins

Washington, except during the seige of Boston, had never commanded an army in the open field. He had to learn generalship by trial and error. He committed a serious blunder in the art of war by dividing his little army, stationing one-half in New York and the other in Brooklyn with a virtually undefended river between them. Admiral Howe, the British naval commander, a brother of General Howe, failed to see what would have happened if he had ordered his fleet into the East River, thereby cutting off Washington's retreat from Long Island. He could have split Washington's army in half and made it an easy victim for British conquest. Fortunately Admiral Howe was in no hurry, and missed the opportunity. General Howe was a brave officer but easy-going, indolent, and generally inefficient, besides being a bon vivant or what is now called a playboy. He was a God-send to American success as he missed several opportunities to crush our armed forces. An interesting item concerning his career was that he was elected as a member of the Parliament on a pledge not to serve against American colonists, but when he was offered a high command by the king, he repudiated his promise. After the war, he was charged with military inefficiency and profiteering while in command of British forces in New York. His treatment of American prisoners in the rotten, disease-infested British hulks, and their death by thousands, will always be a stigma on his name.

The British forces landed in Long Island on the morning of August 27, 1776, and quickly defeated the inexperienced and untrained American army. Washington rushed over fresh regiments from Manhattan, but by the time of their arrival the defeat was an accomplished fact. The thundering and effective British cannon and the attack by the Redcoats and Hessians caused the out-numbered Continentals to retreat. Some did not retreat fast enough and were surrounded and captured. The British captured 900 prisoners, including Generals Sullivan and Sterling.

The prospect for the survival of the Revolutionary Army on August 29th was dim. General Washington, in the opinion of the historian Charles Francis Adams, "had disregarded almost every known principle of strategy or rule of tactics, some of them in an almost grotesque way . . . in reaching his decision. It is not too much to say that Washington betrayed a truly singular ignorance of what cannot be regarded otherwise than the elemental principles of military movement."

Military action of this type could be expected of Washington as it was virtually his first venture in command on the field of battle, and apparently he was more courageous and less cautious than he should have been. However, Washington's retreat in time saved his beaten and disorganized army. It was a remarkable, efficient, and successful maneuver. It took his courageous, inspirational leadership, not only to make the decision to order his dispirited army to recross the river to New York, but to organize a secret and rapid evacuation. He accomplished this by deceiving the British through an old dodge of keeping his campfires burning.

Moreover, George Washington had plenty of help from the heavens in what might be termed celestial interference in the destiny of men. It began to rain at the opportune time—while the Revolutionary Army was retreating to its last line of defense on the heights of Brooklyn. Proper British generals did not like to fight in the rain. They were confident that the rebel army had been disorganized and could be rounded up and captured when the rain stopped. Furthermore, the cannon had to be brought up and put in place for the final assaults. Consequently, the British advance guard was ordered to halt. But it continued to rain on the 29th, interspersed with a heavy fog. This gave Washington the opportunity to assemble his troops on the Brooklyn banks of the East River, to be ferried across during the night in every available type of small scows and boats. The Marblehead fishermen from Massachusetts, under

121

the command of Generals Parsons and Glover, were in charge of this highly successful operation. There was disorder and near panic on the Brooklyn shore, but, between Washington's steadfastness and sound leadership, the American army was saved. "Amid the gloom moved one majestic form, controlling the elements of discord and struggling with inexhaustible courage." Full daylight found Washington still on the Brooklyn riverside until he led his horse onto one of the last boats as the British advance guard appeared.

Washington's masterful retreat and evacuation of his beaten and disorganized army from Brooklyn largely offset his military errors of judgment. The test of real generalship is often greater in encompassing a successful retreat than in a fortuitous victory.

After the American defeat and evacuation of Washington's army from Brooklyn to New York, a council of the generals, presided over by Washington, determined that New York was untenable. It was a sound military move, as his army would have been trapped and destroyed if the city had been defended in force. All of the labor in fortifying New York was worthless.

Two weeks after the evacuation of Brooklyn, hostilities were resumed on the 15th of September. After a heavy cannonading by the British warships on the East River, the British infantry landed in force at Kip's Bay, East 34th Street. The Connecticut militia troops who were stationed there deserted their entrenched positions on the river banks and fled in panic towards the American fortifications at Harlem Heights without firing a shot.

Washington was at his headquarters at the Roger Morris House, at 160th Street on the west side, when he heard the booming of the British cannon on the East River, signaling the landing of their troops. He immediately rode with his aides to the scene of the battle. There he found a disorganized mob of fleeing soldiers—some even without guns because they had discarded them in their flight. This was about where Grand Central Station stands today. He quickly realized that this was not a battle but an ignominous stampede. The panic had spread among all the soldiers and even among the officers. Washington was "livid with rage," but neither he nor his aides could control the panicky rout. He was a general without any army and was "pale, haggard and broken."

Again there seemed to be almost a benign celestial interference in behalf of the American cause. The trouble with the British on that afternoon was that they did not have a general, for all the generals had gone to a party at the residence of the gay Mrs. Robert Murray, whose house was about 39th Street and Park Avenue. After all, what was the reason for haste, the British officers asked, when all the rebels could do was to run? Thus, due to the delay of the British advance, the Revolutionary Army again escaped and retreated to the fortifications at Harlem Heights. This particularly applied to the American troops stationed to guard lower New York, who were enabled to escape by taking the road north on the west side, which the British had stupidly delayed in securing.

The dawn of the next day was to bring about one of the most inspirational reversals in the history of the Revolution. Washington, on the morning of September 16th, having placed his troops on Harlem Heights in a strong defensive position—on a line roughly from 125th Street and St. Nicholas Avenue to 130th Street and the Hudson River, decided to forestall the British advance. He was consumed with anger and remorse at the debacle of the previous day, and his grim determination was easily understood and communicated to his troops. He ordered Col. Thomas Knowlton of the Connecticut Rangers to advance and probe the right wing of the British line. This gallant officer—killed later in the day—

attacked a British advance guard at about 106th Street and inflicted heavy casualties. The British were amazed at this unexpected audacity of the Revolutionary troops.

The signal for the British counterattack was a fanfare of trumpets, including a British bugler who put a horn to his lips and blew a few hunter's signals for the end of the chase, meaning that the fox had been cornered and was about to be taken by the dogs. A wave of anger spread through the Revolutionary line as they heard this hunting insult. During the next few hours, the British advance was checked and driven back by Colonel Knowlton's Rangers and by Major Leitch in command of three Virginia companies. Major Leitch was killed leading his troops in a victorious attack on the British Regulars. The fight, which was really a skirmish and not a full-fledged battle, took place near where Columbia University stands today.

The American victory revitalized the fighting spirit and prestige of Washington's army. Lord Howe recognized that he would have a much bigger job on his hands than he had anticipated to defeat the rebels and pacify the country. The valor shown by the Americans at the skirmish at Harlem Heights was enough to cause Gen. Sir William Howe to send a report to the British secretary of War that "he needed a much larger army if he was to win the war."

The battle, although on a limited scale, was an inspirational blessing to the American cause which was at a very low ebb as a result of the defeat and withdrawal from both Brooklyn and New York.

A month later, Washington, fearing encirclement by the British who controlled both the East and Hudson Rivers, retreated from Harlem Heights about thirty miles to White Plains, in Westchester County. There another hotly contested battle was fought with losses of about 300 on each side. Alexander Hamilton, with his little battery of five guns, played an important and gallant part in the American defense.

After the Battle of White Plains, Washington withdrew northward a short distance to the higher ground, but General Howe led his forces back to New York. On his return, he successfully attacked and captured Fort Washington at West 180th Street, with 2,700 Americans. This was the biggest British victory of the war, with the possible exception later on of the capture of Charleston, South Carolina. The British were generally successful in the battles around New York and New Jersey for the first year of the war. The second year, 1777 brought American victories, at Bennington, Fort Stanwix, and Saratoga and its associated battles in New York State. That included the capture of seven thousand British and Hessian soldiers. The same year also produced significant victories for Washington's army at Trenton and Princeton in New Jersey.

Major Nicholas Fish, aged 18, wrote the following scornful account from Kingsbridge (Harlem, N.Y.) on September 19, 1776, to Secretary John McKesson, at the New York State Convention, then at Fishkill. This letter describes the attack on New York September 15th, by the British at Kip's Bay, East 34th Street, and the cowardice of the Connecticut troops:

> This Phenomenon took place on Sunday morning last when our Brigade which was last in the City, excepting the Guards, marched to the lines back of Stuyvesant's where from Movements of the Enemy it was evident there was a preparation for landing. The Enemy's Ships of War were drawn up in line of Battle parallel to the Shore and Troops to the amount of about 4,000 were embarked in flat bottom boats. A Cannonade from the Ships began, which far exceeded my ideas, and which seemed to infuse a Panic thro' the whole of our Troops, especially the Connecticut Troops who unfortunately were posted upon the left, where the Enemy landed without the least opposition. Upon their near approach

125

to the Shore these dastardly sons of Cowardice deserted their lines & fled in the greatest Disorder and precipitation & I know not but I may venture to say infected those upon the Right, who speedily copied their vile conduct & pursued them in flight. I am sorry to say that the Panic seized as well Officers & those of distinction as men, in so much that it magnified the Number of the Enemy to thrice the Reality & generated substance from their own shadows, which greatly assisted them in their flight to the Heights above Harlem. . . .

We are now in possession of the ground from the Heights of Harlem to the Heights of West Chester, our advance Guard is posted a mile from our Lines. Here it was that our brave and heroic Marylanders Virginians, etc. made a Noble and resolute stand against the Efforts of the Enemy on Monday the 16th, drove them back, pursued and forced them to retire. The Conduct of the Troops on this occasion was so counter to that of some others the preceding Day as nearly to form a Counterpoise.

Our Troops were in a most desponding Condition before, but now are in good spirits. Our Brigade is encamping upon West Chester side.

Your most obedient & very humble Servant

Nich. Fish

P.S. In the action of the 16th we lost about 17 killed and I believe as many wounded. It is remarkable that all our killed were shot thro' the head, which induces the belief that they were first taken prisoners & then massacred. The number of the Enemy killed and wounded is not yet known, but it is generally thought they far exceeded us.

In fairness to the Connecticut troops, the Connecticut Rangers, under the command of Colonel Thomas Knowlton, drove the British advance guard back at Harlem Heights the following day, and restored the military morale of the American army, but in doing so, Colonel Knowlton was killed leading his troops to victory.

126

Later in the war, several Connecticut non-commissioned officers were signally honored by being presented with the Purple Heart, then awarded for exceptional bravery in battle. Only a very few of these decorations were issued during the war.

The Beverley-Robinson house, Garrison, N.Y.

15

The importance of the American Privateers during the Revolutionary War—

The Birth of the United States Navy

Privateering during the Revolutionary War was not a new enterprise. It began 200 years before our War of Independence, in the West Indies. Sir Francis Drake, Sir Walter Raleigh, Hawkins, and Morgan all preyed on Spanish treasure ships in the 16th and early 17th centuries, as did the French, Dutch, and Portuguese corsairs.

Admiral Piet Heim of the Dutch navy, in the employ of the Dutch West India Company which had recently been organized, made one of the greatest treasure hauls in privateering history in 1628. He captured, off of Matanzas in northern Cuba, the entire Spanish treasure fleet of eight galleons with 200,000 pounds of silver and nine others with different valuable commodities. The Dutch West India Company received twelve million dollars for financing the enterprise. This helps to show the reasons for the neglect of the Dutch West India Company toward New Netherlands. There was no gold or silver there, no Spanish pieces of eight, and not even the profitable sugar, cocoa, and fruit crops.

The fur trade in New Netherlands was good, but not in comparison with gold and silver. There were great quantities of beaver skins and other fur-bearing animals. The fur trade continued to be important and profitable for 200 years. New York later on remained as a center of the fur trade operations even while it extended to the Pacific coast. The Astor fortune was made out of the fur trade soon after the Revolutionary War, and continued for a number of years.

The twelve million in successful privateering payments to the Dutch West India Company was probably more than it received from the fur trade during the fifty years of Dutch control of New Netherlands.

In New York State, the Provincial (Patriot) Congress, in 1778, complying with instructions from the Continental Congress, encouraged the equipping of privateers by furnishing funds. Commissions were issued to twenty-four privateers. The better known were the *Washington, General Schuyler, General Putnam, Montgomery, Miflin, Congress, Independence, Revenge, Retaliation, Resolution,* and the *Enterprise.*

The capture of New York by the British on September 15, 1776, made privateering virtually impossible from there. From that time on, these privateers, commanded by New York Patriot captains and crews, were based in Connecticut and New Jersey harbors, although some might have operated from the eastern end of Suffolk County and certainly did after the withdrawal of the British garrisons from Suffolk in 1780.

These New York privateers preyed on British commerce. The *Montgomery,* of 24 guns, under Captain William Rogers, captured eight prizes. The *General Schuyler* and *Miflin* captured a number of prizes, including a brig and a Bermudian sloop. The *Nancy* was a captured British vessel which was fitted out as a privateer. As late as 1781, such vessels as the *Shark, Porpus, Fox,* and *Suffolk* were sent out as privateers from the eastern end of Long Island.

The Patriot privateering raids on Lond Island were carried out in small boats for the purpose of information, capturing important civilians such as the great Loyalist judge Thomas Jones for exchange purposes, and on a much larger scale in attacks on British outposts. These daring raids were not always successful. In one of them, Col. Samuel B. Webb of Connecticut, his officers, and eighty soldiers were captured by a British frigate before they landed. Colonel Webb was afterwards exchanged. He was wounded three times in battle and had a brilliant military career. Immediately after the war, he moved to New York City and became one of its leading citizens and is the ancestor of the well-known Webb family. The British policy regarding captured privateersmen was an abomination of desolation—man's inhumanity at its worst. Thousands of American sailors suffered death from starvation and disease on the vermin infested British hulk *Jersey*.

The United States Navy During the War

The Congress ordered the construction of twenty war vessels (frigates) in 1775, and established a marine committee in order to have representation from each of the colonies. Soon after the Declaration of Independence, the Continental Navy Board was appointed to assist the marine committee. In October, 1779, a Board of Admiralty was created. Its secretary, John Brown, was equivalent to our secretary of the Navy. Robert Morris, a delegate from Philadelphia, was authorized as marine agent to outfit a number of privateers, which he did, partially at his own expense. In November, 1776, Congress determined the relative rank of naval commanders. An admiral would be equal to a major general, and a commodore equal to a brigadier general. The first commander or high admiral of the navy was Esek Hopkins of Rhode Island. He led a small fleet to the Bahamas, captured the town of New Providence (Nassau), and brought back a large number of cannon and a quantity of powder. On the way home, he captured several British vessels off the east end of Long Island and took them safely into Narraganset Bay.

Although our navy was not successful with the warships Congress had ordered, it did not prevent John Paul Jones, and Captains Barry, Biddle, Manley, McNeil, and Hinland and others, from spreading terror and destruction on the high seas among the British merchantmen. They captured many prizes off the American coast. John Paul Jones, on his first voyage from Portsmouth, New Hampshire, which lasted six weeks, captured sixteen British vessels. In 1777, the Congress made him a captain of the new warship *Ranger*, in command of which he raided the British coast, burned several ships, and even destroyed some British fortifications, whereupon he sailed home without losing a single man.

Captain John Paul Jones, in command of a small American fleet outfitted at L'Orient, France, and manned by American and French sailors, prowled the coasts of England and Scotland during the autumn of 1779, taking prizes and even attacking weakly defended British and Scottish harbors. Jones's flagship, the *Bonne Homme Richard,* was an old, weather-beaten warship. But, fortunately for the American cause, was under the command of an experienced and intrepid Scottish-born American who did not know the word "surrender." The battle between his ship and the British frigate *Serapis* was one of the bloodiest and fiercest ever fought. The American warship was such a complete wreck that the British captain called for its surrender and Jones then made his famous reply heard around the world, "I have just begun to fight." He steered his battered ship alongside the more modern frigate and led his men in a bloody conflict that ended in the surrender of the *Serapis*. Jones was forced to abandon the *Bonne Homme Richard,* which sank soon after the battle.

In command of the enemy warship, he sailed his lit-

131

"The Honorable Sir William Howe, Commander in Chief of His Majesty's Forces in America"

tle fleet back to the French harbor where he was welcomed by the entire population. His name and exploit were carried in all the French gazettes and American newspapers. It was a great topic of conversation for a long time in the taverns and coffeehouses, and in the highest circles of both France and the United States. He became an American hero overnight, and not only the foremost naval commander of the Revolutionary War, but among the very greatest in the naval history of the United States.

The record of our navy, particularly the exploits of John Paul Jones, were gallant and at times brilliant. But our Revolutionary navy had an impossible task, confronted by the greatest navy in the world. At the beginning of the war, Britain had 30 warships, with 500 guns and 4,000 sailors, which operated from Halifax and New York. This fleet was increased from time to time as needed, to keep British trade routes open and to patrol the entire coast from Canada to Georgia. The efforts of our navy to defeat or to diminish the vast British naval superiority were ineffective. Except for John Paul Jones's victory over the British *Serapis,* there were no other important naval victories. The British had the ships and the gunpower and we had very little to oppose them with until the French fleet joined the war.

Of our twenty frigates authorized by Congress, four were destroyed in the process of building to prevent their falling into the hands of the British.

The frigates *Warren* and *Providence* were bottled up in Rhode Island for two years, and the *Raleigh* was captured within a year. The *Virginia,* built at Baltimore under Capt. James Nichollson of New York, was captured before leaving the Chesapeake. He was then given the command of the *Trumble,* which was likewise lost. The frigate *Randolph,* commanded by Nicholas Biddle, remained ineffective in Charleston for months because the crew deserted. Finally, in her last fight, she blew up, kill-ing the entire crew. The frigate *Hancock* was captured and renamed the *Grisby* by the British. At the end of the war, the American navy had only one or two ships larger than an armed schooner.

Most Americans believe that George Washington and his army won the war single-handedly and overlook the important part played by our own American privateers, our warships, and the French fleet.

Privateering during the Revolutionary War became a serious and dangerous business on a large scale. All types of boats were used, from whaleboats to ships of considerable size, that attacked the British merchantmen on the high seas and particularly in the West Indian trade.

The Loyalists in New York also organized a privateering fleet of their own on Long Island Sound. Theirs were smaller vessels used in commando raids that kept the people and farmers in Connecticut in fear and turmoil. These small vessels conducted their operations under cover of darkness and raided the farms of the Patriots along the Connecticut coast. The Loyalists had the backing and encouragement of the British High Command in New York, and were permitted to keep what they took. The fleet of associated Loyalists, had its headquarters at Lloyd's Neck, Long Island. Its operations were carefully planned and were for the double purpose of protecting Long Island from the Patriot marauders and for making their own raids. This privateering venture had great appeal to numerous Loyalists who were without employment in New York and vicinity. They brought back cattle, sheep, poultry, and grain which they had seized from the Connecticut farmers. This was manna for the New York Loyalists. Very often the Loyalist privateers captured Patriot prisoners whom they exchanged for captured Loyalists. There were also good-sized British privateers from New York that raided the American coastal trade from Boston to Atlanta.

134

The Patriot privateers, however, had a big advantage, for they had the whole coast from Massachusetts to Georgia to operate from. Despite the fact that it was highly dangerous, the rewards were so great that there were several thousand Patriot privateers, small and large. American privateers reaped a rich harvest. Benjamin Franklin wrote from France in 1777, "that which makes the greatest impression in our favor is the prodigious success of our armed ships and privateers. The damage we have done in the West India trade has been estimated by the Merchants of London at one million eight hundred thousand Sterling, which has raised the insurance rate to 27% higher than at any time in the last war with France and Spain."

Professor Albert Bushnell Hart, the well-known American historian, is quoted as saying: "America, however, not only preyed, but was preyed upon. For the six hundred vessels that our cruisers took before the French alliance, we lost nine hundred vessels to British cruisers. New England coasting trade and fisheries were nearly ruined."

Assuming an average of fifteen sailors on each privateer of the 900 lost, it would amount to thirteen thousand five hundred captured American sailors. However, some were killed, escaped, freed, or traded for Loyalists. Even the whale boats, which were used extensively on Long Island Sound, carried a crew of ten to fifteen.

The whole coast of Connecticut was a hornet's nest of stinging American privateers. In retaliation, Governor Tryon, commanding a large body of Loyalist troops, invaded and burned Fairfield, Norwalk, and the ships in New Haven harbor. Later on, Gen. Benedict Arnold burned the American ships at New London and part of the town, and a Loyalist regiment of his command massacred the American garrison at Fort Griswold.

The activity of the large privateers and the mosquito fleet along the coast played havoc with the British supplies for New York, which was dependent on supplies from London, Halifax, the West Indies, and from the Loyalists on Long Island and in New Jersey.

The history of the American privateers and their destruction of the British commerce to and from New York was an important factor in winning the War of Independence, but is still almost unknown to the American people.

Most of the sailors captured on American privateers were brought back to New York to be imprisoned on the rotting and disease-laden British hulks stationed off the Brooklyn shore, near the recent navy yard. A large part of these sailors came from New York, Connecticut, and the rest of New England. Thousands of them died of starvation and disease as a result of a deliberate and diabolical British extermination policy.

The great New England historians who lauded the Boston Tea Party, Paul Revere's Ride, Lexington and Concord, and "the shot heard around the world," overlooked and ignored the terrible ordeals and the sacrifice unto death of thousands of young, patriotic New York and New England privateersmen.

New York had been the center of privateering during the English and French Seven Years' War for possession of Canada 1756-1763. It was revived immediately at the outset of the Revolutionary War.

The British Parliament in November, 1775, declared the revolting colonists to be rebels and determined to crush them by force of arms. The seizure, destruction, or confiscation of all American vessels was authorized.

A huge land and naval force of 55,000 was voted to crush the rebellion. Later, 20,000 Hessians were hired to kill the American colonists who had petitioned for their rights and had opposed taxation without representation.

Intelligence of the war measures taken by Parliament caused the Congress to take immediate steps to prepare defensive measures. George Washington was appointed to command the American forces at Boston. Privateers were authorized, and private individuals were encouraged under government license to arm and equip privateers to prey on British merchant ships.

Privateer whale boats from Connecticut infested the shores of Long Island. They entered the harbors; captured the wood boats, oyster boats, and fishing boats; took Loyalist prisoners; seized their cattle, horses, slaves, and provisions; and destroyed their crops. The prisoners, sailors and farmers, were exchanged for American prisoners in New York.

A group of Rhode Island Loyalist refugees was granted permission by Governor Henry Clinton, the British governor of New York, to erect a fort at St. George, in Suffolk County, Long Island. Owing to the deprivations of these Rhode Island Loyalists, complaints were made to Governor Clinton, who ignored them. The local inhabitants then appealed to Major Talmadge, an American officer in Connecticut. Whereupon he crossed the sound with 200 Patriot soldiers and privateersmen, and captured the fort and all of its 200 occupants without the loss of one man. On his return, he stopped at Coran and set fire to and destroyed about seventy tons of hay for use of the British army.

The privateers were generally small, swift, graceful ships, well armed, with from 2 to 24 guns, and manned by experienced crews, most of them trained as whalers or fishermen on the Grand Banks. They were bold, effective fighting machines, akin to their earlier cousins, the pirates. These raiders "pounced on unsuspecting British merchantmen, like a falcon on the dove." They swarmed over the sea lanes and around the trading posts in the West Indies. The smaller privateers, that often had only one or two guns, prowled along the coast and bays to cut off supplies to New York. They also acted as scout ships to watch and report the activities of the British patrol boats and frigates whose duty it was to keep the Long Island Sound open for all types of British ships bringing supplies to New York City.

Approximately 1,500 small and large privateers were based on the New England coast, along the New Jersey shores, and the Delaware River. The dramatic story of the Patriot American privateers during the Revolution and the very important part they played in helping to defeat the British is a fascinating story in itself. Even the names of these privateers had a romantic sound and were interesting to the public, such names as *Hornet, Wasp, Tiger, Dolphin,* and *Rainbow.* One of the best-known privateers, the *Ranger,* was built by private subscription at Portsmouth, New Hampshire.

Such was the fighting spirit of the swarms of American privateers which courageously challenged the mighty British navy that they succeeded, by harassment and hit-and-run tactics, in capturing and destroying 600 British merchant ships. About 10,000 Patriot sailors were captured from the privateers or from American naval vessels, and in attacks on their home bases from 1775-1783. It is almost impossible to obtain adequate records of these American privateers and what happened to them and their crews. All that their home folks would know was that the ships did not return to their ports.

The success of the American privateers caused the British navy to order drastic actions against them, and seek in every way to destroy or curb their activities. The infuriated British admirals feared the ravages of these privateers and, when they were captured, treated the sailors even worse than the captured soldiers. In revenge, they sent all sailors to the *Jersey* and other hell ships, to die of starvation, putrid food, and maltreatment.

Such was the patriotism of these privateersmen that they preferred death to disloyalty and treason. They steadfastly and virtually unanimously refused to serve in the British navy or to cooperate with them in any way.

Thousands of American sailors suffered death by extermination in the British prison hulks. These patriotic sailors were the unsung heroes of the Revolutionary War, and bequeathed the legacy of loyalty and patriotism which has been part and parcel of the gallant history of the United States Navy ever since.

In the spring of 1780, General Robinson, then in command of New York since General Howe was with a great part of the Royal Army in Philadelphia, decided to concentrate his troops near New York City for defensive purposes. The British garrisons at Oyster Bay, Huntington, Brookhaven, Southampton, and other posts on eastern Long Island, consisting mostly of DeLancey's Brigade, were withdrawn and the works demolished.

This withdrawal of British Long Island outposts encouraged the American patriots in eastern Long Island (Suffolk County) to outfit a large number of whale boats, commissioned as privateers, and even larger ships.

Connecticut, New Jersey, and all of New England were the bases for patriot privateers against British merchant ships and smaller craft. Privateering was also carried on from hidden harbors all the way down the east coast to Georgia. There were several thousand privateer American ships all the way from southern Georgia to northern Massachusetts which courageously preyed on the British commerce from England, Canada, and the West Indies throughout the war, and suffered very serious losses.

16

Martyrdom of thirteen thousand American Patriots—
The Monstrous Jersey—A Disease-Infested Inferno
A Camouflaged British Policy of Horror
and Extermination

Certainly the truth can now be told without arousing animosity. The historian has a duty to narrate the facts, no matter how gruesome they may be. In this instance, it tells the story of unrivaled American heroism and also reveals the frightful horrors suffered by American prisoners in the disease-infested prison ships in New York harbor. It is one of the most tragic, but little-known, events in our history.

Actually, three times as many American Patriots were liquidated—13,000 on the infamous British prison ships and in New York prisons—than the 4,300 killed in the American armed forces during the entire war. It is only right that the terrible fate of these early American Patriots and heroes, who preferred death to disloyalty, should be publicly known.

If there are still Americans influenced by the Revolutionary War propaganda emanating from New England, let them pause and read impartially the story of the martyrdom of 13,000 American prisoners in the foul, overcrowded jails, in disease-infested, rotting hulks; in the loathsome warehouses and sugar factories in New York City during our War for Independence. New England was fortunate in knowing little of such horrors and atrocities, although many of their sailors died unknown in the British hell ships.

Last but not least were the densely crowded churches, and warehouses where Patriot American prisoners died like rats, of disease and hunger. In the summertime, they suffered from suffocation and, being without covering, froze to death or died of pneumonia in the winter. With little food and scanty water, the health of the prisoners was quickly undermined, which left them no power of resistence to the mass attack of dysentery, typhoid fever, smallpox, yellow fever, tuberculosis, and contagious diseases of all kinds. The food was not only insufficient to keep body and soul together, but was often putrid.

There was obviously a conspiracy among Provost Marshal William Cunningham, Commissary Joshua Loring, and Naval Commissary David Sprout, down to the lowly prison guards, to decimate the rebel prisoners. "Decimate" is not the correct word, as it means taking the death toll of only one of every ten. The proper word should be "annihilation" or "extermination," for that is what it amounted to. It was one of the most horrible and awesome tragedies in American history. There is nothing to compare with it in military history since the religious wars 400 years ago, except the butchery of the Jews by the Nazis. The Black Hole of Calcutta, in which English soldiers in overcrowded prisons were suffocated to death, is the nearest resemblance to what occurred on the terrible prison ships and in other British prisons in New York City, Charleston, and Savannah.

Ten thousand American Patriots, mostly in their early twenties or thirties, imprisoned on board the inhuman British prison ship *Jersey*, were given stinking food and literally starved to death or died of disease. This extermination policy now appears to have been a deliberate conspiracy not only among the prison commissaries, but actually by the British High Command.

These unfortunate victims of the Revolution were buried in the sands of the adjacent shore of Wallabout Bay, where the Navy Yard in Brooklyn was located.

Twenty years after the war, in making walls and building sites, a vast quantity of the bones of these martyrs were dislodged and strewn over the shore. They were, however, collected by Captain John Jackson, the proprietor of the neighboring land, and reinterred at his expense. Later still, public ceremonies were held over this common grave, but even to this day these American Patriots, who preferred death at its worst rather than disloyalty to their country, are still the forgotten heroes of our War for Independence.

The *Jersey* was by far the largest prison hulk, but there were others, and several so-called hospital ships which were almost equally as bad. Captain Freneau, who was confined on board both hospital and prison ships, survived by being exchanged. He put his sufferings into verse, which he entitled "The Prison Ship":

The various horrors of these hulks to tell,
These Prison-ships where pain and penance dwell,
Where death in tenfold vengence holds his reign,
And injur'd ghosts, yet unaveng'd complain;
This be my task
There, the black Scorpion at her moorings rides,
There, swings Strombolo, yielding to the tides,
Here, bulky *Jersey* fills a larger space,
And *Hunter,* to all hospitals disgrace—
Thou, Scorpion, fatal to the crowded throng,
Dire theme of sorrows and Plutonian songs,
Requir'st my lay—thy sultry decks I know,
And all the torments that exist below,
The briny wave that Hudson's bosom fills,

Dripp'd through her bottom in a thousand rills,
Rotten and old, e'er fil'd with sighs and groans
. . . .
No masts or sails these crowded ships adorn,
Dismal to view, neglected and forlorn;
Here, mighty ills oppress'd th' imprison'd throng,
Dull were our slumbers, and our night were long—
From morn to eve along the decks we lay,
Scorch'd into fevers by the solar ray.

The silent acquiescence of Lord Howe and other British generals in the tragic and criminal actions of Provost Marshal Cunningham, Commissary Loring, and Naval Commissary Sprout and their evil subordinates is appalling and difficult to explain. The author has spent considerable time investigating the records of this frightful tragedy, and feels that there is no longer any reason to cover up this mass murder of American heroes by disease, starvation, overcrowding, and the elements.

It can be compared to a more recent and even more horrendous crime, but actually much more merciful, and that was the mass murder by shooting of 12,000 Polish officers by the Communists in Katyn Forest and in other parts of Russia. At least they did not die by degrees—a living death.

Naturally, the British used every propaganda device when they capitulated and evacuated New York City to cover up their responsibility for these prison dens of iniquity and death and for the stinking hulks of abomination and desolation. The evidence is contained in the letters written by prisoners who survived. There is also the word of escaped and exchanged prisoners. Then there is the report made by Elias Boudinot, appointed commissioner by Congress to secure the exchange of prisoners, to provide them with clothing and food, and to investigate the situation in some of the New York prisons, by consent of the British.

Eight years after the prison doors were opened as a

143

result of the American victory, William Cunningham, the notorious former provost marshal, made a pre-hanging confession in writing. He was hanged in England in 1791 for forgery. Cunningham was a thoroughly vicious character. He was the son of a British soldier, brought up in Ireland. He became engaged in the illicit business of shipping indentured servants to Boston and New York under false pretenses. The last shipment was freed by the New York courts.

From that time on, Cunningham developed an intense and bitter hatred of American Patriots. He came to New York and became a leader among a gang of "bully boys" who annoyed and picked fights with the Whigs or Patriots. On one occasion, the retaliation by the Sons of Liberty was instantaneous. Cunningham was beaten and forced to get on his knees and bellow for liberty. The chastisement by the Liberty Boys added insult to injury and increased his intense hatred of the Patriots. Later, when he became provost marshal, he brutally treated the American prisoners who came under his absolute reign of terror. He ingratiated himself with General Howe and other British authorities because of his well-known hatred of the so-called American rebels.

General Howe, as commander in chief, cannot escape his responsibility for appointing Cunningham, a person of the lowest character, to the important office of provost marshal. The appointment of such a ruffian and scoundrel and his bloody acts of reprisals and hangings are a black mark on the record of General Howe and Sir Henry Clinton, before God and man. They not only had a direct responsibility for the acts of their agent, but they obviously knew the terrible situation in the prisons, yet kept Cunningham in office during the entire time of their command.

Howe had a direct link also with Commissioner Loring, whom he appointed. Loring was a Boston Loyalist and a contemptible character second only to Cunningham, in greed, graft, and starvation of prisoners, besides selling his wife to Howe for the appointment. This is not just unfounded gossip, but a fact well known in New York during the Revolution, and related afterwards by the historians of that period. Later, Loring admitted he misappropriated two-thirds of the allowance for prison food, resulting in the starvation of the American prisoners which caused them in their weakened condition to die off like flies before the ravages of disease and exposure. When the American commissioner, Elias Boudinot, asked Cunningham who was responsible for the loathsome conditions of the prisons, he arrogantly replied that he was entirely responsible and that he saw no reason for any change or excuses.

He had an assistant by the name of Sergeant O'Keefe, a cruel, brutal blackguard who treated the prisoners worse than condemned criminals. He was probably the secret hangman or at least in charge of almost 300 private, unofficial hangings ordered and directed by Cunningham without any kind of trial. The public hangings were those of spies, British deserters, and condemned criminals. It is inconceivable that under British army control such bestial and lethal treatment of prisoners of war was permitted and continued almost to the end of the war.

The confession of Cunningham deals with his early life and the reasons for his hatred of American Patriots. The fact that it was made eight years after the war when he was hung is not unusual. The famous trial of Adolph Eichman, the Nazi executioner of the Jews in the German and Polish concentration camps, was held in Israel sixteen years after the end of World War II. Memoirs by participants of that war are still flourishing. It is not surprising, however, that the British authorities did everything in their power to cover it up, and denounced Cunningham's confession as a forgery just as the Nazis tried to hide their iniquities in the concentration and extermination camps. Commissioner Loring, who admitted appropriating the money for the prisoners' food, and who was responsible for the deaths of a large number of them from starvation, escaped hanging and died shortly after the war in England.

Both Cunningham and Loring combined did not cause one-fourth as many deaths of American Patriots as Naval Commissioner Sprout in the old death-trap prison ships. Cunningham and Loring killed off, between them, approximately 2,500 prisoners through starvation, sickness, and privation in the city prisons, warehouses, churches, and in the Provost jail, whereas 10,500 helpless prisoners died of disease and putrid food in the stinking British hulks. The prisoners actually rotted away until death took them out of the dismal hulks. They were virtually murdered, these 13,000, one-third of which were civilians. The lucky ones were those who escaped or were exchanged. If we estimate 1,000 were exchanged, 100 escaped, and 200 more permitted to go free through bribery or parole, the percentage of death amounted to 75 percent, as compared with Andersonville and Elmira prisons of 33 percent in our Civil War. The death rate of French and British prisoners of war in German prison camps was not more than 15 percent, and actually less for American prisoners. The estimated death rate on the *Jersey* was 85 percent. The author places the total American prisoner mortality at 13,000, which is 1,000 less than other estimates.

The following is an extract from the *Life Confession and Last Dying Words of William Cunningham,* formerly the British provost marshal in the City of New York who was executed in London the 10th of August, 1791, taken from his own mouth by the Ordinary of Newgate.

The first part deals with his early life, which is unimportant. He was born in Dublin Barracks in the year 1738, the son of an English soldier, and his early life was mostly connected with the army. In 1772, at Newry, Ireland, he engaged in the business of enticing mechanics and country people to ship themselves to America on promises of great advantages. Then he artfully obtained indentures upon them, the consequence of which was that on their arrival in America they were told of it and obliged to serve a term of years for their passage. Quoting from the *Confession:*

I embarked at Newry, in a ship *Needham*, for New York, and arrived at that port the fourth of August, 1774, with some indentured servants I had kidnapped in Ireland. But they were liberated in New York on account of the bad usage they received from me during the passage. When the war commenced, I was appointed Provost Marshal to the Royal Army, which placed me in a situation to wreck my vengeance on the Americans. I shudder at the murders I have been accessory to, both with and without orders from the government, especially while in New York, during which time there were more than 2,000 prisoners starved in the different churches, by stopping their rations, which I sold.

There were also 275 American prisoners and obnoxious persons executed; out of all this number there were only about one dozen public executions, which chiefly consisted of British and Hessian deserters. The mode for private executions was thus conducted. A guard was dispatched from the Provost about half after 12, at night, to Barrack Street and the neighborhood of Upper Barracks, to order the people to shut their window shutters, and put out their lights, forbidding them not to presume to look out of their windows or doors, on pain of death; after which the unfortunate prisoners were conducted, gagged, just behind the Upper Barracks, and hung without ceremony and there buried by the black pioneers of the Provost.

It is very difficult to estimate the number of American sailors captured by the British on both large and small privateers and on navy warships during the war. It

147

is certainly not fewer than 9,000. A very large percentage of the captured sailors were imprisoned on the *Jersey* or companion prison ships, where they were virtually exterminated.

In the *History of the City of New York,* Charles Burr Todd asserted that "no less than ten thousand six hundred and forty-four American prisoners perished in the 'Jersey' during the war." But what of the other smaller ships, *Whitby, Good Hope, The Prince of Wales, Falmouth, Scorpion, Strombolo,* and *Hunter?* Two of these were so-called hospital ships. The mortality rate on these must have been far less than the *Jersey* because of better conditions or being less crowded. It would seem that the *Good Hope* was reserved for sea captains and other officers. In 1779, nine sea captains overpowered the guard and got away in one of the ship's boats.

Historians of the American Revolution state that 900 American privateers were captured by the British. If that is the case, the average would certainly not be less than 12 per privateer and that would amount to 10,800. It is fair to assume that some escaped, some were killed, some were released, and others were exchanged for Loyalists.

It is almost impossible for a New Yorker or American to attempt in any way to justify the brutal treatment and murder of thousands of American prisoners of war in British prisons or in the murderous prison hulks. There must be some underlying or concealed reasons for such a barbarous violation of the laws of humanity and the custom of warfare. The responsibility in a military organization rests with the top officers. Out of the 20,000 prisoners in New York, there were not more than 5,000 captured soldiers: 3,000 surrendered at Fort Washington, 1,000 at the battle of Brooklyn, a few hundred at White Plains, and in the capture of Forts Clinton and Montgomery, and the rest in skirmishes in Connecticut, New Jersey, and Westchester.

There were about 9,000 sailors captured from the eastern seaboard. The remaining 6,000 were civilian Patriots who lived in New York City, Long Island, Staten Island, New Jersey, Pennsylvania, Connecticut, and Westchester.

General Howe, and Sir Henry Clinton, who succeeded him, apparently for military reasons, secretly adopted a program approaching extermination because there was no place except England to send the prisoners, and probably England did not want them. New York was to some extent a beseiged city and might be attacked at any time. An adequate food supply would then be necessary. Thousands of American prisoners would also have been a serious menace in case of attack.

The author merely suggests possible reasons that may lessen, but which never can condone, the criminality for such murderous acts.

It would not be fair to make such serious charges of cupable neglect or designed cruelty against the commander in chief of the British army or of a criminal thirst for riches on the part of David Sprout, without definite first-hand evidence. Sprout, a Scotsman whose face put his scarlet coat out of countenance, had two assistants: one Scottish and the other a refugee from New Jersey. The general character of the first was harshness and of the second, kindness. The responsibility or blame should not be placed solely on the prison commissaries or deputies for the cruel death of thousands of American patriots.

The following statement is by an officer on board the U.S. Frigate *Confederacy* that was captured by two British frigates: "Being at the time of capture sick, he was put on board one of the hulks in the Wallabout that served as a hospital ship for convalescents, but was as soon as somewhat restored transferred to the 'Old Jersey' to make room for others more helpless." Here he experienced all the suffering, and witnessed the horrors

149

described by the Rev. Thomas Andros for five months. The confinement in so crowded a place, a pestilential air, the putrid and damaged food given to the prisoners (procured by the commissaries for little or nothing, and charged to the English government at the price of the best provisions) soon produced a fever under which this young man suffered without medicine or attendance, until nature, too strong for even such enemies, restored him to species of health, again to be prostrated by the same causes. He said he "never saw given to the prisoners, one ounce of wholesome food. The loathsome beef they prepared by pressing, and then threw it, with the damaged bread, into the kettle, skimming off the previous tenants of this poisonous food as they rose to the top of the vessel."

On the 18th of January, 1777, George Washington wrote to Lord Howe on the subject of naval prisoners:

that I am under the disagreeable necessity of troubling your Lordship with a letter almost wholly on the subject of the cruel treatment which our officers and men in the Naval Department, who are unhappy enough to fall into your hands received on board the Prison ships in the harbor of New York.

From the opinion I entertain of your Lordship's humanity I will not suppose that you are privy of proceedings of so cruel and unjustifiable a nature and I hope that upon making the proper inquiry you will have the matter so regulated that the unhappy persons whose lot is captivity may not, in the future, have the misery of cold, disease and famine added to their other misfortunes.

You may call us Rebels, and say we deserve no better treatment, but remember, my Lord, that we still have feelings as keen and sensible as Loyalists and will if forced to, most assuredly retaliate upon those upon whom we look as the unjust invaders of our rights, liberties and properties.

I should not have said this much, but injured countrymen have long called upon me to endeavor to obtain redress of their grievances, and I should think, myself, as cupable as those who inflicted such severities, were I to continue silent.

The answer of Lord Howe was evasive and a general denial of the charges.

Howe was a poor disciplinarian, and naturally lazy and indolent, who preferred the good things in life and did not want to be bothered with investigations that might take up his time or reflect on the British army's administration in New York.

Judge Thomas Jones, an ardent Loyalist, and in exile with the British, condemned General Howe bitterly in his book on New York during the war for inefficiency and disregard even of the property of the Loyalists, who were constantly being robbed by British troops. General Howe's relationship with the wife of Joshua Loring, whom he had appointed commissary of the prisons, was a scandal well known among the Loyalists. Loring was finally relieved of his position on charges of corruption and sent to England during the war, where he died shortly afterwards, a disgraceful and despicable character.

Bancroft's *History of the United States* drew a tragic picture of the British prison ships in Charleston, South Carolina, and stated, "of more than 3,000 confined in these ships all but 700 were made away with." The situation among the American prisoners in Savannah was almost as bad. It would seem from this that there was a definite policy of extermination of so-called rebel prisoners in these horrible disease-infested British hulks.

The British army commanders, both in Charleston and Savannah, were directly under the control of the commanding general in New York, first Sir Henry Howe, and next Sir Henry Clinton. Fortunately for the officers, many of them were exchanged, and the number of officers incarcerated in the living tombs were few. Most of them were kept in the main provost prison in New York in very cramped quarters, but their chances of exchange or survival were good.

Early in the war, the Continental Congress commissioned Lewis Pintard of New York to try to alleviate the conditions of the prisoners held there, which he did until the funds ran out, but continued with his own money until it was exhausted.

His nephew John Pintard wrote a description in the *New York Mirror* of September 10, 1831, of the treatment of American officers in the Provost Prison during the Revolution:

> Cunningham roamed from cell to cell . . . insulting the noblest of the land. He saw them suffering from cold, and he mocked their cry for bread. For slight offenses he thrust them into underground dungeons. . . .
>
> The North-east chamber, turning to the left on the second floor, was appropriated to officers and prisoners of superior rank and distinction, and was called Congress Hall. So closely were they packed that when they lay down at night to rest, when their bones ached on the hard oak planks, and they wished to turn, it was altogether by word of command, "right-left" being so wedged and compact as to form almost a solid mass of human bodies. . . .

Nathan Hale, just before his execution as a spy, was permitted to write a brief note to his mother and to Miss Adams, to whom he was betrothed, in which he said, "I wish to be useful and every kind of service, necessary to the public good, becomes honorable by being necessary. If the exigencies of my country demands a peculiar service, its claims to the performance of that service are imperious." As he ascended the ladder, he turned to his executioner and said, "I only regret that I have but one life to lose for my country." The brutal provost marshal

Cunningham who was the chief of the execution, upon reading his other letters, destroyed them and exclaimed with an oath "the 'damned rebels' shall never know they had a man who could die so bravely."

It appears that the treatment of American prisoners became steadily worse as the war progressed. Actually, the *Jersey*, the monster of them all, was only used as a prison ship the last four years.

Sometime after the war, in response to a request from our government, the British army archives furnished a partial list of the American prisoners on the *Jersey* to the number of 8,000. Some twenty years after the war, in 1804, the Columbian Society (Tammany Hall) undertook to collect the bones of these Patriots buried at Wallabout Bay and transferred them to a tomb in a wooden building nearby. Seventy years later, the people of Brooklyn built a permanent tomb at Fort Greene Park, and later still, in 1912, a monument was erected there to those early American Patriots who preferred death on stinking prison ships to dishonor and disloyalty to their country.

It is estimated that ten thousand American Patriots paid the supreme sacrifice for their country, mostly in the one "living hell" ship, the *Jersey*, yet there were others, but not as deadly. "Abandon ye all hope who enter here" applies accurately to the infamous *Jersey*.

The most outrageous of all the crimes committed by Cunningham was the hanging of 275 American prisoners of war without trial and in utter repudiation of all existing articles of war. The ignominious and undercover hanging of war prisoners was a blot on the British military government.

All of these Patriots could have betrayed the cause of liberty and independence in exchange for their lives, but preferred death. All they had to do was to sign a document of allegiance to the Crown and receive a free pardon by enlisting in His Majesty's Army or Navy. If we were to single out any group of Americans for out-standing patriotism, it would be the prisoners in the British prison hulks and in the jails. These Patriot prisoners should be placed at the top of the list of sublime courage and sacrifice in support of independence and freedom. This recognition is long overdue.

This chapter is the most ghastly and longest in the book. After 200 years, the America people are entitled to know the blood-curdling truth and to learn about the heroism of our Revolutionary War Patriots, even unto death.

17

The Hudson River Highlands was the fortress and cradle of our Republic, and Washington's headquarters for more than three years

George Washington spent 3½ years, or one-half of the Revolutionary War, in the southern part of New York State, mostly along the banks of the Hudson River.

The title of this chapter is enough to prove that New York State was the center of the Revolutionary War activities and its greatest battleground. Ninety-two official engagements out of 318 in all thirteen states, were fought in New York State.

The Highlands along the Hudson River was a natural fortress during the Revolution, controlling navigation on the Hudson and the Post Roads between New York and Albany and New England, and its vital importance is difficult to overemphasize.

General Washington saw the necessity of using the Highlands as the permanent fortified base for the Continental army early in the war. It was his determined and continuous policy to hold and fortify the Highlands against attacks by the British army in New York City. None of the combined military exploits and political events compared to the 25-mile section of the Hudson River which includes Stony Point; Forts Montgomery,

Clinton, Constitution, and Lafayette; VerPlanck's Point; Continental Village; Peekskill; West Point, the main American stronghold; Washington's chief headquarters at New Windsor and Newburgh; Temple Hill at New Windsor; Fishkill, the depot of supply; the VerPlanck house at Fishkill; General Von Steuben's headquarters; and the site of General Arnold's headquarters at the Beverly Robinson House at Garrison.

Washington sacrificed his fortune and risked the gallows in assuming the leadership of the American rebellion against the armed might of King George III and the British Empire. There is no doubt that patriotism stirred him, but the fires of ambition also urged him on to victory and immortal fame.

Washington is universally considered by most Americans and Europeans as one of the greatest men who ever lived, and rightly so, because of his exalted and almost sublime character and successful leadership of the "ragamuffin" army which achieved victory over the best-disciplined, most-experienced, and bravest soldiers in the world. The British army, hitherto, had been successful in Europe, India, Canada, and in a large part of the four corners of the world.

For some reason, a strange myth has grown up critical of Washington's indecisive military leadership which only in recent years has been exploded by students of history. It is possible that, because of Washington's many great qualities and outstanding character, his military competence has been minimized by historians with the result that public opinion has regarded Washington as a mediocre general.

Recent historians, after intensive research, have refuted this myth by emphasizing that General Washington, who was in command of our armed forces for seven long years during the Revolution, was responsible for winning a final and complete victory from almost certain defeat. He had under him a number of brave generals who were often motivated by ambition, and quarreled with each other, and even with him and the Continental Congress. They were constantly threatening to resign, and it took all of Washington's firm leadership to keep them united and fighting. Nevertheless, he was able, by his authority, patience, and courageous resolution, to keep unity in the army and to out-maneuver and out-fight the enemy, and finally, after great hardships and privations, to force the British army, which out-numbered his own, to retreat from Philadelphia back to New York. Then, with his small army, he succeeded in keeping the British forces off-balance, penned up in New York City and afraid to come out and fight a decisive battle. His final, highly successful maneuver, marching 300 miles from New York with the French army under Rochambeau to Yorktown, brought about the capitulation of General Cornwallis with his army of 6,000 British Regulars, and thereby virtually ended the war.

No other American general, with the possible exceptions of Robert E. Lee and Douglas MacArthur, could have, with such inadequate forces, out-maneuvered one of the largest armies that Britain had ever sent overseas, and won an all-out victory.

In 1778, the British warships and accompanying troops out-numbered the militia defenders of Forts Clinton and Montgomery, located three miles south of West Point. General George Clinton, afterwards governor of New York State, his brother General James Clinton, and a number of the militia escaped in the night to fight again.

General Washington, at his headquarters at New Windsor, ordered General Anthony Wayne to retaliate for the loss of Forts Clinton and Montgomery by attacking a strongly fortified British post fourteen miles south of West Point on the west side of the River.

The storming of Stony Point by General Anthony

Wayne on July 15, 1779, and the capture of the entire British garrison with all the munitions, artillery, and stores, was one of the most daring and successful feats during the war. The following is the official report of General Wayne to the commander-in-chief:

Stony Point, July 16, 1779
2 o'clock A.M.

Dear General: The fort and garrison with Col. Johnston are ours. Our officers and men behaved like men who are determined to be free.

Yours most sincerely,

ANT'Y WAYNE

The army was immediately informed of the victory by General Washington from his headquarters at New Windsor:

The Commander-in-Chief is happy to congratulate the army on the success of our arms under Brig. Gen. Wayne, who last night with corps of light infantry, surprised and took the enemy post at Stony Point, with the whole garrison, cannon and stores, with very inconsiderable loss on our side.

Five hundred British soldiers and their officers were taken prisoners in a gallant, commando-type raid. It ranks as one of the major military victories of the war.

18

West Point—our greatest
Revolutionary War Fortress

It was located fifty miles from New York City, where the river takes a sharp turn in a narrow channel, and was the most logical and strongest possible place for a fortification on the lower Hudson River. On January 20, 1778, on the recommendation of Governor Clinton, approved by George Washington, a brigade of Continental troops under General Parsons began the construction at West Point of the most formidable fortress of the Revolutionary War.

The first recorded visit of Washington to West Point is in Thatcher's *Military Journal,* on the date of July 16, 1778:

> His Excellency, the Commander-in-Chief visited West Point to take a view of the works, which are being constructed there. His arrival was announced by the discharge of thirteen cannons, the number of the United States.

About two months later, Washington visited West Point again and wrote the following letter from there to General Duportail, the chief engineer of the army:

Sir: I have perused the Memorial which you delivered, relative to the defense of the North River at this place, and upon a view of it, highly approve what you have offered upon the subject. Col. Kosciuszko, who was charged by Congress with the direction of the forts and batteries, has already made such progress in the construction of them as would render any alteration of them in the general plan, a work of too much time, and the favorable testimony which you have given to Colonel Kosciuszko's ability prevents any uneasiness on this head.

From July 16, 1778, the date of Washington's first visit to West Point, until the end of the war, five years later, well over half of his time was spent in the Highlands.

To those skeptical people who have doubted that Independence Day is celebrated on the right or correct date, the following order of George Washington, taken from the orderly book, should set their minds at rest:

Sunday, July 4, 1779, New Windsor, N.Y. This day being the anniversary of our glorious independence will be commemorated by firing 13 cannons from West Point at 10 o'clock P.M. The Commander-in-Chief thinks proper to grant a general pardon to all prisoners in the army under sentence of death. They are to be released from confinement accordingly.

The headquarters of the commander in chief was transferred to the Moore House at West Point on July 21, 1779, and remained there until November 28, 1779. The house occupied by Washington was situated in what is now called Washington Valley, about a mile to the north of West Point and near the river. It was designated in general orders as "the Moore House," and was built prior to 1749 by John Moore, a prominent merchant of New York and grandfather of the bishop of Virginia, Richard Channing Moore. The house must have been a large, costly structure, being known in its day as "Moore's Folly." It was during this period that the strong works of the fortress and vicinity were constructed.

While at his headquarters at "Moore House" on July 29, 1779, the commander in chief issued the following remarkable order against swearing:

Many and pointed orders have been issued against that unmeaning and abominable custom of swearing. Notwithstanding which with much regret the General observes that it prevails, if possible more than ever; his feelings are continually wounded by the oaths and imprecations of the soldiers whenever he is in hearing of them. The name of that being from whose bountiful goodness we are permitted to exist and enjoy the comforts of life, is incessantly imprecated and profaned in a manner as wanton as it is shocking. For the sake, therefore, of religion, decency and order, the General hopes and trusts that officers of every rank will use their influence and authority to check a vice which is as unprofitable as it is wicked and shameful. If the officers would make it an unavoidable rule to reprimand and if that does not do, punish soldiers for offenses of this kind, it could not fail of having the desired results.

The author, with pardonable pride, asks permission to inject an ancestral note by quoting briefly from the account published by the Marquis de Chastellux in his *Travels in North America* on his visit to West Point, in November, 1780:

On landing or rather on climbing up the rocks which rose on the border of the river, and the feet of which the river washed, we were received by Col. Lamb and Maj. Bowman, both artillery officers, by Maj. [Nicholas] Fish a young man of fine figure, refined and intellectual and by Maj. Frank formerly aide de camp to General Arnold.

During the autumn of 1779, when General Washington had his headquarters at West Point, the garrison consisted of two Massachusetts brigades at the Point, the Connecticut line on the east side of the river between the Garrison house and the Robinson house, and the North Carolina brigade on Constitution Island.

West Point was virtually an impregnable bastion that controlled the Hudson River and guaranteed unmolested transport of troops across the river north of West Point, from the supply depot at Fishkill to the American army encampment at New Windsor, and to Washington's headquarters at nearby Newburgh.

The British valued West Point highly and entered into a conspiracy with Gen. Benedict Arnold, in command at West Point, to surrender it for an appointment as brigadier general in the British army for 6,350 pounds, 500 pounds a year for Peggy, his wife, commissions in the British army for his three sons by a former marriage, and after 1785, 100 pounds a year for Peggy's five children. Benedict Arnold betrayed the young American Republic at a much higher price than Judas Iscariot. The traitorous Arnold might have succeeded in betraying the American cause for which he had previously fought so gallantly at Quebec and at Saratoga where he was wounded, if Major André, the British agent, had not been captured. Because of his wounds, General Washington entrusted Benedict Arnold with the less active command at West Point.

Major John André, the British adjutant general, was commissioned by Gen. Henry Clinton, in command of the troops in New York, to contact General Arnold regarding the plans for surrender. The young and accomplished British officer, just as he was about to reenter his own lines with incriminating documents providing for the betrayal of West Point, was captured by an American outpost.

Arnold, at that time, was at his headquarters, the lovely home which previously had belonged to Col. Beverly Robinson, then a colonel of the Loyal American

162

Major André

Regiment in the British army. It was located two miles
south of West Point on the east side of the river. It afterwards belonged to the author's grandfather, Hamilton
Fish, and was destroyed by fire in 1892. Arnold was
awaiting the arrival of General Washington and his staff,
returning from a visit to General Rochambeau, commander of the French army at Hartford. As Washington
and his staff were approaching West Point, he sent forward two young officers to notify Arnold of his arrival.
While Arnold was breakfasting with these two officers,
he received word of Major André's arrest. He told the

officers he had to go over to West Point immediately on urgent business. He took leave of his wife and fled to what is known as Beverly Dock, one-third of a mile away, where he kept a large barge and crew for his transportation to West Point. He ordered them to take him down the river, twelve miles to the British sloop of war *Vulture*, which they did, not suspecting any treachery. Thus the greatest traitor in American history escaped with his life, to fight on the side of the British against his compatriots, which he did in a brutal and murderous fashion, both in the capture of New London and in the Virginia campaign.

When Washington arrived at Arnold's headquarters, he was dismayed not to find Arnold. He crossed the river to look for him at West Point and, not finding him, again returned to Arnold's headquarters on the other side of the River, known as Beverly. There he learned of Arnold's treason, but it was too late to prevent the traitor's escape. Turning to General Knox, Lafayette, and Hamilton, more in sorrow than in anger he said, "Whom can we trust now?"

This story is told briefly only to show the very great importance which the British High Command at New York placed on the seizure of West Point through the blackest kind of treason in order to obtain control of the Hudson River and divide the New England states from the middle and southern states. It was this strategy that caused New York State to become the most important and the bloodiest battleground of the entire Revolutionary War.

When General Arnold became a British general in New York after his treason, he raised and commanded the American Legion, with which he conducted depredations from Connecticut to Virginia. The powerful American war veterans' organization of today, called the American Legion, would be aghast to learn of the origin of the British American Legion commanded by an American traitor.

West Point and the Highlands

After Arnold's treason was discovered, Mrs. Arnold went into hysterics and, by clever play acting, completely deceived General Washington, Alexander Hamilton, General Lafayette, and Arnold's staff as to her innocence. Washington provided transportation for her to be escorted by Major Frank, one of Arnold's aides, back to her family in Philadelphia.

It wasn't until much later that the facts became known. It might interest the readers to know the truth.

Gen. Benedict Arnold, aged 38, married, while in command at Philadelphia, the 18-year-old Tory socialite Margaret Shippen. He acquired an expensive, lovely, ambitious, pro-British wife. Strong-willed, determined, charming Peggy Arnold was a co-conspirator in the proposed betrayal of West Point. She acted as an intermediary in the secret correspondence with Major André, whom she knew during the glamorous days of the British occupation of Philadelphia. For over a year, Arnold and his young Tory wife sought to sell-out West Point, even in advance of his appointment there, for 10,000 pounds and a British generalship. It was a definite, well-calculated plot that failed by almost providential help when Major André was captured.

Early historians believed that Arnold had sold-out for greed, avarice, ambition, and anger at Washington's stern reprimand over his maladministration as military governor of Philadelphia. But after the war, clear proof that Arnold's young wife was the main instigator of the traitorous conspiracy. She shrewdly feigned ignorance until she rejoined Arnold behind the British lines.

There are those who believe, with a good deal of credibility, that Arnold also planned to capture General Washington and his staff at the time of the proposed surrender of West Point to the British. This could have been accomplished without too much difficulty, as Washington did not have the faintest suspicion of Arnold's treachery. If Arnold had succeeded in surrendering West Point to the British, it would have been a devastating blow to the American cause of freedom and independence. If he had arranged also to capture Washington, and maybe Knox, it would have been a death blow to American war plans and at least set back the hands of victory for many years.

West Point was never attacked after it was actually fortified. In 1778, a chain and boom was installed from West Point to Constitution Island but it was not effective. When the fortifications at and around West Point were completed, it was protected by 28 forts and gun batteries, making it the most heavily fortified post in the United States, and it remained so throughout the war. The garrison at West Point was composed of between 2,000 and 4,000 troops, both New York militia and Continentals who were camped on both sides of the river. The Continental troops were mostly from New York, Connecticut, or from the rest of New England.

After the war, West Point was the headquarters for the enlistment and organization of New York and some Connecticut volunteers for service in the First United States Regiment, sometimes called the First American Regiment. This was the only regular regiment, and composed our entire army except for the militia.

Lt. Col. Nicholas Fish was in charge of the New York and Connecticut contingent, and was second in command to Colonel Harmer of Pennsylvania, the commander of the regiment, a much older officer.

The early histories of the formation of the First United States or American Regiment are erroneous and defective because the extensive correspondence between Lt. Col. Nicholas Fish and Gen. Henry Knox, secretary of War, was destroyed in a fire at the War Department. The author has approximately 100 letters, originals and copies many from General Henry Knox, secretary of War, addressed to Lt. Col. Fish commanding the troops in New York. These volunteers for the First United

Colonel Nicholas Fish, from a miniature by Malbone

States, often called the First American Regiment, were organized at West Point in 1885 and 1886. Other volunteers were organized in Philadelphia by Colonel Harmer.

The author goes into some detail regarding the formation of the first and only regiment in the American army after the disbandment of Washington's army because of the fire that destroyed most of the correspondence between General Knox and his staff with Lt. Colonel Fish. Thirty years ago, the author went to the historical department of the army in the Pentagon Building in Washington, and showed the commanding officer there letters from Knox and the War Department regarding the formation of the regiment and was told then all these letters had been burned in a fire and that the War Department was delighted, even at this late date, to get the true information about the creation of the First United States or First American Regiment, which was the precursor of the Third U.S. Regiment. This is unwritten history. It is therefore of great historic importance, as West Point was the base for at least half of the original regiment, and mostly from New York.

In the chapter on the history of New York State Indians and their participation in the Revolutionary War, there is a letter from General Knox dated April 9, 1786, to Lt. Colonel Fish explaining about Indian policy after the war. Lt. Colonel Fish, who was 27 years of age, after he had been in command of the troops at Fort McIntosh on the Ohio River for several months before Colonel Harmer arrived, wrote him to find out whether the rumor was true that he did not expect to continue in command much longer. It was a friendly letter, but Lt. Colonel Fish had to decide whether he wanted to remain in the regular army with the immediate prospect of promotion as the head of the only regiment, or to accept an offer by Governor Clinton of New York to become the first adjutant general of that state. When he found out definitely that Colonel Harmer intended to remain in the army, he accepted the appointment as the first adjutant general of New York State, and held that office for many years.

Due to the burning of the correspondence between General Knox and Lt. Colonel Fish, the historic part played by West Point almost immediately after the war in the formation of the First Regiment in the service of the United States is confused and little known.

It is also an historic fact, but likewise little known, that George Washington was the first to propose the creation and maintenance of a military academy at West Point, and naturally the memory and name of

Washington will always be held in the highest honor there. History also tells us that General Alexander Hamilton, an artillery captain in the Revolutionary War, and General Henry Knox, as chief of artillery, both recommended the establishment of a military academy at West Point, for instruction in artillery.

Today West Point is generally regarded as the finest and greatest military academy not only in the United States but throughout the world, and among its famous graduates were Generals Winfield Scott, Robert E. Lee, U. S. Grant, William Sherman, Stonewall Jackson, Phillip Sheridan, John Jay Pershing, Douglas MacArthur, George Patton, and Dwight D. Eisenhower.

Major General Henry Knox, First Secretary of War and founder of the Society of Cincinnati

19

The Hasbrouck House at Newburgh, where Washington refused the offer of a crown

The Hasbrouck House, at Newburgh, New York, which is the most important of all of Washington's headquarters, is still standing and justly claims to be among our most famous Revolutionary shrines. The Hasbrouck House has the distinction of being his main headquarters from April 1, 1782, to August 19, 1783, which is far longer than any of his other headquarters. It may even be said that our Republic was born in the Hasbrouck House, as it was here that he refused an offer of a crown and, at the end of the war it was the symbolic White House of the New Republic.

Washington's headquarters at Newburgh may properly claim to be the first White House in America. It was from the Hasbrouck House that Washington wrote his famous letter of advice to the governors of the states, and, as stated, his reply to Colonel Nicola disdaining the offer of a crown. It is probable that his law-and-order speech delivered at the "Temple," or new building in New Windsor, was written in the Hasbrouck House.

Owing to the reputation of Congress for weakness and incapacity, Washington, after Yorktown, was, for all practical purposes, not only the commander in chief of

171

Steuben's headquarters at Fishkill, N.Y., where the Society of Cincinnati was born

the army, but also the true ruler of the confederation. A steady stream of distinguished foreign officers and statesmen sought General Washington at his Newburgh headquarters, surrounded by his well-known generals. General Knox occupied the John Ellison House, which is still standing at New Windsor, until he took command at West Point. General von Steuben occupied the Verplank House across the river at Fishkill, where the Society of Cincinnati was organized on May 13, 1783. The Verplank House, which is often referred to as Mount Gulian, was unfortunately burned down 35 years ago, but has since been rebuilt by the Society of Cincinnati. The Marquis de Lafayette had his headquarters at the Brewster House in New Windsor, and the other generals were all nearby.

The following is an extract from Bayard Tuckerman's book on Lafayette:

As the *James Kent,* in 1824 approached Newburgh, Lafayette said to his old companion in arms, "Nick what has happened to those lovely Newburgh girls we went sleigh riding with?" And Nicholas Fish is reported to have replied, "General, they are all respectable grandmothers now."

The Marquis de Chastellus describes his visit on December 5, 1782, to Washington's headquarters at Newburgh in the following words:

We passed the North River as night came on, and arrived at six o'clock at Newburgh where I found Mr. and Mrs. Washington, Colonel Tilgham [Tilghman], Col. Humphreys and Major Walker. The Headquarters at Newburgh consist of a single house, neither vast nor commodious which is built in the Dutch fashion. The largest room in it (which was the proprietor's parlour for his family, and which General Washington has converted into his dining room) is in truth tolerably spacious, but it has seven doors and only one window. The chinmey, or rather the chimney back, is against the wall; so that there is in fact but one vent for the smoke, and the fire is in the room itself.

Martha Washington spent considerable time at the Newburgh headquarters and helped in receiving the distinguished guests and in entertaining the generals and their wives. It is related that she maintained a flourishing garden in front of the Hasbrouck House. The following letter from Mrs. Washington to General Knox and his reply may be of interest to the American public in these days of bobbed hair:

Newburgh, March 6, 1783

Mrs. Washington presents her compliments to General Knox and begs acceptance of two hair nets. They would have been sent long ago, but for want of tape to finish them and which was not obtained till yesterday.

173

General Knox has the honor to present his most respect-
ful compliments to Mrs. Washington and to assure her
he is deeply impressed with the sense of her goodness in
favor of the hair nets for which he begs her to accept his
sincere thanks.

The Hasbrouck House, cherished for the length of
Washington's residence and made sacred by the events
that occured there, is still in good condition and was taken over by the state when the author's grandfather,
Hamilton Fish, was governor in 1849, and is administered by a nonpartisan commission appointed by the
governor of New York State.

There is apparently some confusion concerning the
indignant answer made by Washington to the offer of a
crown from his disgruntled officers. It was not delivered, as is often stated, in a speech from Temple Hill,
near Newburgh, but was contained in a letter written to
Colonel Nicola, a meritorious foreign officer in the
Pennsylvania line, from the Newburgh Headquarters on
May 22, 1782. He rebuked the attempts of those officers, dissatisfied with the weakness of the incompetent
Congress at Philadelphia, who wished to make him
"King by the voice of the Army" and establish a constitutional monarchy in our country.

The firm rebuke administered by Washington to
those officers with monarchial proclivities was delivered
ten months prior to the well-known Law and Order
Speech at Temple Hill and had no connection with it,
and constituted the mightiest blow struck for the formation of our Republic since the Declaration of Independence was proclaimed at Philadelphia seven years before. Washington's letter to Colonel Nicola concluded
with these words:

Let me conjure you, then if you have any regard for your country, concern for yourself or posterity, or respect for me, to banish these thoughts from your mind and never communicate as from yourself, or anyone else a statement of like nature.

Later, on March 15, 1783, at Temple Hill, New Windsor, before a convention of officers presided over by General Gates, the commander in chief answered the justifiable complaint of his officers for back pay, many of whom had expended their own means and were about to be discharged on empty promises. In one of the most memorable addresses in American history, Washington prevented his officers from open rebellion against the Congress by his wise advice and sagacious leadership. Amid the most profound attention, General Washington commenced reading:

Gentlemen: By an anonymous summons, an attempt has been made to convene you together. How inconsistent with rules of propriety, how un-military, how subversive of all order and discipline; let the good sense of the Army decide.

Pausing a moment, he drew out his spectacles, carefully wiped and adjusted them, and while doing so remarked:

These eyes, my friends, have grown dim and these locks white in the service, yet I have never doubted the justice of my country.

He pointed out the dreadful consequences of following the advice of the anonymous writer, subsequently ascertained to be Major Armstrong (afterwards, secretary of war):

175

Either to draw their swords against their country, or retire, if war continues, from the defense of all they hold dear.

I conjure you in the name of our common country, as you value your own sacred honor, as you respect the rights of humanity, to express your utmost horror and detestation of the man, who wishes, under any specious pretenses, to overturn the liberties of your country and who wickedly attempts to open the floodgates of civil discord and deluge our rising empire in blood.

The convention resolved, unanimously, among other things, that the army have unshaken confidence in Congress and view with abhorrence and reject with disdain the infamous proposition contained in a late anonymous address to officers of the army.

This address of Washington's, upholding military discipline and our existing civil government, is as a sublime a speech as was ever delivered by any American. It was the first law-and-order speech which has become so common today, and had a far-reaching effect on maintaining intact the fruits of victory already won after seven long years of deprivations and warfare.

The famous letter of congratulation and advice to the governors of the thirteen states, pointing out the course he deemed it the duty and interest of the country to adopt, was written by General Washington on June 8, 1783, from Newburgh, and is one of the most important state papers in our history and stands next in general acclaim to the better-known Farewell Address.

The letter to Colonel Nicola refusing the crown, the speech on law and order at the "Temple," and the letter of congratulation and advice to the governors were all composed by Washington at his headquarters at Newburgh.

Congress was at times hysterical, often absurd, and usually impotent. It passed resolutions, gave much advice to the commander-in-chief, and sat forever whistling

176

to the wind. The state governments were filled with jealousy and suspicion, by no means groundless, one of another. They were incapable of effective cooperation without a delegation of their petty sovereignties to the federal government. Congress was in fact bankrupt of executive power, and still more wanting in able men. The need of officers had drawn many away, while foreign missions and state governments had found more congenial employment for others. The finances of the country were in a most dismal state or near exhaustion while profit-making and corruption took a heavy toll upon the meager funds. "Speculation and peculation," in Washington's words, "were deadlier enemies than the fleet and armies of King George."

Is there any wonder that Washington's headquarters at Newburgh after the victory at Yorktown, for a year and a half was the virtual White House of America?

Students and readers may well ask why has the defense of the Highlands and Washington's Newburgh letters and address at Temple Hill, been given so little attention by historians. The answer is that almost all the historians of the Revolutionary War hailed from New England. Lodge, in his *Life of Washington*, although he mentions Washington's refusal of the crown and his speech to the dissatisfied and rebellious officers, does not even indicate that these events took place at Newburgh and vicinity.

The people living in the Hudson Highlands have a right to be proud of the historic landmarks near where Washington's headquarters still stands as a testimonial to the nearness of the Revolutionary War and the far-reaching events that occurred there, affecting the interests, and welfare of the American people and the formation of our republican form of government.

Senator William M. Evarts, speaking at the centennial celebration of the disbanding of the American army in 1883 at Newburgh, said: "Wide however is our land

and vast our population today, these are not the limits to the name, fame, life and character of Washington. No wonder his countrymen celebrated the event and the scene where Washington refused the crown."

Emphasis has been placed on Washington's headquarters at Newburgh for a year and a half. The actual length of time spent by him at his various headquarters, including the Highlands, are as follows: six months at his headquarters in the Roger Morris House in New York City, now owned by the Daughters of the American Revolution. Around 160th Street on the west side, it was occupied by Washington from September 16 to October 21, 1776. Previous to that, it was the old DePeyster house in the lower part of New York. A fair estimate would be that Washington had his headquarters at Morristown, and at other New Jersey locations, including Trenton, Princeton, and Monmouth, which are within seventy miles of New York, for a period of a year and a half. The figures in New York State are strictly accurate; those in New Jersey are estimated. They show that Washington had his headquarters in New York State for 3½ years, and for 1½ years in New Jersey, where his army was still within striking distance of New York City.

These figures are all based on when Washington assumed command of the American troops in New York City in April, 1776. The only time he spent outside of this radius was when he occupied Philadelphia, fought the Battles of Brandywine and Germantown, lost Philadelphia, and encamped at Valley Forge in the winter of 1778-1779.

The Pennsylvania campaign involved about a year's time, and six months was spent going from New York to Yorktown, including the campaign there, and returning to New York. This gives a rough composite of the geographical breakdown of Washington's main headquarters after the Declaration of Independence.

Washington weighed and deliberated all his actions,

but his genius showed in his matured and considered judgment and personal leadership. He, as the public hero of the war, established an enduring precedent when he was elected president. Public heroes in the succeeding wars took over the White House. Andrew Jackson, the hero of the War of 1812, was later elected president. The precedent was followed by Zachary Taylor, the Mexican War hero, and by General Grant, Hayes, Harrison, and McKinley, all of whom served in the Union Army during the Civil War. General Pershing in World War I did not become president, but Capt. Harry Truman did.

World War II produced four Presidents: Eisenhower, John F. Kennedy, Lyndon B. Johnson, and Richard M. Nixon. Those who did not serve in our armed forces in the emergency of war were invariably defeated as aspirants or candidates for the presidency: Thomas E. Dewey, Averell Harriman, Nelson Rockefeller, and Hubert Humphrey.

Washington's humility in understanding that he needed advice and help was a source of his courage. It was this courage—the firm, relentless, sustained courage to carry on through all difficulties—that was his outstanding characteristic, out of which he, more than any other, created a nation.

Abraham Lincoln, who ranks second only to Washington as our greatest and best-loved president, delivered an eloquent and inspired eulogy on Washington, February 22, 1842, when Lincoln was only 33 years of age. It is still unsurpassed in the English language. It contains beautifully worded gems of truth.

Washington, is the mightiest name on earth—long since mightiest in the cause of civil liberty, still mightiest in the cause of moral reformation.

On that name no eulogy is expected. It cannot be.

To add brightness to the sun, or glory to the name

of Washington is alike impossible. Let none attempt it.
    In solemn awe pronounce the name and in its naked
deathless splendor, leave it shining on.

All Americans, young and old, should take to heart this
little known, magnificent eulogy of George Washington.

Washington's Headquarters, Newburgh, N.Y.

20

Alexander Hamilton, the ghost writer of Washington's Farewell Address

Over a long period of time, the author has made a careful investigation, having the benefit of the original letters in his possession, and is impelled in fairness to Alexander Hamilton, one of America's greatest statesmen, to set forth his impartial views on why he is convinced that Hamilton was the virtual author of the famous Farewell Address.

Through the lapse of time, the greatness, glory, and attainments of George Washington cannot be diminished by the fact that he selected Hamilton to ghost write the historic Farewell Address.

The author's great grandfather, Col. Nicholas Fish, was the closest life-long personal friend of Alexander Hamilton, or at least from 1774, when, as youngsters of 16 and 17, they first met in New York, until the day of Hamilton's death, thirty years later in a duel with Aaron Burr. He was named by Hamilton as an executor and a trustee of his Last Will and Testmament, together with John B. Church, Hamilton's brother-in-law, and Nathaniel Pendleton.

Nicholas Fish, who was made a major in the Continental (regular) Army at the age of 18 and three

Alexander Hamilton, after the Wiemar painting

months, was the youngest major ever commissioned in the armed forces of the U.S. up to the present time. The author has the original commission signed by John Hancock, president, dated 1776. He served with distinction throughout the Revolutionary War. He was second in command of the New York Regiment of which Alexander Hamilton was colonel, in the seige of Yorktown.

Fish was commissioned a Lieutenant Colonel by Brevet soon after the victory at Yorktown. When the war was over, he was appointed a Lt. Col. in the First (and only) United States Regiment, which was stationed at Fort McIntosh on the Ohio River, in the midst of Indian territory. He resigned in 1786 to accept an appointment by Governor Clinton as the first adjutant general of New York, which office he held until 1793 when he was appointed by President Washington as the first supervisor of Revenue of New York. He married Elizabeth Stuyvesant in 1803, and occupied the house at 21 Stuyvesant Street, which was a wedding gift from his father-in-law. This was one year before Hamilton was killed in the duel.

As stated in another chapter, Fish declined to serve as second in that duel as he believed it would amount to planned assassination. He urged Hamilton not to accept such a nebulous, politically inspired challenge. However, Hamilton, whose son Philip had been killed in a duel only a few years before, felt he was honor-bound to accept, but stated he would fire harmlessly in the air. Public opinion after the death of Hamilton apparently believed that it was politically inspired, and Burr, although vice-president of the U.S., was outlawed in most of the northern states.

Nicholas Fish outlived Hamilton's two other executors by more than a decade.

Many friends and admirers of Alexander Hamilton wrote him letters inquiring about various phases and events of Hamilton's life. These letters the author inherited, including numerous letters from Hamilton's wife asking Nicholas Fish, as one of his earliest and closest friends, if he would put into writing his recollections of Hamilton's younger days in New York City before he joined the Continental Army, and also about other events in his life. Among the interesting letters was one from Theodore Sedgwick from Stockbridge, Massachusetts, immediately after Hamilton's tragic death, inquiring about an unfinished letter from him. This is the letter in which Hamilton stated the day before the duel that "I have had in hand for some time a long letter to you, explaining my view of the course and tendency of our politcis and my intentions as to my future conduct—But my plan embraces so large a range that owing to much avocations, some indifferent health and a growing distaste for politics, the letter is still considerably short of being finished." This letter, unfortunately, was never found among Hamilton's papers. Theodore Sedgwick was an able lawyer and Federalist leader who became speaker of the House of Representatives and a U.S. senator. He declined an offer from Washington to be secretary of the Treasury.

Nicholas Fish maintained an extensive correspondence from 1822 to 1825 with Timothy Pickering, a close friend of George Washington and Hamilton. Col. Pickering, who came from Salem, Massachusetts, was a prominent Revolutionary War officer, having served both as adjutant general and as quartermaster general in the army under Washington. He also served, later on, as secretary of war and as secretary of state under the Washington administration, and continued for a number of years as secretary of state under John Adams.

His lengthy letters to Nicholas Fish show his intense interest in having an impartial and able life of Alexander Hamilton written and the truth presented concerning the authorship of the Farewell Address.

Limitations of space in this chapter will only permit

quotations of the most pertinent comments and observations made by Colonel Pickering to Nicholas Fish, who at the time of these letters was the sole remaining executor of Alexander Hamilton. In Pickering's first letter, dated Salem, July 30, 1823, he says:

When I had the pleasure of seeing you two weeks ago, we had some conversation about Washington and Hamilton, and writing the life of the latter. . . . Washington's acts which have given him such an unrivaled reputation, are so blended with the efficiency of Hamilton, that I fear it will be difficult to find a biographer bold enough to do justice to the latter; it would so derogate from the generally supposed transcendant abilities of the former. . . .

The day after I saw you, I saw Mr. King [Senator Rufus King of New York, minister to Great Britain]. We had an hour's conversation, *tete a tete;* Washington and Hamilton two of the subjects. I repeated what I mentioned to you—Mr. Jay's reasons for concluding that the *original draft* of the Farewell Address, was Washington's own. Mr. King answered that he had the letters which Judge Pendleton had put into his hands, by which it would appear that the original draft was made by Hamilton. These letters, I understand, were the correspondence of Washington and Hamilton on the subject. These ought to be in the possession of Mrs. Hamilton to put in the hands of her husband's biographer.

Washington had virtues so extremely rare among men in high public stations as to place him on an eminence elevated, and almost unique, but his intellectual powers were so much below those of many others, on so moderate a scale, that I venture to say you will never find in Hamilton's writings a single expression of eulogy on that ground. *Suum cuious tribuito.* Hamilton's counsels and writings were most material, perhaps I should say essential to Washington's superior fame. Let Hamilton have his share. The sentiments in Washington's Farewell Address ought not to have the less weight, if, instead of Washington's, they are known to have eminated from a

185

superior mind; and to be judged so correct as to be approved and adopted by Washington as his own. You told me that you knew that some letters written for Washington were copied by him and signed as his own. Col. Varick was charged with recording in books all Washington's official letters from the original drafts. It would be as curious, as useful, to know what (if any) were in Washington's handwriting. In 1777 I found Harrison was the secretary and Hamilton his first aide-de-camp; and I know that these two gentlemen were constantly writing for the General when the army was not on a march. Harrison and Hamilton remained with him till some time in 1781. They were succeeded you know, by Humphreys and Jonathan Trumbull—an immense falling off.

To this letter, Nicholas Fish answered:

It delights me to find that you are so sensibly alive on the subject of Hamilton's biography, and retain so correct and perfect a recollection of his distinguished talents and public services. Your letter to me, which I shall present to Mrs. Hamilton as soon as she returns from a tour of Niagara, will doubtless be balm to her drooping spirits, it will renew with confidence the hope of having justice at last done to the memory of her husband in a faithful biography. To you my dear Sir, must this subject be committed, there is no other person so peculiarly circumstanced and so admiraly qualified to write the life of Hamilton; your personal and long acquaintance with him, the high and various public trusts you held during the Revolutionary War and under the Federal Constitution, your particular agency and cooperation with him, in many of the prominent and most important transactions of the Civil and Military Administration of our Government, all point to you as the fit and appropriate biographer of Hamilton.

In another letter from Pickering, dated November 12, 1825, he states:

I perceive that Washington's Farewell Address is noticed in the newspaper, and the question agitated, whether the draft was his own or General Hamilton's. John E. Hall, editor of the Portfolio in Philadelphia, has stated in the newspapers that Washington put his original of this address into the hands of the gentleman in whose newspaper it was first published and who agreeable to his request, was permitted to retain it—and that the gentleman now has it in his possession. Hall says it is in Washington's own handwriting and with his signature, ergo—Washington was the real author of that composition; but you know that this inference is not demonstratively true from the simple fact of the handwriting.

In answer to this letter, Nicholas Fish wrote:

The discussions which have taken place in the newspapers respecting the Hamilton papers, as they are called, I perceive you have seen. The papers you know are said to be a manuscript copy of a draft of General Washington's Farewell Address, and the correspondence between him and Hamilton on that subject; those papers were put into the hands of Mr. King many years ago by Judge Pendleton, one of General Hamilton's executors, and are still in the possession of Mr. King, who being on the eve of departure on his mission to England, was called on by the young Messrs. Hamilton for a surrender of those papers to them, previous to his leaving this country, which he declined doing—whereupon a suit in Chancery was instituted by Mrs. Hamilton for the recovery of those papers.

Mr. Horace Binney has written a very able book entitled *Inquiry into the Formation of Washington's Farewell Address,* and has covered a far larger scope than is possible in a single chapter such as this. According to Mr. Binney, in 1792, Washington, contemplating withdrawal from public life, sent Madison certain suggestions and asked him to put them into the form of an address. This Madison did very briefly, confining himself to the points given to him by Washington. As Washington decided to accept a second term, the paper was not used. In 1796, Washington sent to Hamilton the draft by Madison, together with certain additional paragraphs of his own. These two papers constituted Washington's original draft and Hamilton was requested to re-dress it. Hamilton, first incorporating these suggestions into an abstract of points and adhering strictly to the lines marked out by Washington, made an entirely new draft of his own. This may be called Hamilton's original draft, which was sent to Washington at once. Hamilton then took Washington's original draft and consulted Jay in regard to it. The result of this conference was that Hamilton drew up a paper of changes and corrections, which he sent back to Washington together with the latter's original draft. Washington compared the three papers with his customary care and then wrote that he greatly preferred Hamilton's original draft and returned it to the author for certain changes including a paragraph on education, and asked that it be put in shape for the press. Hamilton, therefore, wrote a second draft, which may be called Hamilton's Revision, and sent it to Washington, September 1, 1796. Washington then made an autograph copy of the Revision, cancelled all those passages which he had told Hamilton he should expunge, and on September 17th, the Farewell Address was given to the world.

Mr. Binney's conclusions are logical and sound: "The thoughts and general idea of the Farewell Address was Washington's. The form, arrangement and the method of argument and presentation are Hamilton's."

It is somewhat the same as if an individual wanted his picture painted and told the artist how he would like it done and prescribed certain specifications. In the final analysis, the artist is recognized as the creator (author) of the finished painting. In the Farewell Address, Washington prescribed the general idea and certain specifications, but in the final analysis, the brain and intellect was Alexander Hamilton. He was the author, master-craftsman, and ghost writer of the Farewell Address, and Washington was its responsible sponsor. This was not by any means the first time that Hamilton drafted or ghost-wrote important state documents and speeches for Washington. It was the usual custom and procedure. The question is not why Washington used extensively the great talents of Hamilton to formulate and expound policies, but why anyone should question the propriety and wisdom of his making the greatest possible public use of Hamilton's genius as a political ghost writer and of such a brilliant mastermind of sound logic, reasoning, and eloquence.

Four years before, in 1792, President Washington wrote to James Madison from Mount Vernon in which he openly asked Madison to ghost write a farewell speech for him. The following is an exact quotation:

> I would fain carry my request to you further than is asked above, although I am sensible that your compliance with it must add to your trouble. But as the recess may afford you leisure, and I flatter myself you have dispositions to oblige me, I will, without apology, desire, if the measure in itself should strike you as proper, or likely to produce public good or private honor that you would turn your thoughts to a Valedictory Address from me to the public . . . . etc., etc.

In fairness to historical truth and accuracy, and without detracting an iota from the grandeur and noble characteristics and achievements of Washington, all the evidence that has been laid bare by time and events apparently substantiate the fact that Hamilton was the real author of the Farewell Address.

No other American was nearly as well qualified through knowledge, experience, rare sagacity, lucid penmanship, and masterly craftsmanship. He was not only the inspired defender of the Constitution but also the mastermind of American finances, and recognized as the foremost lawyer in the nation.

The Farewell Address is one of the noblest public statements in the annals of American history. It is a stern appeal to duty and a solemn warning to his fellow countrymen by George Washington on his retirement from public office, and points out in clear and eloquent words the danger of weakening the Union, the mischief from party strife, the necessity of sound public credit, and the menace of foreign entanglements.

It is a testament of political wisdom and a model of literary excellence. Together with the Declaration of Independence and the Constitution of the United States, it forms the Trilogy of famous American historical documents. Compared to the Declaration of Independence, it has all the earmarks of literary genius and permanacy.

Washington was a great and inspired leader and a man of the highest ideals, patriotism, ability, and practical wisdom, but he did not have a trained legal mind nor was he an intellectual genius. His life was spent largely in the management of his large estate at Mount Vernon, as a surveyor, as an officer in the Virginia Militia, and as commander-in-chief of the Continental Army before he became president.

Alexander Hamilton, on the other hand, was remarkable for his extraordinary intellect, his unprecedented genius in writing innumerable brilliant, political pamphlets and letters from the age of 17 to his death at 47. At the immature age of 17, he acquired early fame for writing two anonymous pamphlets: "Full Vindication" and the "Farmer Refuted," both in defense of American liberties. He became known as the infant prodigy. The most famous and best known are the *Federalist Papers,* signed "Publicus," on the formation of our constitutional government. In his letters to Phocion, he courageously and ably argued for a more humane and

190

honorable treatment of Tories and refugees. In "The Continentalist," he expounded his theory of statesmanship. He emphasized in these six essays the lack of power by the Continental Congress and proclaimed:

> In a government framed for durable liberty no less regard must be paid to giving the magistrate a proper degree of authority to make and execute the laws with rigour than to guard against encroachments upon the rights of the community; as too much power leads to despotism and too little leads to anarchy and both eventually to the ruin of the people.

From that time on, except when he was engaged in military duty, he continued to expound his views on governmental problems and on foreign affairs in a long series of essays under many pseudonyms, mostly Roman or Greek, such as "Pacificus," "Americanus," "Horatius," and "Camillus." The latter was one of his best. Although quite lengthy, it was written on foreign policy as was the other above mentioned from 1793 to 1795. These letters set forth the broad principles which were the foundations of our foreign policies that lasted until World War I. Many of the principles enunciated in these papers were later incorporated into the Farewell Address.

Alexander Hamilton was the first, most brilliant, versatile, and greatest American political pamphleteer, essayist, columnist, and ghost writer. He was the father of all ghost writers. He seemed to delight in issuing pamphlets under assumed names, an early form of anonymity.

A study of his innumerable letters to George Washington clearly prove his aid in formulating and writing many of the important policies of the Washington administration. This again is no reflection on the statesmanship of Washington. In truth, it is the highest commendation for a president to use the best available brains in expounding his policies for which he alone is responsible.

The name of ghost writer was unknown in the early days of the Republic. Today, ghost writers are part and parcel of the presidency. Franklin D. Roosevelt surrounded himself with experienced and extremely able ghost writers who were largely responsible for his popularity, policies, and fame. With his melodious voice, he won popular applause by reading extremely well, the speeches off the production lines of his highly competent ghost writers. This is not a reflection on F.D.R. Instead, it is to his credit for making maximum use of his own assets in his radio talks and his careful selection of his experienced ghost writers.

From Washington to Franklin Roosevelt is a long span of time. But governmental problems are fundamentally the same today as at the outset of our Republic. Washington never knew he originated the now recognized use and system of ghost writers. At the time the Farewell Address was proclaimed by Washington, and for many years thereafter, it was probably thought best to minimize or cover-up Hamilton's brilliant craftsmanship and authorship. This was undoubtedly done with Hamilton's acquiescence. It does seem strange, however, that Judge Pendleton, without the consent of Mrs. Hamilton or any of her family, should have transferred the letters between Hamilton and Washington, and Hamilton's drafts of the Farewell Address, to Rufus King, a leading Federalist. This rather unethical transaction was obviously taken to cover up Hamilton's authorship of the Address, by oblivion.

In summing up, there seems to be no dispute of the facts that Washington asked Hamilton to "redress and then draft a Valedictory Address." Time and events have conspired to disclose and prove the attempts, 179 years ago, to cover up Hamilton's authorship of the Address. No one disputes that Washington was its originator, editor, and sponsor, and was officially responsible for its proclamation. It was accepted by the American people as the testament of a beloved president and war hero who served his country with great success in war and peace.

It is almost impossible to separate Washington and Hamilton in the total authorship of the Address. The political principles of these two outstanding men are virtually identical. No one should have reasons to doubt that Washington had ample wisdom to have written a noble and memorable document unaided. But he was sagacious enough and of great enough stature to select Alexander Hamilton to consummate his Farewell Address. In truth, it was a joint testament of both men in spirit and in words of advice to all the American people and to future generations.

Elizabeth Hamilton, the wife of Alexander Hamilton, was 47 when her husband was killed, and lived for fifty years to mourn his death. She always maintained that her husband was the author of the Farewell Address and stated emphatically she could recall his reading parts of the speech to her.

In 1840, she was deeply disturbed by the claims of some political enemies who tried to belittle Hamilton. She therefore issued a public statement regarding her husband's authorship of the Farewell Address:

He was in the habit of calling me to sit with him that he might read to me as he wrote, to discover how it sounded upon the ears, making the remark, "my dear Elizabeth, you must be to me what old Moliere's nurse was to him." Nearly all of the address was read to me by him as he wrote it and the greatest part in my presence. The original was forwarded to General Washington who approved it with the exception of one paragraph, on the subject of public schools, which was stricken out. It was afterwards published as "General Washington's Farewell Address." Shortly after, my husband and myself were

193

walking on Broadway when a soldier accosted him with a request to purchase General Washington's Farewell Address. He did and turning to me said, "That man does not know he has asked me to purchase my own work."

The whole circumstances are at this moment so perfectly in my mind, that I can recall his bringing General Washington's letter to me and his remarking on the only alteration which he [General Washington] had requested to be made.

Elizabeth Hamilton was a woman of the highest integrity and honor all of her long life. Her testimony, naturally slanted, was, by force of character, fundamentally truthful.

Veritas magna est et prevalebit—the truth is mighty and will prevail.

The author has a profound admiration for the integrity and heroic leadership of George Washington, our first and most revered, and by consensus, our greatest president. He nevertheless regards Alexander Hamilton as having the finest intellect among all of our public officials up to the present time.

There is no denying that Hamilton was one of the greatest Americans who ever lived. He was, however, less known, less understood, and, consequently, less appreciated than other statesman much his inferiors. He was the immortal genius and champion of the Constitution and its master spirit and mind. He was the first secretary of the Treasury and founder of our financial system. He struck the financial rock and golden streams poured forth. He would turn in his grave at the astronomical present-day deficit spending and national debt. He was the alter ego of George Washington.

When he resigned from the Cabinet in 1793, he immediately became the foremost attorney in the nation, and the recognized leader, and "the little lion" of the Federalist Party.

194

Judge Ambrose Spencer, a Jeffersonian opponent in numerous political contests, commended his legal talents and creative genius in the highest possible terms:

> Alexander Hamilton was the greatest man this country has ever produced. I knew him well. I was in situations often to observe and study him. I saw him at the bar, and at home. He argued cases before me while I sat as Judge upon the bench. Webster had done the same. In power of reasoning, Hamilton was the equal of Webster, and more than this can be said of no man. In creative power, Hamilton was infinitely Webster's superior. It was Hamilton, more than any other American who thought out the Constitution of the United States, and the details of a Government of the Union; and out of the chaos that existed after the Revolution, raised a fabric every part of which is instinct with his thought. I can truly say hundreds of politicians and statesmen of the day got both the web and woof of their thoughts from Hamilton's brains. He, more than any other man, did the thinking of the times.

A prophet is sometimes without honor in his own country. The renowned and famous French diplomat, Talleyrand, who knew all the statesmen of his era intimately, placed Alexander Hamilton at the head of the list.

When President Washington supported the foreign policy advocated by secretary of the Treasury Alexander Hamilton, the secretary of State, Thomas Jefferson, resigned from the Cabinet in wrath. Hamilton, the watch dog of the Treasury, won a mighty victory. He remained in the Cabinet for another year and devoted his time to fiscal and domestic affairs. When he resigned, he said, "My enemies do not realize how much money I have sacrificed by giving up my law practice and taking a $3,500 a year government job. I have made a fortune for my country and I have impoverished myself."

195

The Jeffersonians rightly called Hamilton "the colossus of the Federalists," and feared him accordingly for his outstanding courage, integrity, versatility, sagacity, ability, and brilliance as a writer, orator, political economist, and statesman.

Marc Anthony, at Caesar's funeral, began his oration by saying "I come to bury Caesar not to praise him." Inverting Anthony's remarks, the author admits that he delights in praising Hamilton and defending him, although he needs no defense against his envious and misguided enemies.

"The elements were so mixed in him that nature could say to all the world—this was a great man."

Alexander Hamilton became New York State's most famous adopted son, and ranks in the annals of American history as one of the greatest of all time.

21

The first twenty-five years of the life of Alexander Hamilton
New York's adopted son and greatest genius

It was the original intention of the author to write a short profile on the life of Alexander Hamilton. But on reconsideration, it seemed advisable, in view of the fact that there have been so many biographies of Hamilton written in the last quarter of a century, and because of the chapter on Hamilton as the ghost writer of Washington's Farewell Address, to confine this profile to his less-known early life and activities. It covers his first 25 years, his marriage, the battle of Yorktown that virtually put an end to the fighting, and his election to Congress in 1782, more than a year before the British army evacuated New York City.

Alexander Hamilton was one of America's greatest, if not the greatest, intellectual and political genius. He was born out of wedlock in the British island of Nevis, in the West Indies, on the 11th of January, 1757, the son of James Hamilton, a younger child of Alexander Hamilton of Grange, the family seat in Scotland. He, like many younger sons, had left his home to seek his fortune as a merchant in the prosperous West Indies, where slave labor helped to make large plantations profitable.

His mother, Rachel, was the daughter of John Faucette, a successful Huguenot physician and wealthy plantation owner whose family had been driven out of France by the Edict of Nantes. He settled on the Island of Nevis and later Anglicized his name to Fawcett. His daughter, Rachel, a charming, beautiful young girl of 16, was urged against her will to marry John Lavine, a much older, wealthy Danish plantation owner of Jewish origin. The marriage was unhappy and unfortunate, probably due to the difference in age. She left him after a few quarrelsome years because of mutual antipathy. She later met, and either married or lived openly with, James Hamilton, who was about the same age, attractive, intelligent, and well born but unsuccessful in business affairs.

She was a woman of "superior intellect, highly cultivated, of elevated and generous sentiments, and of unusual elegance of person and manner." Such were the words used by Alexander Hamilton's son in writing his life. From this union of France and Scotland, Alexander Hamilton derived from his parents the superior intelligence, intellectual qualities, independent spirit, self-reliance, energy, industry, amazing ambition, charm, character, and good looks. He had an older brother named James Hamilton and a step-brother, the child of his mother and John Lavine. His mother, to whom he was greatly devoted, died when he was about ten years old.

Alexander Hamilton, at the age of twelve, entered the accounting house of Nicholas Cruger, a merchant at St. Croix where, due to his industry, tact, and exactness of figures, he eventually took over the conduct of the business and ran it successfully. At the same time, he came under the influence of the Rev. Hugh Knox, who supervised his studies in the ancient classics and encouraged his taste for history and literature.

When he was only thirteen years of age, he wrote

his West Indies friend, Edward Stevens, at New York, a personal letter in which he related his consuming ambition for advancement in these words:

My ambition is prevalent, so that I condemn the grovelling condition of a clerk as the life to which my fortune condemns me and would be willing to risk my life though not my character to exalt my station. I am confident, Neddy, that my youth precludes me from any hope of immediate preferment nor do I desire it but I mean to prepare the way for futurity. I am no philosopher, you see and may be justly said to build castles in the air. My folly makes me ashamed and beg you, to conceal it. Yet, Neddy, we have seen such schemes successful when the projector is constant.

This remarkable letter from such a young boy shows a clear understanding, good common sense, ambition, and a firm and fixed purpose to prepare himself for future opportunities and advancement. This was the key secret of Hamilton's success.

At fourteen, he attracted the attention of most of the reading public of Nevis by writing a glowing description of the disastrous effects of a hurricane that swept over the West Indies in 1772. His narrative was so lucid, graphic, and descriptive that it caused the leading citizens and his aunts to contribute funds to send him to New York to obtain a better education which they thought his talents warranted. They made no mistake. No contributions of such a nature ever received greater dividends in intellect and achievement. Hamilton soon became the greatest product of the Island of Nevis, and has kept it in the limelight ever since. He arrived in Boston in October, 1772, and immediately went to New York and, after a short stay there, moved to Elizabethtown, now Elizabeth, New Jersey, where he entered Barber's School in preparation for Princeton.

However, President Witherspoon of Princeton refused to acquiesce to his request for permission to go through the course there in a shorter time if he had the ability to do so. Hamilton then decided to return to New York and entered King's College, located in back of Trinity Church which, after the end of the war, became known as Columbia College. He lived the rest of his life as an adopted son of New York, and eventually became its foremost citizen and intellectual leader in the United States.

Alexander Hamilton, having been brought up in the West Indies where there was no resistance or active opposition to the Parliament and the king, was naturally undecided for some time after his arrival in New York regarding the rights of the colonists in their contest against the king and parliament. In Columbia, he joined a debating club of six members: Robert Troup, Richard Varick, Robert Berrien, Nicholas Fish, Edward Stevens, and himself. They were all ardent, hard-headed Patriots, but, at the outset, Hamilton had not yet shaken off his West Indian traditions and was disinclined openly to oppose the king and Parliament. It was at this time that Nicholas Fish became an intimate friend and ardent admirer of Hamilton who was a year older. It was a mutual friendship that lasted thirty years, until Hamilton's tragic death in 1804. With the possible exception of Robert Troup, Fish was Hamilton's closest personal friend. The debating club gave an opportunity to these youngsters between 17 and 18 years of age, in 1775, to express their views on current events and read prepared articles on subjects nearest to their hearts, such as liberty versus tyranny, taxation without representation, the rights of colonists, and the denunciation of the American Tories and King George. Because of his outstanding ability in writing and eloquence in speaking, Hamilton was the acknowledged leader. All of them knew they were living in serious and dangerous times. Fish said of Hamilton at that early age, "He could write prose as well as poetry and there was no melancholy about him. He was a fountain of humor, and satire." Troup, referring to Hamilton, said, "He was equally attentive to social and religious duties and a believer of the fundamental doctrines of Christianity."

What did Hamilton look like as a collegian? He was of slender build, medium height, on the small side, 5 feet 7 inches, fair complexion, with reddish-brown hair, handsome, and with high spirits, wit, and intelligence. He was an industrious student, and must have read much and widely. He made notes and even an outline of a proposed book on the political history of the British Colonies in America.

During the years 1774-1776, while he was in college, New York City was in a turmoil of dissension between the Whigs and Tories who were gradually giving way to Patriots and Loyalists, on the vital issues of taxation without representation and the rights of the colonists.

Americans do not realize that the Revolutionary War was unpopular in England. The author studied under Professor Albert Bushnell Hart at Harvard who was one of the greatest authorities on American history. He was most emphatic in insisting that the Revolutionary War was caused by the uncompromising, obstinate, and imperious character of King George III, a militarist who believed in the use of force to punish the American colonists who rebelled against the acts of Parliament.

The Whigs in Parliament openly opposed war with the American colonists: Chatham, Fox, Burke, and Barre. Chatham, in his great speech of 1775, expressed the sentiments of American colonists better than they themselves. His language excited and strengthened the American Whigs: "The spirit with which your taxation is opposed in America," he said, "is the same as we formerly opposed loans, benevolences and ship money in England." This vigorous Whigism animated millions in

201

America who preferred poverty with liberty to gilded chains.

Alexander Hamilton's conversion to the cause of liberty was not instantaneous. He studied closely the issues from the Stamp Act of 1765, the tax on tea five years later, and the closing of the Port of Boston. He was not the type of remain neutral long, or to take halfway measures. The moment he was convinced that the American Patriots were right in principle and that their cause was just, he ceased to be a West Indian and became a champion of the rights of the colonists against the Crown. He revolted against illegal and unwarranted oppression. With his remarkable capacity even as a youngster to determine issues on the basis of logic and sound reasoning, he must have reached the conclusion that it was the king's war and not the people's.

Gertrude Atherton, in her interesting book on Hamilton entitled *The Conqueror,* a best-seller seventy years ago, gives a vivid description of King's College:

> King's College had a fine building facing the North River, back of what is now Trinity Church, surrounded by spacious grounds, shaded by old sycamores and elms. There were many secluded corners for thought and study. A more favorite resort of Alexander Hamilton was Bateau Street, under whose great elms he formed the habit of strolling and preparing his speeches and muttering his lessons to the concern of the passersby. In his hours of leisure, he rollicked with Stevens his old friend of the West Indies and with his new friends, Nicholas Fish and Robert Troup.
>
> These youngsters did not have much time for leisure. Sundays, Hamilton dined at the homes of either Stevens, Troup or Fish.

At the latter house, he must have enjoyed the animated, one-sided conversation of young Nicholas Fish against his father, mother, and sister—all three Tories.

Hamilton and his college friends all foresaw the necessity of military training as they anticipated armed resistance and had the wisdom to anticipate the onrushing event.

Hamilton, Troup, Varick, Berrien, Stevens, and Fish, a year before the Declaration of Independence, had been quietly and secretly training under the guidance of former British officers. When the news came of the Battle of Lexington, they voluntarily joined the military organizations aided and advised by John Morin Scott, the legal firebrand of the rebellion against British despotism. They became lieutenants in Malcolm's and Lasher's provisional regiments.

These young Patriots continued their studies during 1775 at King's College, but they soon threw all caution to the winds and strutted openly in their new militia uniforms as all young officers are accustomed to do. When the war came, these young college boys had a certain amount of military training. That is why they were all commissioned within six months after the Declaration of Independence, in the Continental Army as captains and majors. There was obviously a dearth of officer material. Hamilton, Troup, Berrien, Varick, and Fish all made excellent officers, and served with distinction during the war.

On July 6, 1775, a great multitude of the New York Patriots assembled in the fields where City Hall is now located, to choose delegates for the Continental Congress in Philadelphia. It was presided over by Alexander McDouglas, afterwards a distinguished general in the war, who had recently been imprisoned for his outspoken views against British usurpations of American liberties. Gertrude Atherton, in *The Conqueror,* gives a vivid description of this meeting:

Nicholas Fish and Robert Troup pushed their way through the crowd to where Alexander Hamilton stood,

203

his uplifted face expressing his thoughts so plainly to those who knew him that his friends determined to force him to the platform. At first he protested; and in truth, the idea shaping concretely, filled his very legs with terror; but the young men's insistance added to his own surging thoughts, conquered, and he found himself on the platform facing a boundless expanse of three cornered hats. . . . He recovered his poise and as ideas swam from his brain on the tide of a natural eloquence, he forgot all but the great principles which possessed him, the determination to inspire the people to renewed courage and greater activity. He rehearsed their wrongs, and emphasized their inalienable rights under the British Constitution. He insisted that the time had come to revert to the natural rights of man—upon which all civil rights were founded. . . . They had been reduced almost to the level of their own slaves who soon would cease to respect them.

He paused so abruptly that the crowd held its breath. Then his ringing thrilling voice sounded the first note of the Revolution. "It is war!" he cried. "It is war! It is the battlefield of slavery." When the deep roar which greeted the startling words had subsided, he spoke briefly of their immense natural advantages in the event of war, the inability of England to gain any permanent advantage, and finally of the vast resources of the country and its phenominal future when the waves of rebellion, sparkling with fire, had washed back to the shores of England the wrecks of her power, her wealth and her glory.

Miss Atherton, in her own eloquent style, goes on to say:

His manner was as fiery and impetuous as his discourse was clear and original. The great crowd was electrified. It was as if a blade of lightning had shot down from the hot blue sky to illuminate the doubting recesses of their understanding. They murmured, repeatedly "It is a collegian, a collegian," and they thundered their applause when he finished.

204

Troup and Fish bore him off in triumph to Fraunces Tavern where Stevens joined them immediately, hot but exultant. Fish, leaned across the table at Fraunces Tavern and looked penetratingly at Hamilton, who was flushed and nervous. "You have committed yourself, Hamilton," he said. "That was no college play. Whether you fight or not does not so much matter, but you must give us your pen and your speech. I am no idle preveyor of compliments but you·are extraordinary and there isn't a man living can do for the cause with the pen what you can do: write pamphlets and they will be published without an hour's delay."

"Ah, I see!" cried Hamilton gayly, "I was a bit bewildered. You think my new Patriotism needs nursing."

"You have read my thoughts," said Fish with some confusion, "I have never known anyone whose brains worked at so many things at once. I am selfish enough to want you to give a good bit of it to us."

"I never was one to make fierce demonstrations," said Hamilton, "but fill up another bumper, the first to calm my nerves which were like to jump through my skin—and stand up and I will drink to you a pledge."

"Stand on the table," cried Troup. "It is where you belong; you're the biggest man in New York today."

As Hamilton, although self-confident was modest, Troup put down his bumper, seized the hero in his big arms and swung him to the middle of the table. Then the three, raising their glasses again, stood in a semicircle. Hamilton threw back his head and raised his own glass. His hand trembled and his lips moved for a moment without speaking, his habit, when excited. "The pledge!" cried Fish, "the pledge. We want it."

"It is this," said Hamilton. "I pledge myself, body and soul and brain to the most sacred cause of the American Colonies. I vow it to all my best energies for the rest of my life. I swear to fight for it with my sword; then when the enemy is driven out, with all my brain to help to reconstruct these tattered Colonies and unify them into one great state, or group of allied states, which shall take a respectable place among nations, to give her all that I have learned and all that my brain is capable of

205

learning and conceiving. I believe that I have certain abilities and I solemnly swear to devote them wholly to my country. And I further swear that never, not in a single instance, will I permit my personal ambitions to conflict with what must be the lifelong demands of this country."

The speech of the young collegian, Hamilton, was the sensation of New York, particularly among the Patriots. Not long afterwards, Hamilton wrote a number of pamphlets in reply to the attacks made on Congress by the ablest Tory leaders of that time. Hamilton's pamphlets were entitled: "A Full Vindication of the Measures of Congress from the Calumnies of their Enemies" and "The Farmer Refuted." These pamphlets were so sound and logical that they created a profound public sensation, and were attributed to John Jay and William Livingston, two of the ablest Patriots in New York. Hamilton's friends did not hesitate to let the public know that he was the author of these pamphlets. Dr. Cooper, president of King's College (Columbia University) was annoyed and shocked that one of his students was the author of the most logical and compelling arguments against the illegal actions of the Parliament. The bitterness against the president of King's College by the students and fellow Patriots was so great that they invaded the college grounds, and attacked the residence of Dr. Cooper. Alexander Hamilton intervened by making a speech to the crowd which enabled Dr. Cooper to escape through the back door and seek protection on the British warship *Asia*. This was a typical act of Hamilton, who was utterly fearless on questions of principle but abhorred violence and lawlessness.

It was about this time that Hamilton was made a captain of the Provincial Company of Artillery which was later incorporated into the Continental Army.

Gertrude Atherton dramatized the disgraceful retreat of American troops from New York on the 15th of September, 1776:

The retreat was under the command of General Putnam and guided through all the intricacies of those thirteen winding miles by his aide-de-camp, Aaron Burr. The last man in the procession was Alexander Hamilton and his small battery. "So, you're covering again, Alexander," said Fish as he passed him on his way to his regiment of the New York Militia of which he was Brigade Major. "You can't complain that your adopted country doesn't make use of you. By the way, Troup is in the Jersey prison ship safe and sound."

"Can't we exchange him?" asked Hamilton eagerly. "Do you think General Washington would listen to us?"

"If we have a victory. I shouldn't care to approach him at present. God! This is an awful beginning. The whole Army is ready to dig its own graves. Well, I hate to have to leave you here, the very last to be made a target of. You won't be rash?" he added anxiously.

"No, Granny," said Hamilton, whose gaiety had revived as he heard of Troup's safety. "And I do not exchange my position for any. Good-bye."

Handshakes in those days were solemn. Fish feared that he never would see Hamilton again and his fear was close to being realized.

Hamilton's little unit, with three cannon, played important parts in the Battles of Brooklyn, White Plains, Trenton, and Princeton. He came under the observation of Gen. Nathanael Greene who was so impressed with his bravery and military efficiency that he introduced him to the commander in chief, George Washington, suggesting that he was well qualified to serve as the general's aide. This is how he started his famous career as the close friend, the military aide, and the secretary for George Washington.

Hamilton was already one of Washington's aides when Lafayette joined Washington's staff. Lafayette admired Hamilton's intellectual and conversational talents and soon became Hamilton's friend.

Hamilton, who was the illegitimate child of a

younger son of an ancient Scottish family, was attracted to the gallant French nobleman. They had much in common. Hamilton spoke French fluently and was brought up on the nearby island of St. Croix, in the West Indies. He was now fighting against the tyranny of the British king in Washington's army. Lafayette was a wealthy French nobleman who had volunteered, at the risk of his life, in the cause of liberty in America. These two youngsters, Lafayette just 20 and Hamilton 21, were to become the foremost statesmen in their respective countries and to achieve greatness and glory that is destined for few in history.

Lafayette became the greatest crusader for liberty and freedom in his generation, if not in history. Hamilton became the recognized genius of the Constitution and the first secretary of the Treasury.

This mutual friendship between Lafayette and Hamilton was cemented by time, association, and similar views and objectives. It is easy to trace them in their numerous letters, as they were both given to extensive and prodigious correspondence. Lafayette admired and loved Washington as if he were his father, but Alexander Hamilton was one of his closest companions and friends in America.

Lafayette excited Hamilton's interest by telling of his life in France, of court activities, and his friendships and relationships with important army and governmental officials. Hamilton was deeply impressed and quickly envisioned making Lafayette into an intermediary to persuade France to send an expeditionary force to fight in America.

From the time Hamilton became Washington's aide to the day of his death, his public activities are well known and are part and parcel of American history except for his plan, with Lafayette's cooperation and that of General Washington, to persuade the French government to send an expeditionary force to the U.S. In

Lafayette (1757-1834), a painting by Francisco Guiseppe Casanova

this project, Hamilton was eminently successful.

After the decisive victory at Saratoga, Washington selected Hamilton as the officer to go on the important mission to General Gates, now riding high and refusing to send Washington the soldiers he needed desperately in the New Jersey campaign. The task assigned to Hamilton combined diplomacy, tact, and great persuasive powers. Gates envied and disliked Washington and hoped to replace him. It took all of Hamilton's great powers of logic, reasoning, and persuasion to finally get Gates to send the much-needed reinforcements to Washington. Probably no other officer in the army could have gotten such successful results. Obviously, neither Hamilton nor Washington had much confidence in General Horatio Gates. Later they both protested his appointment to the command of the Southern Department by the Congress, but in vain. Hamilton wrote several members urging the appointment of Gen. Nathanael Greene in place of Gates. Later, on September 6, 1780, after the disastrous battle of Camden, Hamilton wrote to Duane, who was a member of Congress from New York, as follows:

> But was there ever an instance of a General running away as Gates has done, from his whole army? And was there ever so precipitious a flight? One hundred and eighty miles in three and a half days. It does admirable credit to the activity of the man at his time of life. But it disgraces the General and the soldiers. For God's sake, overcome prejudice and send Greene.

There is no question but that Hamilton was hard-hitting, caustic, and fearless when necessary, and thereby often made enemies.

The story of the early life of Alexander Hamilton would not be complete without an account of his marriage and a description of his charming and intelligent wife, Elizabeth Schuyler.

Just a year before his marriage, he wrote in December, 1779, a bantering note to his great friend, Colonel John Laurens, who was tragically killed in a skirmish in his own state of South Carolina shortly after the surrender of Cornwallis at Yorktown. In this letter, he said:

I empower and command you to get me a wife in the Carolinas. Such a wife as I want will, I know, be difficult to be found, but if you succeed, it will a stronger bond of zeal and dexterity. Take her description—she must be young, handsome (I lay most stress upon a good shaped face), sensible (a little learning will do), well bred and tender (I am an enthusiast in my notion of fidelity and fondness), of some good nature, a great deal of generosity (she must neither love money nor scolding for I dislike equally a termegent and an economist); in politics I am indifferent of what side she may be on. I think I have arguments that will even convert her to mine. As to religion a moderate stock will satisfy me. She must believe in God and hate a Saint.

In the remaining part of the letter he said, "What could have gotten into my head to hazard this jeu de folie. Do I want a wife? No. I have plagues enough without desiring to add to the number, that greatest of all."

Yet within one year, Hamilton was married, on December 14, 1780, at Albany, to Elizabeth Schuyler, the second daughter of Major General Philip Schuyler. He belonged to one of the great patroon families of New York, allied with the Van Cortlandts and the Van Renssalaers. He owned a large estate near Albany, and was highly respected. A close, personal friend of Washington, he was later elected after the war as a Federalist to the United States Senate.

Colonel Tench Tilhman, one of Washington's aides, described Elizabeth Schuyler "as a brunette with the most good natured, dark lovely eyes that I ever saw, which blew a gleam of good humor and benevolence over her countenance."

The marriage was one of the greatest social events in New York State during the war. Hamilton had won not only a brilliant and accomplished wife, but also a family relationship with the Schuylers which gave him a prestige and a position that were of inestimable value to him in his future career. He was no longer a stranger from the West Indies, but was now allied with one of the oldest, wealthiest, and most influential families in New York State. He formed a warm attachment to General Schuyler, who welcomed him into the family and became one of Hamilton's strongest supporters.

Gertrude Atheron in *The Conqueror* gives a fine description of the wedding, and called it the most notable (social) private event of the Revolution. She described the Schuyler mansion at Albany as being large and commodious, with white columns. It was decorated with holly for three nights before the wedding, and illuminated by hundreds of wax candles while the young people danced to three in the morning. Most of the important Patriot families of New York were there: the Livingstons, Morrises, Sterlings, and Boudinots were all there; also his close military friends. "Troup was there full of youth and honored." He had received the thanks of Congress for his service at Saratoga and had been appointed secretary of the Board of War. Nicholas Fish came with Lafayette. Fish was known as a brave and gallant soldier, and so excellent a disciplinarian that he won the approval and confidence of Washington. Lafayette, who had bought a box full of clothes that had dazzled Paris, embraced Hamilton with tears, but they were soon deep in conjectures of the next campaign. Laurens, looking like a king in exile, wrung many hearts.

The bride wore the white which became her best, made with a long pointed bodice, and paniers and lace that had been worn by the wife of the first patroon. However, she had risen to the dignity of a wig, and her mass of black hair was twisted mercilessly tight under the spreading white monstrosity to which her veil was attached. Hamilton wore a black velvet coat as befitting his impending state. Its lining and the short trousers were of white satin. His shapely legs were in white silk, his feet in pumps with diamond buckles, the present of Lafayette. He, too, wore a wig, a close one with a queue—but he got rid of it immediately after the ceremony for it heated his head.

The world vowed that never had there been so pretty a couple nor one so well matched in every way. Both were the perfection of mates and the one as fair and fresh as a Scot, the other a golden gypsy, the one all fire and energy, the other docile and tender, but with sufficient spirit and intelligence. It is seldom that the world so generously gives its blessings but it might have withheld it for all that Hamilton and his bride would have cared.

This is a fascinating description of the wedding and of the bride and groom by Gertrude Atherton who, in her day, 68 years ago, was the most famous writer of dramatized biography and has not had an equal since.

After a minor misunderstanding, the proud and sensitive young Hamilton resigned as Washington's aide. However, Washington approved his appointment to head a corps of light infantry with Nicholas Fish as his second in command during the Yorktown campaign. There Hamilton succeeded in persuading Washington to place him in command of the attack on British Redoubt Number 10, which was several hundred yards outside of the British fortification on their left flank. Hamilton, under the command of General Lafayette, led three battalions, one of which he commanded, Major Fish a second, and Lt. Colonel Laurens the third. This famous and daring commando attack with only bayonets and un-

213

loaded rifles succeeded in capturing the British Redoubt Number 10 on October 14, 1781, just three months before Hamilton's 25th birthday. Both Hamilton and Fish, and a French officer named Gimat, were officially praised by General Lafayette for their bravery in the capture of the British redoubt.

Soon after the surrender of Cornwallis's army on October 19, 1781, Hamilton resigned from the army to go to Albany where his wife lived and, within six months, by arduous study, he qualified to become a lawyer and to start one of the most famous careers in the legal profession of our country. Soon thereafter he was appointed to help raise the funds in New York State that were necessary for the Congress to carry out its wartime obligations. He was so successful in the financial and economic administration of his office that he was elected to Congress at 25 years of age, where he immediately came into prominence because of his wide grasp and experience in handling financial and monetary issues. It was in Congress that he first started his brilliant political and administrative career.

If anyone should question the close friendship between Hamilton and Nicholas Fish from 1774 to 1804, when Hamilton was killed in a duel with Burr, let him read the following letters. The first was written shortly after the battle of Yorktown where both Hamilton and Fish participated in the famous commando raid on the British Redoubt Number 10. When the letter was written, Hamilton was 25 years of age and was living with his wife at General Schuyler's mansion in Albany. Fish was a year younger than Hamilton. From this letter it would seem that Hamilton was trying to be a matchmaker for his young friend. It merely shows that history does not change and that there were broken hearts and broken engagements then, as now, and into eternity. These letters are included to show the early friendship between Hamilton and Nicholas Fish, which continued until Hamilton's death in 1804.

214

My dear friend

I am sorry you seem to have broken your resolution so finally respecting a certain matter; as since I have been here I have had reason to believe you were mistaken in your original suspicion—Several officers have reported here that you have openly professed to renounce the connection—I imagine it has reached the family and I am told Miss is in great distress—'Tis probably by this time your doubts are removed—Mr. G. went lately into the Jerseys. I conjecture his errand was to see you; and I dare say you will understand each other. At all events you must be cautious in this matter or your character will run some risk, and you are sensible how injurious it might be to have the reputation of levity in a delicate point—The Girls have got it among them that this is not your first infidelity.

I have been very sick—I am still alternately in and out of bed—How are you after your Southern fatigues?

I will thank you to take up my bedding and forward them care of Major Kearse at Kingston for me.

Adieu Yrs Aff.

A. Hamilton

Albany, December 29, 1781
Major Fish
2nd New York Regiment
Pompton, N.J.

April 11, 1782

Albany, N.Y.

Dear Fish

I am sorry that for want of a person to send them with I have been obliged to detain your horses til now. The articles I shall want—are four fine decanters if to be had, if not two quart bottles, a dozen wine glasses, two ale glasses, to hold about a pint each, if not to be had two tumblers.

You will much oblige me by procuring these articles as soon as possible having them carefully packed up in a small box and forwarded to Major Kearse. I shall also thank you to speak to him on your way to camp about forwarding them as soon as they arrive by water. Beg his particular care, I shall not be able to give a friend a glass of wine til these arrive, for they are not to be had here. Let me know what they cost by the first opportunity, adieu my dear friend,

Yours,

A. Hamilton

Perhaps you may meet with some friend coming directly up whose pormanteau may not be too much crowded to receive them. Send my horses by return of the bearer unless they should be in too bad a plight to travel. In this case be so good as to put them out where they will be taken care of and at the same time will not cost much for keeping.

This letter was from Lt. Colonel Alexander Hamilton, six months after the surrender of General Cornwallis.

Hamilton resigned shortly afterwards as the fighting was virtually over. He had married Elizabeth Schuyler a year before at Albany and returned there to study law. His letter was written asking Nicholas Fish to forward his horses and obtain additional supplies for him. It was addressed to Major Fish at Poughkeepsie, N.Y., where he was commissioned to represent the 2nd N.Y. Regiment in regard to obtaining their back pay from the New York Legislature, then in session there.

During the year following the surrender of the British at Yorktown, Hamilton became a father and a lawyer. "I have been employed in the last ten months," he wrote, "in rocking the cradle and studying the art of fleecing my neighbors" (an old definition of lawyers).

The author has attempted to fill in and emphasize Hamilton's earlier, far less known life up to his marriage, the battle of Yorktown the following year, and his election to Congress at 25 years of age.

This chapter covers the first 25 years of the life of youthful Alexander Hamilton, the adopted son of New York. During the next 22 years, before his death in a duel with Aaron Burr in 1804, he was to become a very great political, legal, and financial genius, the architect of the Constitution, and one of the greatest, if not the greatest, statesmen in the history of the United States.

22

The history of the New York State Indians and their participation in the Revolutionary War

It is amazing how little is known by our generation of Americans about the Indians who inhabited New York State. The actual origin of American Indians has baffled our historians for a long period of time. The controversy still continues regarding their origin—whether they were Mongolians, Malasians, Israelites, Phoenicians, or Egyptians. Moreover, the controversy over the first discovery of the Indians in North America is still a moot question. However, quite a few historians believe that our Indians are indigenous.

Scandinavians, Welch, Irish, and others lay claim to be the earliest discoverers. The general opinion is that from the black hair and eyes of the Indians, they originated from similar people who crossed from Siberia to Alaska and migrated south. The truth may never be known, as the New York State Indians, the same as most others in the United States, left no monuments, stone edifices, nor literature.

Giovanni da Verrazano, an Italian navigator in an English ship, sailed into New York harbor in 1524, 85 years before Henry Hudson. Verrazano, in the service of

King Henry VII of England, described the Indians in New York harbor as wearing deerskins and feathers, "of good proportion, broad across the chest, strong of arms and well formed. In size they exceed us. Their complexion is tawny inclining to white, their faces sharp, their hair long and black, their eyes black and sharp and their expression mild and friendly."

Henry Hudson who discovered the Hudson River in his famous ship the *Half Moon,* sailed all the way to Albany in 1609. He traded with the Mohicans, Delawares, Lenni Lenapes, Hackensacks, Wappingers, Esopus, Mohawks, and other river Indians. He first met the Manhattoe Indians near the Narrows in New York harbor, where they came on board "clothed in mantles of feathers." Many of the river Indians Hudson met were friendly. At Catskill, they brought to the *Half Moon* large quantities of corn, pumpkins, beans, potatoes, and tobacco. The Hudson River Indians were generally peaceful, but suspicious and quick to take offense.

When the Dutch traders arrived in 1614, the Hudson River Indians and the Mohawks gladly exchanged maize (corn), vegetables, game and beaver skins for beads, trinkets, knives, hatchets, blankets, and cooking utensils. This barter trade was necessary because the Indians had no use for money then. In 1624, Fort Orange, at Albany, and New Amsterdam became centers for an extensive trade in furs that continued actively for 200 years, until long after the Revolutionary War.

There were more Americans killed or scalped in Indian and Tory raids and massacres in New York State during the Revolution than there were Americans killed by the British in all of New England.

The western and northern part of New York State was occupied by the famous Iroquois Indians, the Romans of the western world. They originally consisted of five nations in a confederacy, composed of Mohawks, Oneidas, Onondagas, Cayugas, and Senecas. The confederacy was also known as the Longhouse, with the Mohawks on the eastern end and the Senecas on the western. The total population of Indians in the confederation approximated 50,000, but due to incessant warfare with neighboring tribes, it remained stationary for a long period of time. The confederacy was established around 1540 as a united defense against the surrounding Indian tribes, their northern and western enemies.

About 1714, the Tuscaroras from the south joined the five nations, which then became known as the six nations. They were not only united, but were exceedingly warlike, brave, and skillful warriors. They succeeded in defeating their enemies by constant fighting, and reached as far south as Virginia and into Canada to the north. Their territory, which took in conquered and allied tribes, extended 300 miles west from the Mohawk River and 300 miles north and south. It was the constant Indian tribal wars that kept the Indians from becoming much more numerous—not the whites.

The entire Iroquois confederacy, except for half of the Oneidas and some of the Tuscaroras, were united in support of the British throughout our Revolutionary War. These Indians allies of the British were a formidable force considering that their population was more than one-fourth of the Americans in New York State. In no other state were the Indians and Tories so combined and active in waging a bloody, guerilla warfare, particularly along the Mohawk River and on the western frontier of New York. They burned villages, scalped the inhabitants, took prisoners, destroyed livestock and farm property, and perpetrated terrible massacres. Eighty percent of the Indians, including most of the Iroquois, were hostile, but the Hudson River Indians aided the Americans.

Chief Daniel Nimham of the Wappinger Indians, located in lower Dutchess County, now Putnam, had been wrongfully dispossessed of his tribal lands by

Adolph Philipse prior to the Revolutionary War. The Philipse family were ardent Tories and fled to New York City when the war began. Chief Nimham and his Wappinger Indians joined the Americans in the conflict. He bravely led his Indians warriors against the British in lower Westchester. In a local battle, he compelled Colonel Emerick and his British troops to retreat. But Lt. Colonel Simcoe came to his assistance with a much larger British force and drove the Indians back. The heroic elderly Chief Nimham, refusing to retreat, was killed fighting to protect his warriors and, by his fearless action, saved the lives of many of the Indians who were able to escape through the nearby woods.

The great cruelty of the Mohawks induced the Jesuits to call the beautiful vale of the Mohawk "the mission of the martyrs." The illustrious DeWitt Clinton, governor of New York, in an address before the New York Historical Society about the Indian confederacy, said, "They employ all the crafty wiles of the Carthagenians, the cunning of the fox, the ferocity of the tiger and the power of the lion."

The wily Mohawk Indian chief Joseph Brant, in October, 1779, led a raiding party of 65 Indians and 29 Tories disguised as Indians against Minisink, Orange County, only seventy miles from New York City. Brant and his warriors burned several farmhouses, destroyed crops and livestock, and killed a few of the settlers. The inhabitants of the small village successfully resisted by rifle fire from two small, well-defended stone farmhouses used as forts, known as Forts Gumaer and DeWitt.

On the withdrawal of the Indians, who took some prisoners and livestock with them, the nearby Goshen and Warwick militia under Colonel John Hathorn of Warwick and Lt. Colonel Tusten of Goshen pursued the Indians. The militia caught up with the Indians several days later in wild mountainous country where they were ambushed, suffering heavy losses. Brant had received reinforcements and out-numbered the militia who were approximately 120. Lt. Colonel Tusten was killed, and only forty of the brave militia soldiers returned to their families. It was a tragic example of the terrible Indian raids of New York State during the war. Minisink was 100 miles from the Mohawk Valley, the southern boundary of Indian territory, and much less distance from New York City.

Tryon County, west of Albany in the Mohawk Valley, was devastated and depopulated. The following villages were raided and destroyed: German Flats, Cobbleskill, Springfield, Johnstown, Andrustown, Unadilla, Fonda, Wawasing, Shawangunk, Canajoharie, the Schoharie Valley, Cherry Valley, and across the border in Pennsylvania, Wyoming, where the terrible massacre occurred in which 250 Americans were scalped.

Joseph Brant, the Mohawk chief, is often depicted in history as responsible for the scalping, murders, and massacres, but this is far from the truth. He was a friend and close ally of Sir William Johnson, the famous British Superintendent of the Indian confederacy. Brant spoke English fluently and visited England and Canada. He lived at Johnstown at Sir William's castle where his sister, Molly Brant, was the mistress of Johnson for many years. Johnson's headquarters was located a few miles north of the Mohawk River. Sir William died there in 1774, just before the outbreak of the war. Brant had the complete confidence and support of the Loyalists, and of Sir Guy Johnson, who succeeded his uncle as the superintendent. Brant, after the war, retired to Canada where he translated part of the Bible for Indian use and died there at the age of 65. His son became an officer in the British army and fought against the United States in the War of 1812.

The Loyalists, mostly Scotch Highlanders, tenants of the Johnsons, served in the Royal Green Regiment under Guy Johnson and in Butler's Rangers under the murderous Colonel John Butler and his equally cruel son, Walter Butler, both of whom participated in the worst Indian raids and massacres.

Settlement after settlement was plundered, and burned, and the people killed by repeated Indian and Tory raids. Iroquois warriors, numbering 500, fought in the bloody battle of Oriskany where General Herkimer, the New York militia commander, was killed.

In the spring of 1779, Colonel Van Cortland's Second New York Regiment was stationed at Wawasing (Black Bird's Nest), near the present town of Marbletown in Ulster County, to provide protection against Indian raids. Major Nicholas Fish, second in command, received reports that Indians under Brant were murdering the inhabitants at Fautine Kill, five miles up the road from Ellenville. He immediately organized and led a rescue detachment. The Indians had destroyed and burned out all the inhabitants except Jesse Bevier, who was valiantly defending his farmhouse and family. The rescue force arrived just in time and the out-numbered Indians fled.

Mrs. Nicholas Fish used to thrill her grandchildren with an account of the saving of the Bevier family, naturally making her husband the hero of the tale. There apparently was more truth than fiction or vainglory to the story.

Soon afterwards, the Second New York Regiment joined Brig. Gen. James Clinton's command in the expedition against the Iroquois Indians under General Sullivan. It totaled 3,500 troops and invaded Indian territory for 300 miles, destroying all Indian villages, orchards, livestock, corn, and all crops except those belonging to the friendly Oneidas and half of the Tuscacoras. The Indians and some Tories made an attempt at Elmira to stop the invasion and destruction of the Indian villages, but were out-numbered and put to flight.

223

Forty Indian villages were destroyed, as were 160,000 bushels of corn. The American losses were one percent, or approximately forty killed. The Indians were driven into the forests without food or shelter, and were forced to seek aid at Fort Oswego and Fort Niagara from the British.

General Sullivan had been ordered to capture both of these British outposts, which would have ended the Indian and Loyalist raids. For some reason, he did not carry out his orders as these posts continued to provide the Indians with guns, powder, and other provisions to enable them to conduct their terrible raids.

History does not relate why General Sullivan turned back before reaching his objectives. He did succeed in shattering the Iroquois confederacy temporarily, and in extending our western frontiers. Unfortunately, with the help of the British at Fort Oswego, Indian and Loyalist raids recommenced on a bloody scale the following spring.

The Mohawks, who were the cruelest and most aggressive enemies of the Americans, were compelled at the end of the war to leave New York State and take refuge in Canada. The other Iroquois tribes were allowed to remain. However, fifty years later, they sold their land and moved across the Mississippi.

The Rev. Dr. Kirkland, an American Patriot, lived for a number of years among the Oneida Indians and exerted a great deal of influence over them. As a result, most of the Oneidas and part of the Tuscaroras sided with the Americans against the British.

Many of the Hudson River Indians, such as the Wappingers, Stockbridge, Eopus, some members of the Lenni Lenape tribe, and the Mohicans, were friendly and often acted as guides and scouts for the American militia in the border warfare. However, there were quite a few Indians who regarded the conflict between the U.S. and Britain as a white man's war and remained neutral. Of all the Indians who lived in New York State during the Revolutionary War, only a few thousand remain within the boundaries of the state. There are not many Indians left east of the Mississippi.

Their leaders were often fluent and able orators, yet most of the Indians were uneducated, lived in teepees and bark huts, and hunted game, fished, and made war. As warriors, the Iroquois of New York excelled all the rest of the eastern Indians.

Hunting and war were their pastimes. Young braves often died a warrior's death in battle and were scalped by their Indian enemies. If captured, tortured, or burned at the stake, they endured such tortures with amazing courage by singing and shouting defiance unto death.

However, many of the Indians who survived the constant tribal wars attained a very old age. Those who study longevity and its causes should analyze the reasons for the exceedingly long lives of many of the greatest Indian chiefs and most eloquent orators.

The last battle of the Revolutionary War in New York State was fought on October 25, 1781, near Johnstown, a week after the American victory at Yorktown. Walter Butler, with 600 Loyalists and Indians outfitted at Oswego, attacked Warren Bush, the first home of Sir William Johnson, and burned twenty houses and destroyed a large quantity of grain. Colonel Willet, with 400 Americans, caught up with the raiders near Johnstown where, after a fierce and savage battle, the Loyalists and Indians fled to Jerseyfield. There the Americans were again successful. It was here that an Oneida Indian, after wounding Walter Butler, the brutal British Ranger officer, scalped him and carried his scalp on a stick as a token of victory in pursuit of the defeated Indians and Tories. This was the end of Indian and Tory raids and massacres.

For the first time in seven years, the settlers along

the Mohawk could sleep in peace and work their farms, free from fear of being shot and scalped. During the entire war, the firebrand, scalping knife, and tomahawk had hung "like the scaythe of death" over New York's long and unprotected Indian frontier.

When peace was signed with the British in 1783, the Iroquois Indians buried the hatchet and smoked the peacepipe. The Congress ordered General Henry Knox, acting as secretary of War in 1785, to organize the First United States Regiment, whose mission was to guard the Ohio River frontier against Indian and British aggression.

The following letter from General Knox to Lt. Colonel Nicholas Fish, dated April 9, 1786, explains our Indian policy after the war:

> You will repair to Fort McIntosh on the River Ohio, with all convenient speed, and there assume command of the troops of the United States.
>
> It is the expectation of Congress that the troops will be able to keep the public lands free from incumbrances of lawless settlers. You will therefore immediately apply yourself to prevent or remove all intruders.
>
> You will endeavor to conciliate the Indians by all practical means. You will visit the several posts to the Muskeghan and confirm or introduce the most perfect order among the troops in the garrison. You will transmit to me the earliest information of any hostile or improper design or measures which may be entertained or acted by the Indians or British troops.
>
> I wish you a pleasant journey, I am,
>
> H. Knox
>
> War Office, April 9, 1786

The instructions from Knox are clear that every effort should be made to maintain friendly relations with the Indians. This was done successfully for a few years

226

until Tecumseh, the great Indian chief, through his relentless and determined efforts organized the Ohio and Illinois Indians to fight to prevent the encroachments of the white American settlers on their hunting grounds. Tecumseh succeeded in defeating General St. Clair and decimating his army. But General Anthony Wayne, who succeeded him, finally defeated and killed the brave Tecumseh and many of his warriors, and enforced firm peace terms.

Soon after Lt. Colonel Fish's arrival at Fort McIntosh, a delegation of Wyandott and Delaware Indians came there for a peace conference. The conference or council was held at the Fort on May 29th, 1786, with Scotash, a Wyandott Indian, son of the half-king of that nation, and two Delaware chieftans and one Mingo.

The following speech was delivered by Scotash. The officers of the garrison were present, and Pierre Droullier, whom the Indians brought with them, was the interpreter:

Brothers—

When we sat in council with our American Brothers last year we opened our minds, we kept nothing concealed, we declared our strong disposition to live in peace and to consider the United States as our good friend and Brother. We are still of the same mind and have now come to assure you of the continuance of the friendship of our nation, the Wyandotts. We had it in mind when we left home to call particularly at McIntosh and to assure you Brothers of the warm attachment and good will, also of our nephews, the Delaware Indians. We wish to keep the path open between us and you.

We are sorry that some hostilities have been committed by the Indians, but we assure you that the Wyandotts and Delawares had no hand in it. We are determined to keep our word and live in peace with you Brothers. The western Indians are bad men. We cannot be answerable for their conduct and we have nothing to do with them. Many stories have been told us at Detroit to prejudice

227

our minds against the United States and make us break our word but we always shut our ears and will not hear what the bad men say.

Brothers we have brought you this string of wampum as evidence of the truth of what we tell you and to brighten the chain of friendship.

Colonel Fish replied briefly as follows:

You assured us of the friendship of your nations, Wyandotts and Delawares. We rejoice in it. It is necessary for the happiness of you and us. Some of the western and southern Indians have behaved very badly and have killed our people. You must not believe the stories told at Detroit by bad men who want to impose upon the Indians and turn them against us. We want to continue to be your friends and to accept the string of wampum as assurance of mutual friendship and peace.

The report of this Indian conference at Fort McIntosh was found among the author's old family papers.

Pontiac and Tecumseh did succeed, after several years of arduous campaigning, in uniting the Ohio, Illinois, and other nearby Indians and raising a fighting force of about 2,000. This was the top number of Indians ever to fight against the Dutch, French, British, or American forces. Even in the far west when General Custer and his entire cavalry command were exterminated by the Sioux Indians and their allies, the Indians were not more than 2,000 in actual fighters, and all on horses. This is quite different from the large armies of the Incas and Astecs of 50,000 in Peru and Mexico.

In transporting the Cherokees beyond the Mississippi, we were guilty of causing a serious loss of life from cold and hunger which was a disgraceful and inhuman action, and also guilty of a few shameful massacres. Despite the unfounded and false propaganda that Americans slaughtered millions of Indians, there

228

never was more than one million and there are still 652,000 according to the latest U.S. Census. *The main Indian casualties came from their tribal wars.*

The Indians in northern New York State before the Revolutionary War lived in teepees and huts and were confronted with starvation and bitter cold weather in the winter months. They had no trained doctors or hospitals. They suffered from smallpox and scarlet fever. However, physically, they were strong and often long-lived.

It may surprise the public that the great Winston Churchill had Indian blood in his veins through his American mother. Miss Leslie, the great-neice of Winston Churchill's mother, stated in a biography of her, entitled *The Lady Randolph Churchill,* that she was part Iroquois Indian of New York State. They were a strong, rugged, warlike race, and their leaders were often great orators and lived for over four score years and ten. It may be that Winston Churchill inherited his strong physique, his famous oratory, and the fact that he lived to be over ninety years of age from his American Indian blood. Big Chief Winston Churchill also inherited a brave and fighting spirit.

Among well-known Americans with Indian blood were: Charles Curtis of Kansas, former vice-president of the United States, and Cordell Hull from Kentucky, a former secretary of State; Joseph J. Clark, a four-star fighting admiral, and a Cherokee from Oklahoma; Senator Clairborne Pell, an able and popular member of the Senate from Rhode Island and a representative of a famous New York family; former Senator Robert Owen of Oklahoma; Will Rogers; William W. Keeler, chairman of the Phillips Petroleum Company; Jim Thorpe, one of America's greatest athletes; Chief Bender, famous baseball pitcher; Johnny Bench, present-day top baseball catcher, and Allie Reynolds, who pitched two no-hit games.

229

It might be interesting to conclude the chapter on Indians by a brief account of the life and descendents of Pocahontas.

Pocahontas was the daughter of Powhatan, the Indian Chief in Virginia. As a young girl, twelve years of age, history tells us that she saved the life of Captain John Smith from being executed by her father. Later she met John Rolfe, a young Englishman of good family. He instructed her in letters and religion, and, with the consent of Powhatan, she received the rite of Christian baptism and became the wife of Rolfe in April, 1613. This union brought peace with the Indians as Powhatan was afterwards a consistent friend of the English.

John Rolfe became a successful and rich tobacco plantation owner. He took his wife on a visit to England where she was received by the king and queen and welcomed by the English people.

In early 1617, Pocahontas died in England at the age of 22, as she and her husband were about to return to Virginia. She was buried in the church graveyard in Gravesend, forty miles below London on the Thames. Her monument is still there and was visited by Queen Elizabeth who announced that she was the first person from the New World to embrace the tenets of the Church of England. She left an only son, Thomas Rolfe, who was taken to London and educated by an uncle, Henry Rolfe. Young Rolfe, the son of Pocahontas and John Rolfe, later came to America where he became a person of distinction and possessed an ample fortune. He had an only daughter who married Colonel Robert Boling, and died leaving an only son, Major John Boling. He was the father of Colonel John Boling who had several daughters, one of whom married Colonel Richard Randolph, from whom are descended the distinguished John Randolph and those who bore and still bear that name in Virginia.

The Indians regard Pocahontas as one of their

greatest historic characters. Certainly Americans, and particularly Virginians, are under a debt of gratitude to her for virtually saving the original settlement at Jamestown. History states that she warned the settlers at Jamestown of an impending Indian attack in time to defend themselves.

It seems right and proper that, after 350 years, her remains and tombstone should be brought back to the United States before the celebration of the 200th anniversary of the Declaration of Independence and be acclaimed by both Indians and whites as one of our great American heroes.

It is reported that when Pocahontas met Captain John Smith on her visit to England, she embraced him and called him father and said, "I want you to always call me daughter."

Since the Spanish War, 1898, the American Indians have fought bravely and with distinction in all of our wars. They have held high office in our government— vice-president, members of the U.S. Senate and House of Representatives, judges, governors, and numerous state officials. They are engaged in various occupations in all walks of life. There are no more loyal or patriotic Americans in the United States.

23

The Negro in New York State prior to and during the Revolutionary War—Slavery was an economic issue in New York State

Negro slavery was introduced into Virginia in 1619 and extended through all the British colonies in America. It spread from Virginia to the Carolinas and eventually to Georgia, for use in the big plantations that grew tobacco, rice, indigo, and cotton.

However, Negro slavery prevailed in all the northern colonies up to the Declaration of Independence and even beyond. During this period, white persons also were sold as indentured servants for a term of years until the cost of transportation was reimbursed.

Present-day Americans are apt to overlook the fact that New England, New York, and other northern states were just as guilty of the crime against humanity as those in the South. The greatest of all the rights of an individual is personal freedom. Yet for 200 years that first of all rights was deliberately violated in New York State both by the Dutch and English in support of the brutal system of Negro slavery and by Americans in a modified form until 1820.

Negro slavery started under the Dutch government when a few slaves from the West Indies were brought to

232

New Amsterdam by the West India Company where they served as laborers for the company. But it was not until 1654 that a cargo of slaves from Africa arrived at New Amsterdam.

The slaves were generally used as domestic servants and treated well by the Dutch citizens.

When, in 1689, the slave trade was opened up to private traders, the price of slaves declined and the numbers increased rapidly. New York under the British was no exception, and slavery became a legal and recognized institution there.

The growth of slavery caused a parallel development in servile laws throughout the colonies. New York law prohibited slaves from bearing arms, and assembling of more than four was forbidden, except at funerals when the limit was 12, and the entire status of slavery was harshly regulated in all the colonies, north and south.

New York City was swept by a racial panic in 1741 based on hysteria and the circulation of falsehoods inspired by fear. It was known as the great Negro plot or conspiracy to set fire to New York and seize the government. A veritable reign of terror was begun against helpless Negro slaves in New York by flimsy, unsupported evidence of a disreputable indentured white woman, Mary Barton, that the Negroes planned to burn, plunder, and murder the whites. This created the worst and cruelest miscarriage of justice in the history of New York. The deeds of horror and cruelty perpetrated against the Negro slaves paralleled the evil days of Salem witchcraft.

The Negro slaves, mostly domestic servants, were friendly, peaceful, and had no knowledge of the alleged conspiracy. There were, however, a small number of desperate and violent Negroes, just as we have today, who secretly advocated stealing, burning, plunder, and violence in defiance of the law. But 90 percent or more of the New York slaves had no thought of insurrection. Several fires and robberies in close succession, and one in the governor's mansion, produced immediate alarm and terror among all classes of whites, that a frightful Negro conspiracy was threatening to destroy their property and their lives. Before the hysteria and fear had subsided, and the awful toll of lynchings were ended, four white people were hanged, fourteen Negroes were burned at the stake, eighteen Negroes were hanged, two were gibetted, and seventy-two were deported to the West Indies and sold there.

There are today in the U.S. both white and black extremists who openly urge a violent overthrow of the government. Any attempt by whites or blacks, or a combination of both, would be quickly crushed by the police and our armed forces. Violence begets violence. Ninety percent or more of our population are bitterly opposed to bloodshed, civil war, or rebellion of any kind.

The present unrest among the blacks is not so much racial as the dissatisfaction of blacks with their own economic plight, which involves a great deal of unemployment and part-time work. A vast majority of the blacks deplore and disapprove of violence, although some of their leaders believe that the riots have brought home to the public the need for improving the social and economic conditions of the blacks throughout the nation.

It is historically wrong to forget the tragic involvement of the northern colonies in the shameful luxury of slavery and the slave trade. In 1638, a small merchant ship from Salem, Massachusetts made a trading trip to New Providence (Nassau) and returned with a cargo of salt, cotton, tobacco, and Negroes. This was the first introduction of slaves into New England.

After the English took over the control of New Amsterdam in 1664, more and more Negroes were imported on British ships from the West Indies and from Africa, until the Negro population represented about one-fifth of the total white population. This ratio continued in New York until the Revolutionary War. Negro slaves generally were divided into three categories: field hands, house servants, and craftsmen. The latter included apprentices, carpenters, masons, and blacksmiths. There were a number of slaves employed in the various shops, in ship-building and jobs connected with the New York docks and markets to help in the transportation of commodities of all kinds.

Once slavery was established in New York, it became as much a part of the social, economic, and governmental life as in the South. It became so firmly entrenched that slavery maintained its legal entity in New York for more than a quarter of a century after the Revolutionary War. Despite the Declaration of Independence with its concept of freedom, slavery lingered on in New York City and state until it was officially abolished in 1830.

Most of the Negro slaves lived in the same houses or in adjoining outhouses. They brought in the firewood for the stoves and fireplaces. They did the cooking and fetched the water for drinking and bathing. They served the food, attended the children, and did all the chores of servants. They were generally well treated, and often became attached to their owner's family, which was reciprocated. In those days of the horse and carriage, they took care of the stables, drove the carriages, exercized their masters' horses, and took care of the gardens and greenhouses.

During the Revolutionary War, many of them served on privateers. Slavery at the time of the war had become a pocketbook issue as it was in the South. Most New Yorkers were adverse to freeing their slaves.

Military Service During the Revolutionary War

The employment of Negroes in the American army during the Revolution was a vital issue, as the British High Command sought to enlist slaves with the promise they would be freed. Lord Dunmore of Virginia and Sir Henry Clinton of New York attempted to form Negro combat units by freeing slaves. The British naturally saw an opportunity, by offering the slaves their freedom, to turn them against their masters. There were in the U.S., at the time of the war, half a million slaves out of a population of less than three million. The ratio between whites and blacks was then about five to one. Today it is ten to one.

Sir Henry Clinton, British commander in New York, issued a proclamation inviting all Negroes to desert and "take refuge with his army" in New York. Some 3,000 Negroes took advantage of this offer, but mostly to become refugees on British relief to the end of the war. Two thousand joined the Loyalists in exile.

At the beginning of the war, many free Negroes enlisted and fought in the American army. However, the southern members of Congress protested so vigorously that it was disapproved temporarily. The Congress finally yielded by permitting free Negroes to reenlist and to receive the same benefits as white soldiers. But Congress was adamant because of the opposition of the southern states to enlistment of the slaves. Finding it impossible to persuade Congress, resort was had to the state legislatures. This had the support of General Washington, and Negro battalions of slaves were organized in Rhode Island and Connecticut. Many free Negroes were recruited from Massachusetts and New Hampshire.

In 1778, General Varnum proposed that the two Rhode Island white battalions at Valley Forge should be united, and that the officers of one, Colonel Green, Lt. Colonel Olney, and Major War be sent with their subalterns to Rhode Island to enlist a battalion of Negro slaves for Continental service. This plan was agreed to, and the Rhode Island Assembly voted to raise a regiment of slaves who were to be freed upon enlistment and their owners to be paid by the state. Over 300 enlisted under Colonel Green and served with great gallantry in the battle of Newport, three times driving back a much larger force of attacking Hessian troops.

Colonel Humphreys, later general, who was then serving as one of Washington's aides, recruited a small regiment of Negroes in Connecticut, who served bravely and efficiently throughout the war.

In New York, it was not until 1781 that freedom was given to all slaves who served for three years, and the enlistment had to be with the consent of the owner who received a land bounty. It came too late, as the war was virtually over. Nearby New Jersey steadily refused any enlistment of slaves.

Governor Eustis of Massachusetts, an officer in the war, was an outspoken supporter of Negro military service. He stated that the free colored soldiers participated with courage and fidelity, as did the slaves who were purchased from their masters and entered the service that they might be free.

The number of free Negroes in the American army as of August 24, 1778, was 755, and a large number of them were from Massachusetts, Connecticut, and New Hampshire. This does not include the battalions of slaves formed in Rhode Island and Connecticut. Many more free Negroes enlisted, from August, 1778, to October, 1781, in the south as well as the north.

Slavery did not end in New York State when the British army evacuated New York City on November 25, 1783. John Jay, of Huguenot origin, first chief justice of the U.S., and governor of New York, urged his fellow members of the first N.Y. State Convention held in 1777, at the outset of the war, to abolish slavery. However, in his absence, it was voted down by a vote of 24 to 12. Ten years later, a law was passed prohibiting the importation of slaves for sale in New York State and making it easier to free slaves by certificate or will. In 1788, the purchase of slaves for removal to other states was forbidden, and trial by jury was allowed in all capital cases.

The Quakers of Germantown, Pennsylvania, as early as 1690 urged the emancipation of all slaves, and over 100 years later, in 1798, the manumission of slaves by the Quakers in New York State was legalized. At that date, there were still 20,000 slaves in New York State, with a population of 300,000.

On March 29, 1799, the N.Y. State Legislature enacted a law for the gradual abolition of slavery. Any child born of a slave after July 4th of that year was to be free at the age of 25 for a girl and 28 for a boy. That was the beginning of the end of slavery in New York State. It was finally officially abolished in 1830.

The credit for the final victory over man's inhumanity to man in New York belongs to such fearless and persevering anti-slavery leaders as John Jay, Alexander Hamilton, Major General Lafayette, Nicholas Fish, Matthew Clarkson, General Thaddeus Kosciuszko, John Lawrence, Leonard Cutting, John Murray, Jr., and Malancthon Smith of Dutchess County, for their outspoken defense of the rights of all men and women to be free. General Kosciuszko, the famous Polish engineer who constructed the fortifications at West Point, established a fund of $20,000 for the education of Negro children.

Alexander Hamilton, at the request of his close friend the Marquis de Lafayette, who was bitterly opposed to slavery, accompanied him to a meeting in 1786 of the Emancipation Society in New York City. Hamilton did not mince words and came to the point as usual, saying: "In token of our sincerity let every person here, emancipate his slaves now."

Hamilton, perceiving the consternation and disapproval of his proposal, withdrew from the meeting along with Lafayette.

Slavery was first abolished by the French Convention on February 4, 1794, in the West Indies and in all the French colonies. The famous French orator, Danton, declared that the proposal was equivalent to the proclamation of universal liberty (freedom): "By casting liberty into the new world it will there bear abundant fruit and will sink its roots deep." It was appealing oratory, but the United States did not abolish slavery for seventy years.

The English had, for more than a century, participated in the slave trade and were responsible for the spread of slavery more than any other nation. However, William Wilberforce, the great anti-slavery leader in England, finally succeeded in persuading Parliament to abolish the trade in slavery and slavery itself in 1807, which was approximately sixty years before the U.S. took official action to wipe out that stain on the American record of freedom.

The author, having served as an officer in the 369th Infantry Regiment in the American Expeditionary Force during World War I, was inspired by an equally earnest desire as best expressed by Whittier: "to rescue from oblivion" the record of that gallant Regiment composed of volunteers from New York State whose flag was decorated with the Croix de Guerre for heroism on the battlefield. With this in view, the author respectfully submits the following quotations from two well-known Americans:

I cannot commend too highly the spirit shown among the colored combat troops who exhibit fine capacity for quick training and eagerness for the most dangerous work."

—John J. Pershing

I congratulate all colored men and women and all their white fellow Americans upon the gallantry and efficiency with which the colored men have behaved at the front and the efficiency and wish to render service which have been shown by both the colored men and the colored women behind them in this country.

—Theodore Roosevelt

Appendix A

A partial list of patriot civilian and military refugees from New York and Long Island

Later on in this appendix is a partial list of New York's Patriot civilian and military exiles during the Revolutionary War. These American refugees voluntarily left their homes and properties in New York just before the British army, under General Howe, captured the city on September 15, 1776. For seven long years they lived wherever they could find shelter: in Newburgh, Fishkill, Poughkeepsie, Kingston, and in the small towns of Westchester, along the Hudson River, and in Connecticut and parts of New Jersey. Like refugees everywhere, they eked out a difficult and precarious living, which is their usual fate.

This list of self-imposed exiles is far from complete. It is divided between officers who served in the American army, both militia and continental, mostly the latter, and citizens, mostly property owners. It is a list of honor which their descendents might well be proud of. It is composed of the better-known American Patriot families of New York and vicinity. If they had remained in New York City, many of them might have suffered a lingering death in the infamous British prisons there. This list of early American Patriots is far more historic than any society list 100 years later, such as the Four Hundred or the Social Register.

The author hopes, with additional research and the cooperation of interested readers, to add considerably to the list of patriot refugees from New York City.

The author has spent many hours in research with very little constructive results except from a book *Refugees From Long Island,* by

F. G. Mather, in which he has a chapter on some of the refugees from New York City.

It is difficult to explain why historians have overlooked writing about these 6,000 Patriot exiles who, for seven long, harrowing years, suffered hardships and privations. Strangely enough, there are at least a half-dozen well-documented books on the history of Loyalists in New York City, including those from Connecticut and New Jersey, and several books including the Loyalists throughout the United States.

There is practically no available data for students or historians regarding the names of these Patriot exiles. It is to be hoped, however, that some dedicated historian might, by intensive study and research, be able to compile a more complete list.

There were no Patriot militia within the boundaries of what is New York City or in lower Westchester, Queens, Richmond, Kings, and parts of Suffolk County and nearby New Jersey from the time of the British occupation until the end of the war.

Bronx County was then a part of Westchester. The lower part of Westchester was under British control during most of the war as far north as Tarrytown. It is interesting to note that, at the beginning of the war, Albany was the biggest county of the state in population, followed by Dutchess, New York, Westchester, Suffolk, and Queens, all of which had about the same number of inhabitants. Kings, Richmond, Orange, Ulster, and Tryon Counties were considerably smaller.

The following well-known American families were generally favorably disposed towards the British while they were in command of New York City and vicinity. Actually, nearly all of them signed the pledge of allegiance to King George, both for social interests and in order to preserve their properties and business: Amiels, Ardens, Apthorpes, Barclays, Brevorts, Buchanans, Cortelyous, Delanos, Dashs, Downes, Duncans, Edgars, Fowlers, Grims, Kissams, DeForests, Desbrosses, Lispenards, Gerards, Lows, Lorrilards, Lydigs, Marstons, Millers, Moores, Murrays, Nathans, Nichols, Rhinelanders, Roomes, Ruggles, Slidells, Stewarts, Stuyvesants, Wadells, Waltons, Winthrops, Weatherheads, Rapeljes; and Walter Franklin, a Quaker, father-in-law of DeWitt Clinton; Baches, Cuylers, Wilkins, Clarks, Gregs, and Griffiths.

Among these were quite a few who were neutral. There were also many small merchants and storekeepers, particularly those engaged in trade with England, and a number of wage-earners and others, for family and various reasons, who preferred not to take sides openly and did not want to fight for either side.

The following were ardent Loyalists and prominent office-

242

holders under the British government in N.Y. during the war. Most of them fled to Canada or back to England before the return of Washington's victorious army into New York City: Antils, Axtells, Bayards, Bellopps, Coldens, Crugers, DeLanceys, Days, Elliots, Ellisons, Fannings, Folliots, Hechts, Hendrickses, Horsmandens, Jaunceys, Philip John Livingston, Lloyds, Ludlows, Pells, Philipses, McAdams, Sherbrooks, Wallaces, Watts, Whites, Wickhams, Augustus Van Cortlandt, Roger Morris, Beverly Robinson, William Franklin (the son of Benjamin Franklin), DePeysters, Jones (the historian), and others who held office under the Crown, and most of the Anglican ministers; also, Myles Cooper, president of King's College.

Incomplete List of Several Hundred Patriot Refugee Property Owners from New York City and Vicinity During Occupation By the British Army from 1776 to November 25, 1783 (No More Than Two From Each Family)

Abeel, John	Brinkerhoff, Abraham
Ackerman, Aaron	Buchanan, Thomas
Allicoke, Joseph	Bull, Joseph
Alsop, John	Campbell, John
Alsop, Richard	Camptbell, Thomas
Anderson, John	Carghill, Henry
Anthony, Theosopolus	Childs, Francis
Ask, Thomas	Clarkson, David
Bancker, Flores	Clarkson, Levinus
Bancker, Everett	Coe, Benjamin
Bassett, Frederic	Cozene, John
Beck, Joseph	Conklin, Charles
Beekman, James	Constable, William
Benedict, Joseph	Cook, Isaac
Benson, Judge Robert	Cotton, Joseph
Berrien, John	Crane, Thaddius
Bicker, Victor	Cruger, John
Birdsall, Benjamin	Curtenius, Rev. Authoreus
Bish, John	Currie, Archibald
Blackwell, Joseph	Delafield, John
Blackwell, Robert	Delancey, John
Rogert, Nicholas	Demerest, David
Bookhauser, William	Denning, William
Bowne, Richard	Desdrosses, John
Boreum, Samuel	Devenport, John
Boreum, William	Duane, James
Bradford, Cornelius	Duer, William

Duryee, Abraham
Duncombe, Daniel
Duncombe, James
Duyckinck, Gerardus
Egbert, Benjamin
Embree, Lawrence
Fisher, Hendrick
Floyd, William
Furman, Cabriel
Garland, George
Gelston, David
Gibson, John
Gilbert, John
Gilbert, Sr. William
Goelet, Peter
Goforth, William
Gosman, John
Gouveneur, Herman
Gouveneur, Nicholas
Graham, Daniel
Graham, David
Gray, John
Hallett, Joseph
Hammersley, Andrew
Hardenbrook, Gerardus
Hardwick, John
Harper, Richard
Harpur, Robert
Harrison, Richard H.
Hazard, Ebenzer
Hazard, Nathaniel
Helme, Benjamin
Herring, Abraham
Herring, John
Hicks, Dennis
Hitchcock, Daniel
Hobart, John Sloss
Hoffman, Nicholas
Holt, John
Honeywell, Israel, Jr.
Hunt, Jesse
Hunt, Ward
Imlay, John
Imlay, William

Isaacs, Moses
Ivers, Thomas
Jarvis, Arthur
Jay, Fred
Jay, Sir James
Johnson, David
Johnson, George
Jones, Samuel
Josephson, Manuel
Kent, James
Ketcham, William
Keteltas, Garrett
Keteltas, Peter
Kingsland, Edmund
Kingsland, John
Kip, Samuel
Kep, Henry
Knapp, Joseph
Knapp, Nicholas
Lang, William
Lawrence, William
Leaker, John, Jr.
Ledyward, John
Lee, John
Le Foy, Thomas
Lefferts, Jacobus
Leight, Edward
Le Rue, Samuel
Lewis, Francis
Lehommedieu, Ezra
Lispenard, Leonard
Livingston, Edward
Livingston, Philip
Lockwood, Ebanezer
Louden, Samuel
Ludlow, Gabriel
McCormick, David
McKesson, John
Mandeville, John
Marston, John
Meyer, John
Miller, Eleazer
Morris, Lewis Gouveneur
Morris, Richard

Moses, Isaac
Mulligan, Hercules
Murray, John
Myer, Andrew
Myers, Jacobus
Myers, Manuel
Nichol, William
Nicholas, Charles
Nixson, Elias
Norton, Isaac
Ogden, John
Ogden, Samuel
Pearce, John
Peet, Thomas
Peterson, Simon
Pintard, John
Pintard, Louis
Platt, Jeremiah
Platt, Zepher
Ray, Robert
Reed, Frank
Remsen, Henry A.
Rhoads, Hope
Riker, James
Robinson, James
Roosevelt, Claeo Martenzon
Roosevelt, Isaac A.
Rose, James
Rutherford, John
Sands, John
Sands, Joshua
Schuyler, John
Seaman, Zebulon
Seaman, Water
Sears, Joshua
Sears, Richard
Seton, William

Shaddel, David
Sharp, Richard
Sherbrooke, Miles
Siers, John
Sleight, John
Smith, Justus B.
Smith, Thomas
Stagg, John
Stewart, John
Stoutennburg, Grave
Stoutenburgh, Isaac
Taylor, John
Thomas, John
Townsend, Samuel
Tredwell, Thomas
Tucker, Thomas
Tyler, James
Van Cortlandt, Pierre
Van Der Vort, Peter
Van Dyke, Francis
Van Ham, Courant
Van Horne, Augustus
Van Varck, (Varrick) James
Van Voorhees, Jacob
Van Zandt, Jacobus
Varian, Richard
Verplanck, Gulian
Verplanck, Samuel
Ward, Stephen
Walton, Gerard
Wickes, Thomas
Williams, Henry
Wilimot, George
Wood, Isaac
Woodwards, John
Young, Hamilton

A Fairly Complete List of Several Hundred American Patriot Officers, Mostly Continental, Who Were Refugees from Their Homes in New York City and Vicinity During Occupation by the British Army from 1776 to November 25, 1783.

Abeel, James, Capt. Lasher's   Addoms, Jonas, Lt., 2nd. Art.

Alling, Stephen, Lt., 2nd art.
Alner, James, Major, Malcom's
Aroson, Aaron, Capt., 1st, N.Y.
Armstrong, Edward, Lt., Malcolm's
Ashton, Joseph, Capt., 2nd Art.
Anspack, Lt., 2nd Art.
Bagley, Josium, Lt., 1st. N.Y.
Baldwin, Bezekiah, Capt., 2nd. Regt.
Bancker, John, Capt.
Barnes, John, Capt., N.Y. Rangers
Baumann, Sebastian, Col., 2nd Art.
Beekman, Theophilius, Capt., Lasher's
Beekman, Thomas, Lt., 2nd Dragoons
Beekman, Tjerck, Lt., 2nd. N.Y.
Bicker, Henry, Col., Militia
Bleecker, Anthony, Maj.
Bleeker, Leonard, Capt., 1st. N.Y.
Bliss, Thomas, Capt., 2nd. art.
Brogdon, John, Lt., 1st. N.Y.
Benson, Robert, Lt. Col., Aide
Bowen, Prentice, Capt., 4th N.Y.
Brasher, Ephraim, Lt., 1st. N.Y.
Bradhurst, Samuel, Capt.
Brasher, Abraham, Lt., 1st. N.Y.
Brewster, Caleb, Capt., 2nd Art.
Broome, John, Lt. Col.
Broome, Samuel, Capt.
Brooks, David, Lt.
Bull, William, Capt., Spencer's
Burnett, Robert, Jr., 2nd Lt., 2nd. Art.
Bydanck, Petrus, Lt., Militia.
Campbell, Donald, Col., Quar-
termaster's
Campbell, John, Lt.
Cape, Capt.
Cheeseman, Jacob, Capt. (Killed at Quebec)
Clarkson, Mathew, Major
Codwise, Christopher, Lt., 2nd N.Y.
Codwise, George, Capt., 2nd. N.Y.
Connelly, Michael, Lt., Paymaster
Copp, Belton A., Jr., Capt., 1st N.Y.
Copp, John, Capt.
Crimshire, John D., Lt., Paymaster
Curtenius, Peter T., Col., Aud. Gen.
Dennis, Patt. Capt.
Dickson, Charles, Capt.
Drake, Samuel, Lt. Col. (Westchester)
Duncomb, Edward, Capt., 2nd. N.Y.
Doughty, John, Capt., 2nd Art.
Drake, Joshua, Lt., Malcom's
Dowe, Alexander, Lt., Malcom's
Duryea, Dirck, Capt., 1st Regt.
Elliott, John, Surgeon
Eliott, John, Jr., Lt.
Fairliee, James, Lt., 2nd N.Y.
Fenno, Ephraim, Capt., 2nd. N.Y.
Finch, Andrew, Capt., 1st N.Y.
Fish, Nicholas, Major, 2nd. N.Y.
Fondy, John, Ensign, 1st N.Y.
Fowler, Thedosius, Capt., 2nd N.Y.
French, Abner, Capt., 1st. N.Y.
Francis, Samuel, Capt.
Furman, John, Lt., 1st N.Y.
Gano, Daniel, Capt., 2nd Art.

Gano, John J., Chaplain
Gates, Horatio, Maj. Gen.
Gildersleve, Finch, Lt., Spencer's
Giles, Aquila, Major, Aide
Gilliland, William, Lt., 1st N.Y.
Giles, James, Lt., 2nd Art.
Glenny, William, Lt.
Graham, John, Major, 1st N.Y.
Graham, Charles, Lt., 2nd. N.Y.
Gilliland, James, Capt., Spencer's
Gregge, James, Capt.
Green, John, Capt., Navy
Guion, Isaac, Capt., 2nd Art.
Hallett, Jonah, Lt., Malcolm's
Hallett, Jonathan, Capt., 2nd. N.Y.
Hamilton, Alexander, Lt., Col. Aide
Hanson, George, Capt.
Harper, Joseph, 2nd. N.Y.
Harvey, Elvsha, Lt.
Hazard, Samuel, Lt., 2nd Dragoons
Henry, Nathaniel, Lt., 1st N.Y.
Herring, Benjamin, Lt., 1st N.Y.
Hicks, Benjamin, Capt., 1st N.Y.
Hughes, James H., Lt. Col.
Hughes, Timothy, Lt., 1st N.Y.
Hunter, Robert, Lt., Malcolm's
Jackson, Daniel, Lt.
Janeway, George, Capt., Militia
Jansen, Cornelius, Capt., 2nd Regt.
Jay, John, Lt. Col.
Johnson, John, Lt., 1st N.Y.
Johnson, Samuel, Lt.
Johnson, William, Capt., Art.
Keese, John, Capt., Quartermaster

Ketlehost, Wynant, Capt., 1st Regt.
Lamb, John, Brig. Gen., 2nd. Art.
Lasher, John, Col.
Lawrence, Daniel, Capt.
Lawrence, John, Judge Advo. Gen.
Lawrence, Jonathan, Capt., Malcolm's
Lawrence, Oliver, Lt.
Leaycraft, George, Lt.
Leaycraft, William, Lt., 2nd Art.
Ledyward, Benjamin, Major, 1st N.Y.
Ledyward, Isaac, Surgeon
Leonard, William, Capt.
Lewis, Morgan, Col., Quartermaster General
Lewis, Samuel, Lt., 1st. N.Y.
Livingston, Robert G., Col.
Livingston, Brockholst, Lt., Col. Aide
Livingston, Robert H., Lt., 2nd. Regt.
Livingston, William S., Lt., Col. Aide
Lott, Abraham P., Col., Aud. Gen.
Lush, Major
Machin, Thomas, Capt., 2nd. Art.
Magee, Peter, Lt., 1st. N.Y.
Malcolm, John, Lt., Malcolm's
Malcolm, William, Col., Malcolm's
Marriner, Capt.
Marshall, Elihu, Capt., 2nd. N.Y.
McCoed, Stephen, Capt., 2nd. N.Y.
Maxwell, Anthony, Lt., Spences
Merrill, Joseph, Ensign, 1st.

N.Y.
Middleburger, Oliver, Lt.
Moodie, Andrew, Capt., 2nd Art.
Morreel, Thomas, Capt.
Morriss, Lewis R., Lt., 2nd. N.Y.
Morris, Lewis, Brig. Gen., Militia
Morris, Lewis, Jr., Maj., Aide
Morris, William Walton, Lt., 2nd Art.
Mott, Greshon, Capt., 2nd Art.
Mc Dougall, Alexander, Maj. Gen., Continental Army
Mc Dougall, John, Lt., 1st. N.Y.
Mc Dougall, Stephen, Major, Aide
Mundy, William, Lt., 2nd N.Y.
Mc Knight, Charles, Surgeon
Nesier, Abraham, Lt.
Nestel, Peter, Capt., 2nd. Art.
Neely, Abraham, Capt., Spences
Newkirk, William, Capt.
Nicholson, James, Capt., Navy
Oakley, Elyth, Lt., 1st. N.Y.
Oliver, Richard, Lt., Malcolm's
Parsons, Charles, Capt., 1st N.Y.
Pell, Samuel T., Capt., 2nd. N.Y.
Phoenix, Daniel, Capt.
Pintard, John, Lt.
Platt, Richard, Major
Post, Anthony, Capt., 2nd. Art.
Post, John, Commissary
Quackenbush, Nicholas
Randell, Thomas, Capt.
Reed, Jacob, Capt., 2nd Art.
Regnier, Pierre, Lt. Col., 2nd Art.
Remsen, Abraham, Capt., Militia

Remsen, Henry, Col., Militia
Remsen, William, Capt.
Ricker, Abraham, Militia
Rogers, Rev. John, Chaplain
Roosevelt, Nicholas, Major
Rutgers, Henry, Lt. Col.
Ryckman, Wilhelmees, Jr., Lt., 1st N.Y.
Sackett, Samuel, Capt., Militia
Sands, Comfort, Adj. Gen.
Sands, James, Capt., Militia
Scott, John Morin, Brig. Gen.
Sears, Isaac, Capt., Malcolm's
Shaw, John, Lt., 2nd. Art.
Smith, John, Lt., 2nd Art.
Smith, Isaac, Lt., 2nd. Art.
Smith, Robert, Capt.
Smith, William Stephene, Lt. Col., Aide
Snow, Ephriam, Lt., 1st. N.Y.
Stagg, John Jr., Lt., Malcolm's
Steel, Stephen, Capt.
Steele, John, Capt., Malcolm's
Sterling, Alexander, Maj. Gen.
Standford, John, Capt., Spence's
Steinmetz, Frederick, Lt.
Stewart, William, Militia
Stewart, James, Capt., Malcolm's
Sotenburgh, John, Lt.
Stout, John, Lt., Militia
Stockholm, Andrew, Lt. Col.
Stockton, Benjamin, Lt., Surgeon
Stutenburgh, Peter, Capt.
Scudder, William, Lt., 1st. N.Y.
Swartwout, Berradus, Lt.
Sweet, Coleb, Surgeon, 1st. N.Y.
Sytez, George, Capt., 1st. N.Y.
Tappan, Peter, Lt., 2nd. N.Y.
Tapp, William, Quartermaster
Taylor, Andrew, Lt.
Tiebout, Henry, Capt., 1st.

N.Y.
Thorne, Samuel, Lt., 1st. N.Y.
Thompson, Andrew, Lt., Spences
Throup, Robert, Lt. Col., Aide
Throop, J. R., Lt., 2nd. Art.
Troop, Robert, Lt.
Tylee, Nathaniel, Capt.
Van Cortlandt, Philip, Col., 2nd. N.Y.
Van Duersen, Abraham, Capt.
Van Dyke, Abraham, Capt., Lasher's
Van Dyke, Cornelius, Lt. Col., 1st. N.Y.
Van Wagenen, Garret, Lt., 1st. N.Y.

Van Wagenen, Tonio, Lt., 2nd. N.Y.
Van Wyck, Abraham, Capt., 1st. N.Y.
Van Zandt, Peter, Major
Van Zandt, Wyner, Capt.
Varick, Richard, Lt. Col., Aide
Waldron, Capt.
Warner, Thomas, Lt.
White, John, Lt.
White, Andrew, Lt.
Wilcock, William, Capt.
Wiley, John, Major
Walker, Benjamin, Lt. Col.
Willett, Marinus, Col., 3rd N.Y.
Wright, Jacob, Capt., 2nd. N.Y.

Large numbers of Patriot refugees, including most of the Long Island militia, crossed over to Connecticut in 129 ships, 48 of which were commanded by Long Island refugees. Most of them became active privateers. Many of the Long Island refugees enlisted in the 3rd and 4th N.Y. Continental Regiments, and quite a few served an officers throughout the war.

Among the militia officers were: Col. Jacob Blackwell, Col. William Floyd, Col. David Mulford, Col. Josiah Smith, Col. John Young, Maj. Jesse Brooks, Maj. Richard Thorne, Capt. Ephraim Bayles, Capt. Benjamin Birdsell, Capt. William Boerum, Capt. Benjamin Conkling, Capt. David Fordham, Capt. John Foster, Capt. Joseph Halleck, Capt. Robert Harris, Capt. Selah Strong, Capt. John Weeks, Capt. Thomas Wickham, Lt. Benjamin Coe, Lt. Thomas Dering, Lt. David Gilston, Lt. William Havens, Lt. Barnett Miller, Lt. Andrew Onderdonk, Lt. Henry Scudder, and Lt. Thomas Treadwell.

Among the Long Island Patriot refugees who went to Connecticut were numerous adult male members from the following families who must have increased and multiplied in almost 200 years and spread throughout the nation. They are listed numerically: Conkling 40, Reeves 20, Rogers 20, Topping 20, Halsey 15, Halleck 13, King 12, Sayre 12, Bayley 10, Corwin 10, Gardiner 10, Gildersleeve 10, Griffing 10, Howells 10, Hedges 10, Terry 8, Gelston 7, and Sanford 6.

Those readers who had ancestors living in Long Island during the Revolution and are interested in obtaining detailed information can find a vast amount of documented facts in *The Refugees of 1776 from Long Island to Connecticut,* by F. G. Mather, published in N.Y. in 1909. This excellent book of reference is available in the New York Public Library (Astor) and the New York Historical Society. There is also a book by Henry Onderdonk regarding Revolutionary incidents in Queens, Kings, and Suffolk Counties which is interesting historic reading.

The departure of the Patriot families to Connecticut, particularly from Kings and Queens Counties which were even Loyalist before the war, turned these counties into Loyalist strongholds. Suffolk County, however, was, from the beginning and remained to the end of the war, on the Patriot side. A small British garrison was maintained at Southhampton, but was withdrawn before the end of the war.

At the end of the war, Lt. Colonel Fish was ordered by Governor George Clinton to convey a message to General Haldimand, governor of Canada, requesting the withdrawal of the British troops from certain frontier posts. The message was delivered, but the British general was reluctant to act without orders from the War Office in London.

Lt. Col. Nicholas Fish
New York 19th March 1784

Sir

You will immediately proceed to Canada and deliver the inclosed letter to General Haldimand, Commander in Chief of the British Troops in that Province.

You will confer with him on the subject matter of that letter a copy of which is inclosed and endeavour to find the exact time when the British Troops shall evacuate the Posts within this State, which they now hold, and make such arrangements with him for the transaction of that business and our taking possession, as may tend to promote the mutual convenience and interest of both parties.

If however you shall find, that for want of the necessary instructions from his Court, or for any other reason, General Haldimand is unwilling or refuses to find the exact time of delivery of the post above mentioned, you will at least endeavor to make such arrangements with him that whenever the British Troops do evacuate those posts timely notice will be given for the Troops of the State to receive them at the *dispatch.*

In the course of your conference it may not be amiss to inform General Haldimand of the amicable manner in which matters were conducted in the evacuation of this place, and of the good consequences which followed from it. If he should make any inquiries with respect to inhabitants who may be settled in the vicinity of the Garrisons to be evacuated, you may in general terms assure him of the disposition of the State to do every thing that may tend to promote harmony between both parties, and that you have no doubt the State will not only abide strictly by the terms of the Treaty but where particular cases require it, and where the honor and safety of the State, will admit—they will ever extend their indulgences beyond them.

Impressed as you must be with the necessity of my being early acquainted with the result of your mission—I have no doubt you will use all the dispatch in your power to accomplish the business. Wishing you therefore a pleasant journey,

I am
Sir
Your most Obedient
Servant.

Geo. Clinton

To Col. Fish
Instructions from His Excellency, Gov. Clinton relative to the negotiations for the delivery of the western posts—March 19th, 1784.

Appendix B

Americans of German origin fought in all of our wars and were builders of America

After the English, including Scots, Welch, and northern Irish, Germans in the United States, mostly in the west, are the second in population and, through industry and ability, have contributed in a great measure to its growth and wealth.

The German participation in the Union Army during the Civil War represented a higher percentage than native-born Americans. Reputable figures based on military records disclose 176,817 Germans listed in the Union Army which totaled approximately two million men.

There were many high-ranking German officers: Wetziel, Sigel, Carl Schurz, Heintzelman, Steinwehr, Osterhaus, Kautz, Wagner and Schimmelpfenning. Another high officer of German descent was the Union chief of staff, Henry W. Halleck. Moreover, one of the outstanding heroes of the war was the young cavalry general with long golden hair, George Armstrong Custer, who was later killed with his entire command fighting the Sioux Indians. The American public has generally believed that Custer was of English origin, but actually his grandfather was one of the Hessians who either deserted or surrendered during the Revolutionary War.

The following is a letter to General Baron de Steuben from his adjutant, Major Nicholas Fish, aged 22, from West Point, N.Y., July 1, 1780:

Dr. Baron—
Pleasure and Pain often take rise from comparison, and Prejudices do frequently exist without any apparent Cause—we who have spent a most active and itinerent Life, one Day be-

holding the Beauties of Jersey, the next partaking the sweets of Pennsylvania, and then enjoying the agreeable Society of our New York Friends, have been led to imagine from a comparison of our situation with that of those at West Point, Fort Schuyler &c, that we were peculiarly fortunate, they are singularly unhappy.

I know not whence our aversion to this Post [West Point] took Birth so is the Fact however, that myself with others had formed the most despicable Idea of it; and to my agreeable Disappointment I find it not only tolerable but upon the whole somewhat Pleasant; our amusements indeed are few, and rather circumscribed, but we enjoy the constant Luxury of beholding one of Natures most magnificent, tremendous and variegated Landscapes.

There is so solemn a Pomp and Grandeur in the vast prodigious Piles that environ us, that I am constantly impressed with ideas of a *serious* and contemplative kind—

I would not however Sir, wish you to imagine that I am so absorbed in *Contemplation* as to relax in the Duties of Gratitude and Friendship; I would embrace every occasion of evincing this, and should have done myself the pleasure of waiting on the Baron when he was at this Post, had I known it in season, and had not his temporary stay put it out of my Power—

Our Troops Sir you will readily suppose have had a severe Tour since we left Morristown.

One Regiment has visited Fort Schuyler, one Fort Edward, the other two were Posted on the Mohawk River near Fort Plank—We have received no Supply of Clothing excepting Shoes. You will therefore Sir easily figure out our situation—

I have appointed Wednesday next for the Inspection of the Brigade. I should be exceedingly happy to have any Instruction the Baron may wish to give. I would thank Capn. Walker [aide to Washington] or Mr. Fairlie to send by the Bearer a Form that I may copy after in my Returns—If they will send a Return of one of the Pennsylvania Regiments I will very carefully preserve the original—

With my Compliments to the Gentlemen—

I am
Dr Baron most respectfully
Your Obedient Servt.
Nichs. Fish

The Honble Maj Gen
Baron de Steuben

Baron Steuben

The author was always under the impression that General Pershing, whose name was originally Pfoerschin, was of English origin but apparently he was of German descent. Certainly General Eisenhower, who was commander-in-chief of the American forces in World War II, was of German origin as were some of our most courageous and successful fighting aviators in World War I: Lt. Frank Luke, Jr., and Lt. Joseph Wehner. They both shot down numerous German planes and balloons. Both paid the supreme sacrifice in battle for the United States against their motherland. Luke received the Medal of Honor and so did Captain Eddie Rickenbacker who survived. Admiral Nimitz, General Spaatz, General Krueger, General Eichelberger, General Gruenther, General Stratemeyer, and General Wedemeyer were all of German origin in World War II.

Americans of German descent stand high among the builders of America in various occupations. They compare favorably with any other group as leaders of industry, finance and government—Jacob Leisler, Peter Minuit, John Peter Zenger, Flaglers, Astors, Rockefellers, Frelinghausens, Fricks, Wyerhaeusers, Havemeyers, Damroschs, Drexels, Drisers, Dirksens, Girdlers, Hearsts, Heintzes, Carl Schurz, Schwabs, Spreckels, Steinmetzes, Vilards, Westinghouses, Wideners, Wanamakers, Rittenhouses, Roeblings, Yerkes, Anhauser-Buschs, Doelgers, Ehrets, Pabsts, Rupperts, Menckens, Clarks, Gables, Atgetls, Reuthers, Schleys, Zieglers, Babe Ruth, Beineckes, Bergers, Borahs, Debs, Heffelfingers, Wilkies, Kaisers, Kresses, Kresges, Meyers, Ridders, Ritters, Rhinelanders, Studebakers and Wagners.

During World Wars I and II, Americans of German origin were stupidly harrassed and suspected of disloyalty because, along with many other citizens, they opposed our entrance in foreign wars unless attacked. But the record shows that their sons served with honor and distinction on the battlefields of Europe.

The pro-Nazi Bund under Fritz Kuhn's leadership before Pearl Harbor was a small fiasco and had little appeal among Americans of German origin. Ninety-five percent of them were loyal Americans during World Wars I and II.

Appendix C

The Irish Catholics in peace and war, builders of America

The Irish Catholics have always been loyal and patriotic citizens of the United States. There were a number of Irish regiments from New York in the Union Army, and the celebrated Irish Iron Brigade under General Meager served with gallantry and distinction. The most heroic officers of Irish origin in the Civil War were General Phillip Sheridan and the brilliant Phillip Kearny. In World War I, General John O'Ryan commanded the famous 27th Division from New York, and Colonel Bill Donovan commanded the equally famous 69th Regiment.

In 1880, William R. Grace was elected as the first Catholic mayor of New York, followed by many others: William J. Gaynor, John Puroy Mitchell, John F. Hylan, James J. Walker, Joseph V. McKee, John P. O'Brien, and William O'Dwyer.

American citizens from Ireland have prospered in all walks of life in the United States, including literature, poetry, the fine arts, industry, and commerce, and in New York State many of them made great fortunes as industrialists and financiers: Anthony Brady, William R. Grace, Clarence Mackey, John Raskob, and Thomas Fortune Ryan.

Among the outstanding Americans of Irish origin in public life in New York were former Governor Alfred E. Smith, able, popular and a great American; Bourke Cochran, one of the most eloquent orators in the history of our country; former Postmaster General James A. Farley, well known throughout the nation, a mastermind in the art of politics and a candidate for president; former President John F. Kennedy, who lived in New York during part of his youth,

256

and his brother Robert F. Kennedy, elected Senator from New York. This list should also include Ambassador Joseph Kennedy, the father who accumulated a fortune of 200 million dollars and had an office for years in New York; he became a controversial ambassador to the Court of St. James at London. And the able and patriotic James Forrestal, former secretary of Defense. There are distinguished Irish Catholics now holding the two most important positions in New York State—Hugh Carey, governor, and James L. Buckley, U.S. Senator.

Probably the most influential Irish Catholics in New York State have been a long line of highly distinguished cardinals and bishops who have done so much to uphold and defend not only their own creed but the welfare and morality of the city and the nation.

George Meany, the outstanding and able leader of the powerful AFL-CIO has taken a strong stand against Communism as the enemy of freedom, just as Samuel Gompers, the organizer of the AFL-CIO in his day, took a determined stand against Socialism. Peter Brennan has served well as secretary of Labor, and Thomas Gleason, head of the Longshoremen's Union, advocates a strong national defense.

Eugene O'Neil was one of the best-known American playwrights. F. Scott Fitzgerald is among the foremost novelists, Augustus St. Gaudens ranks as one of the top sculptors of the nation and Richard Berlin as a distinguished journalist.

There are more Irish Catholics in New York City than in Dublin, and almost as many in New York State as in the Irish Republic.

Appendix D

American Jews in war and peace, builders of America

One hundred years ago there were only 80,000 Jews in New York City, less than ten percent of the population, and nearly all of them from Germany. The big migration of Russian and Polish Jews began about 1870 and, in the next 45 years, approximately a million and a half Jews entered New York, or thirty percent of the population. The Russian, Polish, and Eastern European Jews now out-number the German Jews by about fifteen to one. Many of them amassed large fortunes and have been successful in various walks of life. Today there are 2½ million Jews in New York City, more than any single ethnic group.

In the Civil War, seven Jews won the Congressional Medal of Honor, the highest award available. During World War I, forty percent of the famous "Lost Battalion" were Jews from New York City. Sam Deben, a Jewish soldier of fortune, became a legendary hero in World War I for attacking and capturing machinegun nests. There were 500,000 American Jews in our armed forces during World War II. They received over 1,000 awards for bravery on the battlefield. Among their outstanding generals were Maj. General Morris Rose, a brilliant commander of armoured troops who was killed at Paderhorn, Germany, towards the end of the war; Maj. General Melvin Krulewitch of New York, who fought in the Marine Corps during both World Wars I and II with honor and distinction and was awarded many decorations; Brig. General Julius Ochs Adler, likewise of New York, who had a fine military record overseas and was decorated with the Distinguished Service Cross and the Silver Star. Among the outstanding and distinguished naval officers were: Admiral Ben Morreel, who organized and commanded the famous Seabees. He rendered conspicuous service in the war and became the highest ranking Jewish officer in Naval history. R/Admiral Louis L. Strauss of New York, as assistant to the secretary of the navy, had a distinguished war career, and the brilliant Admiral H. H. Rickover, creator of our vital nuclear submarines.

The record of the Americans of Jewish origin in all of our wars for military service and bravery on the battlefields ranks high. The fighting ability of the Jews has recently been made known throughout the world by the gallant and victorious defenders of Israel, in two wars although greatly out-numbered. Other officers who served with distinction were Maj. General Irving Phillipson, Maj. General Samuel Lawton, and Brig. General Edward Morris.

Bernard Baruch was of Portuguese origin, but his father came from South Carolina and was a medical colonel in the Confederate Army. Baruch moved to New York and was educated there. He became an extremely able and successful industrialist and was a friend of four presidents.

The following is a list of fifty Americans, mostly of German Jewish origin, who have been prominent in New York in finance, law, and government as builders of America: Baruchs, Belmonts, Benjamins, Brandeis, Cardozas, Cohens, Delacortes, Dillions, Franks, Goldbergs, Goldsteins, Goldwaters, Gimbels, Gompers, Goulds, Guggenheims, Hays's, Herberts, Holtzmanns, Isaacses, Javitses, Kahns, Kuhns, Lefkowitzes, Lehmans, Leidesdorfts, Levitts, Levys, Loebs, Lopez's, Macks, Marshalls, Mendeses, Meyers, Morgenthaus, Nathans, Ochses, Ottingers, Pintos, Rickovers, Proskauers, Pulitzers, Roses, Rosenwalds, Schiffs, Seixas, Seligmans, Steinguts, Silvers, Solises, Solomons, Speyers, Strausses, Sulzbergers, Tobiases, Untermeyers, Wises, and Warburgs.

The Jewish population in New York State is approximately that of Israel.

The author was sponsor of the American Balfour Resolution in 1922 in the House of Representatives which passed the Congress and was signed by the president. This resolution was the cornerstone of the foundation of the State of Israel, as a result of which hundreds of millions of dollars from the United States went to make Palestine a land of milk and honey from Dan to Beersheba.

Ted Berkman, author of *Sabra,* the bestseller on the Six Days Israeli-Arab War of 1968, wrote on the flyleaf of his book the following to the author of this book: "Maker of history and lifetime friend of Jewry without whom the Sabra dream (Israel) would never have been achieved."

Appendix E

New York State Indians

The Rev. Johannes Megapolensis was a highly educated, Dutch Minister stationed at Albany in 1642 who learned to speak the Mohawks' language and became their friend. He wrote an interesting short account of the living conditions and habits of the Mohawk Indians. Due to lack of space, only a few extracts are used in this book.

Prostitution was well known in ancient times in Greece, Rome, and in the Bible. Even burning at the stake was practiced by the Romans against Christians, gladiators, and enemies of Rome. The Inquisition also indulged in burning at the stake.

Scalping was indigenous to Indian customs. But the English government encouraged it by paying the Mohawks, Senecas, and other Indians for the scalps of American Patriots, mostly farmers, their wives, and their children, in spite of the protest of some members of Parliament. A news item referred to a shipment of American scalps by the Iroquois Indians to London—43 soldiers, 98 farmers killed in their own houses, 97 farmers killed in the fields, 102 farmers killed in different places, 88 scalps of women, 193 of boys, 211 of girls. This amounted to over 800, indicating that scalping was a profitable business. The English bounty payers were even more responsible for this nefarious and cruel practice than the Indians.

According to Dominie Megapolensis:
In the summer the Indians go naked, having only their private parts covered with a patch. The children and young folks to ten, twelve and fourteen years of age go stark naked. In winter they hang about them simply an undressed deer or bear or panther skin; or they take some beaver and otter skins, wild

260

cat, raccoon, martin, mink, squirrel or such like skins, which are plentiful in this country and sew some of them to others, until it is a square piece and that is then a garment for them; or they buy of us Dutchmen two and a half ells of duffel, and that they hang simply about them, just as it was torn off, without sewing it, and walk away with it. They look at themselves constantly and think they are very fine. They make themselves stockings and also shoes of deer skin or they take leaves of their corn, and plait them together and use them for shoes. The women, as well as the men, go with their heads bare. . . .

They generally live without marriage; and if any of them have wives, the marriage continues no longer than seems good to one of the parties, and then they separate, and each takes another partner. I have seen those who had parted, and afterwards lived a long time with others, leave these again, seek their former partners and again be one pair. And, though they have wives, yet they will not leave off whoring; and if they can sleep with another man's wife, they think it a brave thing. The women are exceedingly addicted to whoring; they will lie with a man for the value of one, two or three schillings and our Dutchmen run after them very much.

The men have great authority over the concubines, so that if they do anything which does not please them and raises their passion, they take an axe and knock them in the head, and there is an end of it. The women are obliged to prepare the land, to mow, to plant, and do everything; the men do nothing but hunt, fish and make war upon their enemies. They are very cruel towards their enemies in time of war; for they first bite off the nails of the fingers of their captives, and cut off some joints, and sometimes even whole fingers; after that, the captives are forced to sing and dance before them stark naked; and finally they roast their prisoners dead before a slow fire for some days and then eat them up. The common people eat the arms, buttocks and trunk, but the chiefs eat the head and the heart.

The Iroquois and northern Indians evidently burned some of their captives and ate them. But this unnatural practice did not prevail in the south and west.

It is a wonder how they survived the terrible northern winters, yet they did and if not killed while young in battle, survived to a very ripe old age, often over 100 years. This was probably due to an abundance of fresh air, physical exercise, not over-eating, a diet of vegetables, fish, venison, wild fowl, and fruits, and drinking only water until the white traders made rum and hard liquor available.

The white fur traders introduced rum (firewater) which soon became an item of payment for furs. It did more harm to the Indians than soldiers' bullets, and more than present narcotics do to our generation.

There is no denying that the white traders caused a great deal of trouble with the Indians throughout the nation. The government of the United States should provide adequate food, clothing, and relief for all American Indians who are destitute and in need. However, more important is to procure for them a good education and worthwhile employment. The American Indians throughout the United States have been fractionalized for hundreds of years by belonging to various tribes, often involved in blood feuds.

The following letter from Lincoln's secretary of the Navy, Gideon Wells, written to the author's grandmother during the Civil War is interesting, as Unadilla, N.Y., was one of the towns destroyed by the Indians and Tories during the Revolutionary War. The Unadilla River ran into the Susquehanna and was not only very beautiful, but historic as the battleground between the settlers and the raiding Indians.

Mrs. Hamilton Fish, to whom the letter was written, was the daughter of Sarah Morris and Peter Kean. She was the granddaughter of Lewis Morris who signed the Declaration of Independence. Her mother was brought up on 1,000 acres of pioneer wilderness land near Unadilla in Otsego County, N.Y. This was assigned to the Morris family because of the losses to their property in Morrisania, Westchester County, N.Y., by the British during the war. Lewis Morris's son, General Jacob Morris, was the pioneer of the Morris Patent and established his home there when there were no roads or nearby towns. His place, called the Butternuts, afterwards named Morris, is still occupied by descendents of the family.

Navy Department
20 August 1861

Madam,

It affords me pleasure to inform you, that instructions have been issued from this Department, to designate one of the new gun boats for the Navy, after the name of the Indian River "Unadilla" in compliment of your suggestion.

I have the honor to be
very obediently your servant
Gideon Wells
Secretary of the Navy

Mrs. Hamilton Fish
New York

This is a clipping from a newspaper at that time:

THE FIRST OF THE NEW GUN BOATS

The First of the New gun boats launched for the Navy at New York, has been named by Mrs. Hamilton Fish, "Unadilla" from an Indian river falling into the Susquehanna. The "Unadilla" is to be armed with the first of Dahlgren's 150 pounder rifled guns.

The following letter written by the wife of secretary of State Hamilton Fish on June 7, 1870, to her daughter, Mrs. Sidney Webster, describes a White House reception by President Grant to a number of Indian chiefs. She refers to Red Cloud, who was one of the most hostile Sioux Chiefs who, five years later, led the Indian attacks on white settlements and Armed Forces.

In the evening we went to the President's to see the Indian Chiefs received. Nothing could be more curious than the scene as these savage fierce looking Indians with their war paint and feathers and their blankets sat on one side of the East Room which was brilliantly lighted. The Corps diplomatique, the Cabinet and the Committees of both houses on Indian Affairs were the only persons asked to meet them. They all came up to the President and Mrs. Grant after we got into the East Room and each in turn shook hands saying "How" as they passed and then shook hands in turn with each one of the group around the President. They then returned to their seats. In a few moments, the State Dining Room was thrown open and the Indians went in first. The President taking Spotted Tail who is the friendly chief. After the Indians Mrs. Grant followed with your Father and then we all went in procession. Everthing had been done to make the table as superb as possible. The rarest flowers, the most exquisite fruit, the greatest variety of forms of ices. You can imagine how singular it was to see these dusky savages standing around the elegant table. They ate their ice cream with gold spoons and drank champagne from beautiful glasses as if they had always been accustomed to such luxuries and evinced no astonishment at the beauty of the scene. I stood near Red Cloud, the most cruel and troublesome of these Indians. Seeing that he was encumbered by a curious looking stick (something between a club and a scepter) and his fan and tobacco pouch, I offered to hold them for him. He gave me a searching look and then seemed satisfied and handed them to me. I held them while he ate supper and when he took them again he gave me a smile and a courtly bow, which is said to be the only gracious thing he had done since he had been in Washington.

He complains that he had eaten many things here which have not been given to the Red Men's rations, that he has seen many things which have not been sent by his Great Father as presents to the Red Men. He measured the 15 inch gun at the Navy Yard the other day and then complacently remarked that they could not carry that out on the plains.

All this of course through an interpreter as the only English word any of them say is "how," an abbreviation of How do you do. There were four squaws with them; they seemed amused at looking at the ladies' dresses, examined their feet and admired Miss Cascoigne's little white satin slippers very much.

Appendix F

Bill before Congress to Commemorate the Military Service of four American Negro regiments during World War I

These remarks were made by the author primarily to commemorate the military service of the 15th N.Y. volunteer regiment composed of Negroes mostly from New York and vicinity, and mostly led by white officers. This regiment was later called the 369th when it was taken into the U.S. Army and sent overseas, where it was among the first American regiments to serve in the trenches during World War I. It had a fine war record, heavy casualties, and was decorated by the French Government with the Croix de Guerre.

The quotation is from the *Congressional Record* for April 28, 1926. The resolution was adopted by the House by a large margin.

The CHAIRMAN. The House is in Committee of the Whole House on the state of the Union for the consideration of the bill II. R. 9694, which the Clerk will report.

The Clerk read the bill, as follows:

Be it enacted, etc., That the American Battle Monuments Commission is hereby authorized and directed to erect near Scchault, France, a suitable monument to commemorate the valiant services of the Three hundred and sixty-ninth, Three hundred and seventy-first, and Three hundred and seventy-second American Infantry Regiments, attached to the French Fourth Army, at a cost not to exceed $30,000, from appropriations heretofore or hereafter appropriated by Congress.

The CHAIRMAN. The gentleman from New York [Mr. Fish] is recognized.

Mr. FISH. Mr. Chairman, this bill (H. R. 9694) authorizes the expenditure of $30,000 to erect a monument to commemorate the gallant services of four colored regiments of the provisional Ninety-third Division of the American Expeditionary Forces, and I am glad to see that no Republican in this House voted against the consideration of this bill to-day. [Applause.]

Mr. O'CONNELL of New York. Will the gentleman yield?

Mr. FISH. Yes; I yield.

Mr. O'CONNELL of New York. I would also like the gentleman to say that there were some Democrats who voted with him on this proposition.

Mr. FISH. I will be glad to say that some of the Democrats voted in that way, but a great many more who should have voted for its consideration did not so vote.

Mr. GREEN of Florida. And I am glad to say some of them did not vote for it, sir.

Mr. FISH. Mr. Chairman, these colored soldiers, I will say to my friends on the Democratic side of the House, were good enough to be accepted as volunteers in time of war; they were good enough to be drafted; they were good enough to be killed for their country; but they are not good enough to permit the consideration of a bill to commemorate their gallant services. [Applause.]

The four regiments included in the bill are the Three Hundred and Sixty-ninth, formerly the Fifteenth New York National Guard—and I will say to my Democratic friends that they had white officers, and of these 60 white officers 15 of them were killed on the field of battle. The Three Hundred and Seventieth was a National Guard regiment from Chicago; the Three Hundred and Seventy-first a drafted regiment from the South; the Three Hundred and Seventy-second composed of a separate battallion from Ohio, another from the District of Columbia, and separate companies from Massachusetts, Connecticut, and Maryland. The casualties of these four regiments were 40 per cent of their effectives. I have letters in my pocket from officers who served in the regiment drafted from the South, a white officers' association, and they are for this bill, and I am proud of it. [Applause.]

Mr. CONNALLY of Texas. Will the gentleman yield?

Mr. FISH. I will.

Mr. CONNALLY of Texas. Will the gentleman explain why General Pershing, chairman of the battle commission, is against it, and Senator REED on the commission is against it, and why the gentleman from Maryland [MR. HILL] is opposed to it?

Mr. FISH. I do not think the gentleman from Maryland [MR. HILL] is opposed to the bill; he is on the floor of the House and can speak for himself. As far as the other gentlemen are concerned, I will answer the question. The Battle Monuments Commission made a rule that no unit under a division should be considered. Therefore these regiments could not be included under that regulation for a battle monument. But the bill was amended after Senator REED had been before the committee. It was given careful consideration. The bill was amended in committee to obviate some of the objections of Senator REED. In order that the appropriation would not be taken out of the battle monuments fund a special authorization of $30,000 was provided for in this bill. Both amendments were made in committee; they were not offered by me, but accepted unanimously by the committee, and I think that answers the statement of the gentleman who wanted to know why we reported the bill. This is the second time in two years, after careful consideration, that this bill has been reported. [Applause.] The Battle Monuments Commission is a creature of Congress, and it is not only right but just that we instruct them to provide a separate monument for the provisional Ninety-third Division.

The four regiments that make up this division served with the French Army. They were understrength, having about 2,500 men in a regiment. Three of the four regiments had their flags decorated with the French croix de guerre. Very few other American regiments had their flags decorated with the French war cross. There was no dispute by the opponents in the committee as to the heroism, gallantry, and courage of the negro fighting soldiers of the provisional Ninety-third Division. [Applause.] The facts were admitted by witnesses before the committee; even the opposition admitted that these four regiments had conducted themselves gallantly on the battle fields of France, and one of these regiments claims that it served in the line longer than any other American regiment.

Mr. COOPER of Wisconsin. Will the gentleman yield?

Mr. FISH. I will.

Mr. COOPER of Wisconsin. I think the gentleman has omitted an important fact as stated to me by a Member sitting by my side. He expressed surprise when I told him that the distinguished gentleman now addressing the House was an officer of one of these regiments. [Applause.]

Mr. FISH. My friends, I would be derelict to the memory of these colored soldiers in my own regiment and the white officers who were killed in that regiment if I did not do everything in my power to see that they got proper recognition. [Applause.]

There were 400,000 negro soldiers in our Army. There are 12,000,000 of colored people in the country, and everyone is interested in seeing that recognition is given to the soldiers of the colored race who made the supreme sacrifice. [Applause.] There were 457 killed and 3,468 wounded in these four regiments out of a battle strength of approximately 10,000 soldiers. With the exception of the First and Second Divisions, there were not many American divisions which had a higher percentage of killed and wounded. All we ask here is to do away with this unjust discrimination against the heroism of negro soldiers and erect this monument in France, which will be for all time an inspiration to patriotism, loyalty, and heroism for all the colored people of America. [Applause.]

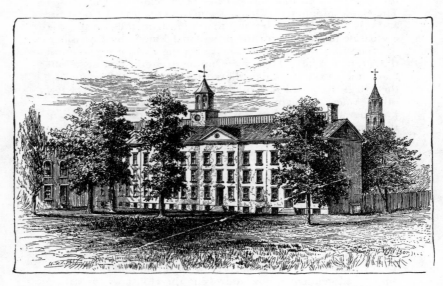

King's College 1756-1783, subsequently Columbia College

Bibliography

Armstrong, Margaret. *Five Generations*. New York: Harper & Bros, 1930.

Atherton, Gertrude. *The Conqueror*. New York: Macmillan Co., 1902.

Atherton, Gertrude. *A Few of Hamilton's Letters*. New York: Macmillan Co., 1903.

Bailey, Thomas A. *The American Pageant*. Lexington, Mass: D.C. Heath & Co., 1961.

Banet, Walter. *The Old Merchants of New York*. 5 Vols 1862.

Birmingham, Stephen. *Real Lace*. New York: Harper & Row, 1973.

Bliven, Bruce, Jr. *Battle for Manhattan*. London: Penguin Books, 1964.

Bloom, Sol: *The Story of the Constitution* 1863.

Boynton, Edward C. *History of West Point*.

Centennial Celebration and Washington Monument at Newburgh, N.Y. Report of the Joint Select Committee, Washington, D.C.: 1889.

Craven, Wesley Frank. *The Legend of the Founding Fathers*. Ithaca, N.Y.: Cornell University Press, 1965.

Davis, Burke. *Heroes of the American Revolution*. New York: Random House, 1971.

Delteil, Joseph. *Lafayette*. Minton, Balch & Co., 1928.

Desmond, Alice C. *Alexander Hamilton's Wife*. New York: Dodd, Mead & Co., 1952.

First New York State Constitution, 1777. Loudon, Fishkill, 1777.

Fish, Hamilton, Jr. *George Washington in the Highlands*. Newburgh, N.Y.: The Press of the Newburgh News, 1932.

Fish, Stuyvesant. *The New York Privateers 1756–1763*. George Grady Press, 1945.

Fiske, John. *The American Revolution*. 2 vols. Boston: 1891.

Flick, Alexander C., ed. *The American Revolution in New York*. 1926.

Flick, Alexander C. *Loyalism in New York during the American Revolution*. 1901.

Fredman and Falk. *Jews in American Wars*. 1946.

Gottschalk, Louis and Maddox, Margaret. *Lafayette in the French Revolution*. Chicago: University of Chicago Press, 1969.

Gronowicz, Antoni. *Gallant General Tadeusz Kosciuszko*. New York: Charles Scribner's Sons, 1947.

Headley, Joel T. *The Great Riots of New York, 1712–1773*. 1873.

Heitman, Francis B. *Historical Register of Officers of the Continental Army*.: F.B. Heitman, 1893.

Herring, Hubert. *And So To War*. New Haven, Conn.: Yale University Press, 1938.

History of the War in America between Great Britain and Her Colonies. Printed for R. Faulder, 1780.

Jefferson, Thomas. *The Jefferson Bible*. New York: Fawcett Publications, 1961.

Judge Jones' Loyalists in America, 2 vols.

Konefsky, Samuel J. *John Marshall and Alexander Hamilton*. New York: Macmillan Co., 1967.

Lossing, B.J. *Pictorial Field-Book of the Revolution,* 1859.

Loth, David. *Alexander Hamilton, Portrait of a Prodigy.* New York: J. B. Lippincott, 1939.

Loth, David. *The People's General. The Personal Story of Lafayette.* New York: Charles Scribner's Sons, 1951.

Marbois-Barbe, Marquis. *Our Revolutionary Forefathers, Letters of Marquis Barbe-Marbois.* Duffield & Co., 1929.

Mather, Frederic G. *The Refugees of 1776 from Long Island to Connecticut.,* 1913.

Morris, G. *Diary and Letters of Gouverneur Morris, 2 vols.* New York:, 1888.

Muzzey, David Saville. *An American History.* Boston: Ginn & Co., 1920.

New York History. New-York State Historical Association. New York, 1944.

New York State Historical Society. *Correspondence of Governor George Clinton,* 10 vols.

Order of Colonial Lords of Manors in America. *Patroons and Lords of Manors of the Hudson.,* 1932.

Paine, Thomas. *Rights of Man.* Freethought Press Assn.

Parkman, Francis. *The Seven Years' War.* New York: Harper Torchbooks, 1968.

Parton, James. *Life and Times of Aaron Burr.,* 1858.

Pennsylvania State Society. *General Society of the Cincinnati with the Original Institution of the Order.,* 1848.

Raiford, William R. *West Point and the Society of Cincinnati.* Washington, D.C.: U.S. Library of Congress, 1967.

Schachner, Nathan. *Alexander Hamilton.* New York: McGraw-Hill, 1952.

Scheer, George F. and Rankin Hugh F. *Rebels and Redcoats*. New York: New American Library, 1972.

Scoville, Joseph A. *The Old Merchants of New York City,* 5 vols. 1862.

Sichel, Edith. *The Household of the Lafayettes.:* Archibald Constable Co., 1897.

Sparks, Jared, ed. *George Washington's Writings,* 12 vols., 1835.

Syrett, Harold C., ed. *American Historical Documents.* New York: Barnes & Noble, 1960.

Thatcher, James. *Military Journal during the American Revolution.* Boston:, 1823.

Trevelyan, George O. *The American Revolution,* 6 vols.

Tuckerman, Bayard. *Peter Stuyvesant.* New York: Dodd, Mead & Co., 1893.

U.S. Hereditary Register Association. *Hereditary Register of the United States.,* 1973.

University of the State of New York. *The American Revolution in New York* Division of Archives and History, 1926.

Van Loon, W.H. *Life and Times of Peter Stuyvesant.* New York: Henry Holt,

Veteran Corps of Artillery, State of New York. *Veteran Corps of Artillery, State of New York, Instituted 1790.,* 1965.

Wharton, Anne. *Through Colonial Doorways.*

Wilson, Woodrow. *George Washington,* reprint of 1893 edition. New York: Schocken Books, 1969.